Dana Louagie
Noun Phrases in Australian Languages

Pacific Linguistics

Managing editor
Alexander Adelaar

Editorial board members
Wayan Arka
Danielle Barth
Don Daniels
Nicholas Evans
Gwendolyn Hyslop
David Nash
Bruno Olsson
Bill Palmer
Andrew Pawley
Malcolm Ross
Dineke Schokkin
Jane Simpson

Volume 662

Dana Louagie

Noun Phrases in Australian Languages

A Typological Study

DE GRUYTER
MOUTON

ISBN 978-1-5015-2570-4
e-ISBN (PDF) 978-1-5015-1293-3
e-ISBN (EPUB) 978-1-5015-1287-2
ISSN 1448-8310

Library of Congress Control Number: 2019947920

Bibliographic information published by the Deutsche Nationalbibliothek
The Deutsche Nationalbibliothek lists this publication in the Deutsche Nationalbibliografie;
detailed bibliographic data are available on the Internet at http://dnb.dnb.de.

© 2021 Walter de Gruyter Inc., Boston/Berlin
This volume is text- and page-identical with the hardback published in 2020.
Typesetting: Integra Software Services Pvt. Ltd.
Printing and binding: CPI books GmbH, Leck
Photo credit: Schmidt, Wilhelm. 1919, Die Gliederung der australischen Sprachen:
geographische, bibliographische . . .
/ von P.W. Schmidt Mechitharisten-Buchdruckerei Wien
National Library of Australia N 499.4 SCH
http://nla.gov.au/nla.obj-338367865

www.degruyter.com

For my parents

Acknowledgements

This book is a revision of my doctoral thesis, entitled *A typological study of noun phrase structures in Australian languages* and defended at the University of Leuven (KU Leuven) in March 2017. I want to sincerely thank my thesis supervisor Jean-Christophe Verstraete for his invaluable support over the past years, and for his generosity in sharing knowledge and ideas and commenting on many drafts. Chapter 6 is based on a joint paper, but, needless to say, the other chapters have substantially benefited from his input as well.

The research for this study was funded by the Research Council of the University of Leuven, and this book was finalised during a fellowship funded by FWO (Research Foundation-Flanders), both of which I gratefully acknowledge.

I also want to express my gratitude to Kristin Davidse, Birgit Hellwig, Bill McGregor and Freek Van de Velde, who as members of the doctoral jury provided constructive and detailed feedback on my thesis, and asked motivating questions on several occasions. Jane Simpson and two anonymous reviewers provided much insightful feedback and advice on earlier versions of the book, which has considerably enriched the analysis and argumentation. I am further indebted to Hendrik De Smet, Sarah D'Hertefelt, Holger Diessel, Alice Gaby, Nikolaus Himmelmann, Rachel Nordlinger, Erich Round, Stef Spronck, Nick Thieberger, An Van linden, and other colleagues for the inspiring discussions, comments and questions. Many people also provided information on their languages of expertise, patiently answering all my questions; thank you, James Bednall, Barry Blake, Joe Blythe, Claire Bowern, Margaret Carew, Greg Dickson, Katerina Forrester, Alice Gaby, John Giacon, Clair Hill, Dorothea Hoffmann, Katie Jepson, Ivan Kapitonov, Bill McGregor, Felicity Meakins, Stephen Morey, Ilana Mushin, Rachel Nordlinger, Alan Ray, Erich Round, Eva Schultze-Berndt, Ruth Singer, Stef Spronck, Tasaku Tsunoda, Marie-Elaine van Egmond and Jean-Christophe Verstraete. Finally, I thank Michiel Vanpachtenbeke, who has resolved technical difficulties with the maps, and Kirstin Börgen at De Gruyter, who has guided me through the publication process.

As always, I have been able to count on the love and support of my family, for which I cannot thank them enough. My warmest thanks to Simon and Yasmin for being not only my brother and sister but also my friends. I cannot begin to express my gratitude to my parents. My mum, who sadly only saw the beginning of this project, and my dad are my inspiration. They have passed on their love of language(s) to me, and it is because of their encouragement and enthusiasm that I have been able to do this project, and much else in life. I dedicate this book to them. Finally, my love and gratitude go to Michiel, for always being by my side, and for his encouragement, care and love.

Contents

Acknowledgements —— VII

List of Tables —— XII

List of Maps —— XIII

Abbreviations —— XIV

Overview of the sample —— XVIII

1	Introduction —— 1	
1	Aims and overview —— 1	
2	Data and methods —— 5	
2.1	Language sample —— 5	
2.2	Data —— 14	
2.3	Maps —— 17	

Part I: **Survey of NP features**

2	**Nominal classification —— 23**	
1	Typology of nominal classification —— 23	
2	Noun classifiers and generic-specific constructions —— 29	
2.1	Morphosyntax —— 31	
2.2	Meaning and use —— 38	
3	Verbal and adjectival classifiers —— 45	
4	Noun classes —— 48	
4.1	Morphosyntax —— 50	
4.2	Meaning and use —— 52	
5	In between classifier and noun class systems —— 60	
6	Multiple classification systems —— 62	
7	Conclusion —— 65	
3	**Qualification —— 66**	
1	Adjectives as a word class —— 66	
1.1	Conceptual criteria —— 72	
1.2	Morphological criteria —— 73	

1.3		Constructional evidence: Functional and morphosyntactic criteria —— 76
1.4		Conclusion —— 81
2		Syntactic realisation —— 83
2.1		Direct qualification —— 83
2.2		Complexity of qualifying structures —— 85
3		Conclusion —— 88

4		**Quantification —— 89**
1		Number marking —— 89
1.1		Distribution and obligatoriness of number marking —— 90
1.2		Distinctions within number paradigms —— 99
2		Quantifiers —— 101
2.1		Distribution of numerals and quantifiers —— 102
2.2		Architecture of numeral and quantifier systems —— 104
3		Conclusion —— 107

5		**Determination and NP constituency —— 108**
1		Determination —— 108
2		NP constituency —— 114

Part II: NP constituency and determination

6		**Noun phrase constituency —— 123**
1		Introduction —— 123
2		Parameters —— 125
2.1		External parameters —— 126
2.2		Internal parameters —— 130
2.3		Overview —— 134
3		Results —— 135
3.1		Word order —— 135
3.2		Locus of case marking —— 143
3.3		Diagnostic slots —— 148
3.4		Prosody —— 150
3.5		Conclusion —— 151
4		Discontinuous structures —— 156
5		Conclusion —— 162

7	**The status of determining elements** —— **164**
1	Introduction —— 164
2	Structural determiner slots in the sample —— 166
2.1	Type 1: determiner(s) – HEAD – modifier(s) —— 170
2.2	Type 2: determiner(s) – modifier(s) – HEAD – modifier(s) —— 172
2.3	Type 3: determiner(s) – HEAD – modifier(s) – determiner(s) —— 175
2.4	Type 4: determiner(s) … modifier(s) – HEAD (or reverse) —— 178
2.5	Discussion —— 180
3	Elements which fill determiner slots —— 183
3.1	Articles —— 184
3.2	'Ignoratives', interrogatives and indefinites —— 186
3.3	Third person pronouns —— 187
3.4	Demonstratives —— 190
3.5	Possessive pronouns —— 191
3.6	Quantifiers and numerals —— 192
3.7	Logical and comparative modifiers —— 195
3.8	Conclusion —— 197
4	Languages without determiner slots —— 202
4.1	Languages with mixed evidence —— 202
4.2	Languages without a determiner slot —— 205
5	Conclusion —— 206

8 **Conclusion** —— **208**

Appendix —— **214**

References —— **239**

Language Index —— **255**

Subject Index —— **259**

List of Tables

Table 1	Overview of the sample —— 7
Table 2	Noun class vs. classifier (Grinevald 2000: 62) —— 27
Table 3	Range of generics in some classification systems —— 41
Table 4	N vs. A in 10 languages of the sample —— 70
Table 5	Evidence for a separate adjective class —— 82
Table 6	Parameters for constituency —— 134
Table 7	Results for NP constituency —— 152
Table 8	Determiner slots —— 170
Table 9	Elements filling determiner slots: distribution in determiner versus other slots —— 198
Table 10	Word order in the NE —— 214
Table 11	Locus of case marking —— 218
Table 12	Diagnostic slots —— 225
Table 13	Prosody —— 226
Table 14	Determiners: languages of type 1 —— 227
Table 15	Determiners: languages of type 2 —— 228
Table 16	Determiners: languages of type 3 —— 229
Table 17	Determiners: languages of type 4 —— 231
Table 18	Determiners: languages with mixed evidence —— 233
Table 19	Determiners: languages with (some) evidence against a determiner slot —— 236
Table 20	Determiners: identification of determiner slot unknown —— 238

List of Maps

Map 1	Overview of the sample (numbered) (http://bit.ly/sample-numbered) ——	**XVIII**
Map 2	Overview of the sample (http://bit.ly/sample-pn-npn) —— 13	
Map 3	Nominal classification: overview (http://bit.ly/classification-overview) —— 28	
Map 4	Generic-specific structures (http://bit.ly/generic-specific) —— 30	
Map 5	Number of generics (http://bit.ly/generics-number) —— 39	
Map 6	Number of noun classes (http://bit.ly/nc-number) —— 53	
Map 7	Nouns vs. adjectives (http://bit.ly/N-A-classes) —— 73	
Map 8	Number marking (http://bit.ly/numbermarking-overview) —— 92	
Map 9	Word order in the NE (http://bit.ly/wordorder-NP) —— 137	
Map 10	Locus of case marking (http://bit.ly/case-NP) —— 144	
Map 11	Diagnostic slots (http://bit.ly/diagnostic-slot) —— 149	
Map 12	NP construal: types of languages (http://bit.ly/NPconstrual) —— 156	
Map 13	Determiner slots (http://bit.ly/determiner-overview) —— 181	

Abbreviations

Abbreviations used in glosses

1	first person
2	second person
3	third person
I-VII	noun classes
A	agent-like argument of canonical transitive verb
ABL	ablative
ABS	absolutive
ACC	accusative
ACT	actual
ADV	adverbial
AFF	affective
ALL	allative
AMBIPH	ambiphoric pronoun
AN	animate
ANA	anaphoric
ANAPH	anaphoric pronoun
ANTIP	antipassive
ASS	associative
AUG	augmented
AUX	auxiliary
AVERS	aversive
CAUS	causative
CL	class marker
CLF	classifier
CTEMP	contemporaneous
COLL	collective
COM	comitative
COMPL	complete/completive
CONJ	conjunction
CONT	continuous/continuative
CONTR	contrastive focus
CRD	cardinal pronoun
DAT	dative
DECL	declarative
DEF	definite
DEM	demonstrative
DIST	distal
DISTR	distributive/distributed
DM	demonstrative marker
DO	direct object
DU	dual
DUB	dubitative

DYNM	dynamic
EMPH	emphatic
ERG	ergative
EXCL	exclusive
F	feminine
FOC	focus/focal
FOC/TENS	focus/tense
FUT	future
GEN	genitive
GENRL	general
GO&	associated motion
GO&DO	'go to a place and do verb action'
H	higher object
HAB	habitual
HUM	human
IDENTIF	identifiable
IMM	immediate clitic
IMMPST	immediate past
IMP	imperative
INCH	inchoative
INCL	inclusive
INF	infinitive
INS	instrumental
INTENS	intensifier
INTENTV	intentive mood
IO	indirect object
IPFV	imperfective
IRR	irrealis
ITER	iterative
KIN	kin suffix
KPL	kinship plural
L.ALL	local allative
LA	lower animate
LIG	possessor ligative
LK	linker
LL	land gender
LOC	locative
M	masculine
M-	modal case
MED	medial
MI	middle
MIN	minimal
N	neuter
N_w	w-class neuter gender
N-	non- (e.g. NCOMPL non-complete, NSG non-singular, NPST non-past)
NARR	narrative suffix
NEG	negation/negative

XVI — Abbreviations

NMLZR	nominalizer/nominalization
NOM	nominative
NVIS	non-visible
OBJ	object
OBL	oblique
ORIG	origin
P	patient-like argument of canonical transitive verb
PFV	perfective
PL	plural
POSS	possessive
POSSD	possessed
POT	potential
PRED	predicative
PRS	present
PRO	prominence clitic
PROG	progressive
PROP	proprietive
PROX	proximal/proximate
PST	past
PT	potent case inflection
PTCP	participle
PUNC	punctual
PURP	purposive
QUAL	quality nominalizer
R/A	realis/assertive
RECPST	recent past
RDP	reduplication
REAL	realis
RECP	reciprocal
REF	contextual deictic
REL	relative/relativiser
REM	remote
REMPST	remote past
REP	repetition
S	single argument of canonical intransitive verb
SER	serial
SG	singular
SMBL	semblative
SP.PROX	speaker proximate
SR	same referent
SS	same subject
TEL	telic
TEXD	text deictic
TOP	topic
TR	transitive/transitivity morpheme
UA	unit augmented
UNSP	unspecified tense

VCL	verb class marker
VBLZR	verbalizer
VEG	vegetable food
VE	vegetable noun class
VSM	verbal stem marker
^	focal accent
~	separates reduplicated items
>	X > Y: X is agent-like, Y is patient-like argument of transitive verb

Other labels (esp. in templates and tables)

Parts of speech

art	article
dem	demonstrative
inal.poss	inalienable possessor
indef	indefinite
interr	interrogative
loc	locational nominal
log	logical nominal
num	numeral
poss	possessive pronoun
PR	possessor
pron	personal pronoun
quant	quantifying nominal

Template

G	template provided in grammar
W	word order described in grammar, put in template-format by me
E	template based on examples

Other

NP	noun phrase
NE	nominal expression

XVIII —— Overview of the sample

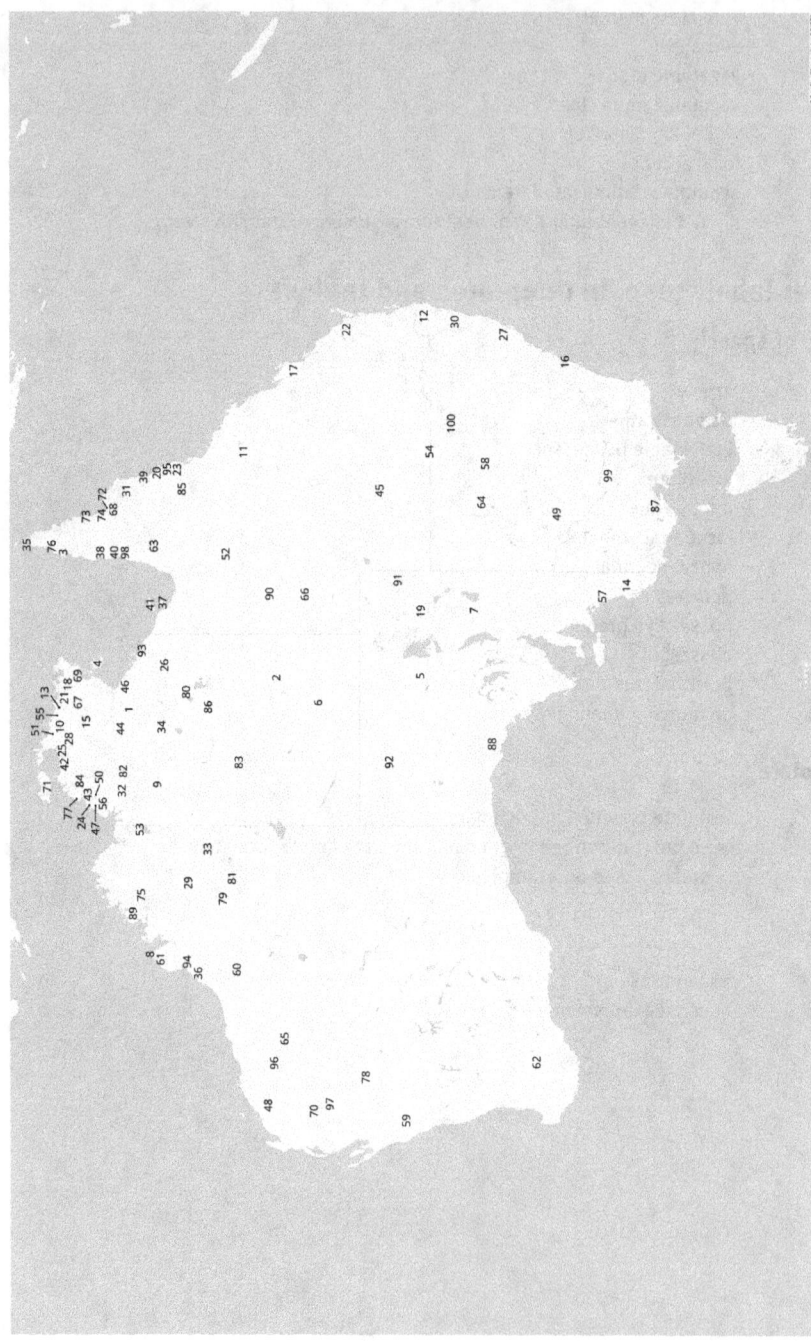

Map 1: Overview of the sample (numbered). For an online, dynamic version of this map, see: http://bit.ly/sample-numbered.

#	Language	#	Language	#	Language
1	Alawa	22	Duungidjawu	43	Malakmalak
2	Alyawarra	23	Dyirbal	44	Mangarrayi
3	Anguthimri	24	Emmi	45	Margany/Gunya
4	Anindilyakwa	25	Gaagudju	46	Marra
5	Arabana/Wangkangurru	26	Garrwa	47	Marrithiyel
6	Arrernte (Mparntwe)	27	Gathang	48	Martuthunira
7	Atynyamathanha	28	Giimbiyu	49	Mathi-Mathi/Letyi-Letyi/Wati-Wati
8	Bardi	29	Gooniyandi	50	Matngele
9	Bilinarra	30	Gumbaynggir	51	Mawng
10	Bininj Kunwok	31	Guugu Yimidhirr	52	Mayi group
11	Biri	32	Jaminjung	53	Miriwung
12	Bundjalung	33	Jaru	54	Muruwari
13	Burarra	34	Jingulu	55	Ndjébbana
14	Bunganditj	35	Kala Lagaw Ya	56	Ngan'gityemerri/Ngan'gikurunggurr
15	Dalabon	36	Karajarri	57	Ngarrindjeri
16	Dharrawal/Dharumba/Dhurga/Djirringanj	37	Kayardild	58	Ngiyambaa
17	Dharumbal	38	Kugu Nganhcara	59	Nhanda
18	Dhuwal (Djapu/Djambarrpuyngu)	39	Kuku Yalanji	60	Nyangumarta
19	Diyari	40	Kuuk Thaayorre	61	Nyulnyul
20	Djabugay	41	Lardil	62	Nyungar
21	Djinang	42	Limilngan	63	Oykangand

XX — Overview of the sample

64	Paakantyi	80	Wambaya	96	Yindjibarndi
65	Panyjima	81	Wangkajunga	97	Yingkarta
66	Pitta-Pitta	82	Wardaman	98	Yir Yoront
67	Rembarrnga	83	Warlpiri	99	Yorta Yorta
68	Rimanggudinhma	84	Warray	100	Yuwaalaraay
69	Ritharngu	85	Warrongo		
70	Tharrgari	86	Warumungu		
71	Tiwi	87	Wathawurrung		
72	Umbuygamu	88	Wirangu		
73	Umpila/Kuuku Ya'u	89	Worrorra		
74	Umpithamu	90	Yalarnnga		
75	Ungarinyin	91	Yandruwandha (Innamincka)		
76	Uradhi	92	Yankunytjatjara		
77	Wadjiginy (Bachamal)	93	Yanyuwa		
78	Wajarri	94	Yawuru		
79	Walmajarri	95	Yidiny		

1 Introduction

1 Aims and overview

The aim of this book is to study noun phrase (NP) structures in Australian languages from a typological perspective, using data from a sample of 100 languages. In the domain of NP structure, Australian languages are probably best known in the typological literature for two characteristics: extensive systems of nominal classification, and noun phrase flexibility. The classic reference on nominal classification in Australia is Dixon (1982), who proposed a basic morphosyntactic distinction between two types of classification, viz. noun class systems and classifier systems. Both types mark nominals as belonging to (largely) semantically based classes, but they differ in their morphosyntactic implementation, as well as their degree of semantic motivation. The first type, noun classes or gender systems, was quite well-known from the study of Indo-European and African languages, but the second type, noun classifiers, had not previously been established as a separate category (Dixon 1982: 159–160, 211–212).[1] The two types are illustrated below in examples from Dyirbal and Yidiny, demonstrating some of the features in which the two systems differ. Example (1) from Dyirbal shows that noun classes are marked by bound forms in agreement patterns, in this case on the demonstratives modifying the nouns, which are marked for one of the four classes in the language (glossed with Roman numerals I-IV). Example (2) from Yidiny shows how classifiers are not marked in agreement patterns, but by free forms juxtaposed to nouns, in this case generic nouns like 'vegetable food' and 'person' classifying the following specific nominals 'yam' and 'girl'.

(1) Dyirbal (Dixon 1982: 161)
    bala   diban   ya-ŋgu-n   yibi-ŋgu   buran
    there.ABS.IV stone.ABS here-ERG-II woman-ERG   look.at
    'The woman here is looking at the stone there.'

(2) Yidiny (Dixon 1982: 185)
    mayi   jimirr   bama-al   yaburu-ŋgu   julaal
    vegetable.ABS yam.ABS   person-ERG   girl-ERG   dig.PST
    'The person girl dug up the vegetable yam.'

---

[1] A third type of classification, viz. numeral classifiers, was again quite well-known from Asian languages (Dixon 1982: 211). This type does not occur in Australian languages.

Dixon (1982) was followed by a whole range of studies on nominal classification in Australian languages (e.g. Dixon 1986; Blake 1987: 94; Johnson 1988; Sands 1995; Harvey & Reid 1997; Wilkins 2000; Singer 2016). Questions addressed in these studies include the degree of grammaticalisation in the system, the semantics of noun classes, and the syntactic analysis of noun classifiers. Aspects of 'Australian-style' classification, including Dixon's basic distinction, have been picked up in the wider typological literature (e.g. Grinevald 2000; Aikhenvald 2003; Corbett 2007: 253–258; Seifart 2010), and are now part of the standard analysis of classification systems (although the basic distinction has obviously not remained unquestioned, see for instance Singer [2016], Corbett & Fedden [2016], Fedden & Corbett [2017]).

The other aspect of NP structure for which Australian languages are renowned is syntactic flexibility, with free word order and the availability of discontinuous NPs; the classic references here are Blake (1983), Hale (1983) and Heath (1986). This is illustrated in an often-quoted set of examples from Kalkatungu in (3), which shows how different word orders are allowed in the NP (3a, d, f) and how different elements can be 'split off' from the rest of the NP (3b, c, e).

(3) Kalkatungu (Blake 1983: 145; cited in Nordlinger 2014: 229)
    a. ***cipa-yi ṭuku-yu yaun-tu*** *yaṇi*   *icayi*
        this-ERG dog-ERG big-ERG white.man bite
        'This big dog bit/bites the white man.'
    b. ***cipa-yi ṭuku-yu*** *yaṇi icayi* ***yaun-tu***
    c. ***ṭuku-yu cipa-yi*** *icayi yaṇi* ***yaun-tu***
    d. ***yaun-tu cipa-yi ṭuku-yu*** *icayi yaṇi*
    e. ***cipa-yi*** *icayi yaṇi* ***ṭuku-yu yaun-tu***
    f. *yaṇi icayi* ***cipa-yi yaun-tu ṭuku-yu***

Such characteristics have played a prominent role in the development of the theoretical notion of 'non-configurationality', which has also found its way into the general theoretical and typological literature (e.g. Jelinek [1984]; the various papers in Marácz & Muysken [1989]; Austin & Bresnan [1996]; Nordlinger [1998b]; Baker [2001]; Rijkhoff [2002: 19–22]; Pensalfini [2004]; see also Croft [2007: 25–27] and Nordlinger [2014: 227–232, 237–241] for overviews). These features have also led to the idea that several Australian languages may lack phrasal structure altogether in the nominal domain (e.g. Hale 1981; Blake 1983; Heath 1984, 1986; Harvey 1992; Evans 2003a: 227–234; Rijkhoff 2002: 19–22). However, this idea is quite problematic in several ways. One is that much of the general literature has a relatively limited empirical basis, usually focusing on the same handful of languages. Another is that individual grammars show a more mixed picture: some confirm the absence of 'classic' NP structure (e.g. Evans [2003a: 227–234] on Bininj Kunwok or Harvey [2001: 112] on Limilngan), while others provide strong evidence in favour of phrasal structure in the nominal domain (e.g. Gaby [2017: 195–197] on Kuuk Thaayorre or Nordlinger [1998a: 131] on Wambaya). Additionally, there are studies which provide alternative functional accounts of phenomena that are traditionally used as arguments against constituency, like discontinuity or phrase fracturing (e.g. McGregor 1989, 1990, 1997; Schultze-Berndt & Simard 2012).

Other aspects of NP structure have received less attention in the Australianist literature, although there are some studies on topics like the status of adjectives as a separate word class (e.g. Dixon 1982, Dixon 2002: 67; also discussed in many individual grammars), number marking (e.g. Dixon 2002: 77; McGregor 2004: 153–154), or the architecture of numeral systems (Bowern & Zentz 2012). In addition, there are some topics that have received little attention in general studies, and are not studied in great detail in reference grammars, like quantifiers in the domain of number, or the entire domain of determination, at least in its syntactic aspects. Thus, our current knowledge of NP structures in Australian languages shows quite a few gaps: there is much work on classification, there are many general claims about NP constituency, but these remain largely unsubstantiated, there is some work on number marking and adjectives, and there is little general work on quantifiers and determiners.

This study tries to fill some of the gaps in the literature by presenting a general analysis of NP structure in Australian languages, with a broad empirical basis. It uses a sample of 100 Australian languages, which represents about 40% of all Australian languages at first contact and about 70% of all Australian languages for which relatively detailed descriptions are available (see section 2 below for details). I develop this analysis in two main parts, each with a different aim and focus. The first part presents a general survey of NP features. In this survey, I try to develop a synthesis of the available Australianist literature, in which I test some of the ideas from the literature on the languages of my sample, and show where Australian languages stand in relation to other languages in the world. The organisation of the survey is inspired by functionalist literature on NP structure, most prominently Rijkhoff (2002), and covers the broad functional domains of classification, qualification, quantification and determination, as well as the overarching question of NP constituency. These domains are to be understood in a broad sense; they are a heuristic tool for organising the data in the survey, rather than a theory of NP structure in Australian languages. In practical terms, the survey consists of four chapters. Chapter 2 deals with nominal classification, which as mentioned above is the best-described aspect of NP structure for Australian languages. Chapter 3 discusses the domain of qualification and includes, for instance, a discussion of the status of adjectives as a separate word class, and some comments on alternative means of modification like compounding, where qualifiers are integrated in the morphological structure of nouns, as illustrated for Bininj Kunwok in (4). Chapter 4 discusses quantification and includes an overview of number marking, which is overall relatively limited for head nouns, but is found more often on the modifiers within the NP, as well as outside the NP; this is illustrated in (5) from Dalabon, where the head noun remains unmarked for number, but the demonstrative as well as the verb have number marking.

(4) Bininj Kunwok (Evans 2003a: 178)
Man-wodj-kare kani-dorrorrke.
VE-log-old   12UA-drag.NPST
'Let's drag the hollow log.'

(5) Dalabon (Cutfield 2011: 123)
[**kanh-ngong** middjinri]   njel=**bula**-h-yeni-nj   **wulad**
DEM:IDENTIF-all missionary   1PL=3PL>O-R/A-accompany-PST.IPFV all
'all those missionaries used to stay with us'

Chapter 5 introduces the domains of determination and NP constituency, which are most poorly understood, due to a general lack of study in the case of determination, and a lack of testing of general claims in the case of constituency.

The second part of this study then takes up the last two aspects, determination and NP constituency, for more detailed analysis. Chapter 6 deals with the question of NP constituency, which as discussed above is a rather problematic issue in the available literature. On the basis of my sample, I show that the idea that Australian languages tend to lack clear phrasal structure is over-stated. I suggest an alternative approach to the question of NP constituency, and argue that it is more interesting to typologise languages on the basis of where and how they allow phrasal structure rather than on the basis of a simple yes-no answer to the question of NP constituency. This alternative approach is followed up in an analysis of discontinuous structures. Chapter 7, finally, investigates the domain of NP determination, which is overall the least well-studied aspect of NP structure for Australian languages. Within this domain, I focus on the syntactic status of determining elements. Australian languages generally lack 'classic' determiner features, like obligatory use in particular (e.g. definite) contexts or a restriction to one determiner per NP. In Ungarinyin, for instance, NPs need not include an element that marks definiteness, specificity or the like, as illustrated in (6a), where the noun *ari* 'man' is used without a determiner and can still be interpreted as definite. When determining elements are included, however, they can easily co-occur, as illustrated in (6b), where both an 'ambiphoric' and an anaphoric pronoun modify the head noun.

(6) Ungarinyin (Spronck 2015: 166)
    a. ***ari***   bern a_1-y_2i   arrangu:: wuran-ra
       man   climb.up 3M.SG-be on.top   tree-LOC
       'The man climbs all the way up the tree'
    b. ***andu***   ***jirri***   ***yila*** nongarrij=karra a_1-ma
       M.AMBIPH M.ANAPH child run.away=MAYBE 3M.SG-do
       'He, this kid might run away'

I show that there is good evidence to identify a determiner slot in approximately half of the languages of the sample, and I discuss which types of elements tend to occur in these slots. Furthermore, I show that there are overall few dedicated determiners, but that at the same time, a whole range of different (non-dedicated) word classes can occur in such a determiner slot.

This ties in with a more general issue that recurs throughout the whole study, viz. the tension between word classes or categories and functional structure in the NP. This is a very basic question, which plays a role in debates on word classes or typologies of word order (e.g. Evans & Osada 2005 and replies by Peterson 2005, Hengeveld & Rijkhoff 2005, and Croft 2005; Dryer 2007b), but also in various theoretical frameworks (e.g. Halliday 1985, Croft 2001). Across the sample, elements are often flexible between different functional roles (and correlating positions), and, conversely, one functional role can often be realised by different word classes. This is not only the case for the determiner role (chapter 7), but also for classifying constructions (chapter 2), or the quantifier role, which can be realised not only by quantifiers but also, for instance, by certain adjectives (chapter 4).

2 Data and methods

2.1 Language sample

Research for this study is based on a sample of 100 Australian languages, which is partly based on convenience and partly on representativeness. The sample is primarily a convenience sample, in two ways: I included only languages for which I could easily access good-quality grammars and other materials, and whenever there was a choice, I favoured languages with more detailed descriptions. It is also partly a representative sample, however, in the sense that it tries to take into account the genetic and areal diversity of Australian languages, covering as many language families and subgroups as possible, and as many regions as possible. Given that only a bit over half of Australian languages have detailed grammatical descriptions, however, proportions are not based on strict measures like Rijkhoff & Bakker's (1998) Diversity Value, but on availability of materials.

In the sample, there are 65 languages representing the large Pama-Nyungan family and 35 representing the various so-called 'non-Pama-Nyungan' families. The large proportion of Pama-Nyungan languages is due to the fact that this family not only includes roughly two thirds of all Australian languages, but also covers almost 90% of the Australian continent (these counts are based on Bowern & Atkinson [2012: 817]). Areally, I have tried to include Pama-Nyungan languages from all over the continent, but the sample contains relatively fewer languages from the regions in the south and southeast that were affected first by European settlement, for which fewer good descriptions are available (see Dixon 2002: 1–3). Genetically, the internal structure of Pama-Nyungan remains uncertain. There is a consensus on many lower-level groupings, but higher-level groupings are often the subject of discussion. The most recent proposal can be found in Bowern & Atkinson (2012). Their highest level of classification shows four main subgroups of Pama-Nyungan, viz. Northern, South-Eastern, Central and Western Pama-Nyungan (these are also mentioned in table 1 below). The sample represents most of the lower-level groupings. The languages that do not belong to the Pama-Nyungan family are traditionally labelled collectively as non-Pama-Nyungan, but in fact they include 24 distinct families and isolates (based on the classification of Evans (2003b)).[2] Almost all of these are represented in my sample,[3] and larger families, like Gunwinyguan, are represented by more than one language (as mentioned, this is largely determined by convenience factors rather than strict methods of calculation).

---

[2] Anindilyakwa, which is traditionally analysed as an isolate (Evans 2003b: 2, 13), has recently been reclassified as Gunwinyguan (van Egmond 2012).
[3] The only three which are not represented are Umbugarla/Ngumbur, Larrakiya and Kungarakany. Their genetic status is uncertain (Evans 2003b: 14).

Table 1: Overview of the sample.

Language name	Genetic status		References
	Pama-Nyungan (PN)		
	Lower-level subgroup	Bowern & Atkinson (2012)	
Kala Lagaw Ya	(unclear)	Northern PN	Ford & Ober (1987, 1991), Stirling (2008)
Uradhi	Northern Paman	Northern PN	Crowley (1983)
Anguthimri	Northern Paman	Northern PN	Crowley (1981)
Umpila/Kuuku Ya'u	Middle Paman	Northern PN	Hill (2018, p.c.), Thompson (1988)
Kugu Nganhcara	Middle Paman	Northern PN	Smith & Johnson (2000)
Umpithamu	Middle Paman	Northern PN	Verstraete (2010, p.c.)
Umbuygamu	Lamalamic	Northern PN	Ogilvie (1994), Sommer (1976, 1998)
Rimanggudinhma	Lamalamic	Northern PN	Godman (1993)
Kuuk Thaayorre	Southwest Paman	Northern PN	Gaby (2017, p.c.)
Oykangand	Southwest Paman	Northern PN	Hamilton (1996), Sommer (1970, 2006)
Yir Yoront	Southwest Paman	Northern PN	Alpher (1973, 1991)
Guugu Yimidhirr	Yimidhirr-Yalanji-Yidinic	Northern PN	Haviland (1979)
Kuku Yalanji	Yimidhirr-Yalanji-Yidinic	Northern PN	Patz (2002)
Yidiny	Yimidhirr-Yalanji-Yidinic	Northern PN	Dixon (1977, 1991)
Djabugay	Yimidhirr-Yalanji-Yidinic	Northern PN	Patz (1991)
Dyirbal	Dyirbal	Northern PN	Dixon (1972)
Warrongo	Maric	Northern PN	Tsunoda (2011, p.c.)
Margany/Gunya	Maric	Northern PN	Breen (1981a)
Biri	Maric	Northern PN	Terrill (1998)
Dharumbal	Dharumbal	Northern PN	Terrill (2002)
Yalarnnga	Kalkatungic	Northern PN	Breen & Blake (2007), Blake (p.c.)

Table 1 (continued)

Language name	Genetic status		References
	Pama-Nyungan (PN)		
	Lower-level subgroup	*Bowern & Atkinson (2012)*	
Mayi	Mayi	Northern PN	Breen (1981b)
Duungidjawu	Waka-Kabi	South-Eastern PN	Kite & Wurm (2004)
Gumbaynggir	Gumbaynggir	South-Eastern PN	Eades (1979)
Bundjalung	Bandjalangic	South-Eastern PN	Sharpe (2005), Cunningham (1969)
Yuwaalaraay	Central New South Wales	South-Eastern PN	Williams (1980), Giacon (2017, p.c.)
Ngiyambaa	Central New South Wales	South-Eastern PN	Donaldson (1980)
Muruwari	Muruwari	South-Eastern PN	Oates (1988)
Gathang	Yuin-Kuri	South-Eastern PN	Lissarrague (2010)
Dharrawal/ Dharumba/ Dhurga/ Djirringanj	Yuin-Kuri	South-Eastern PN	Besold (2012)
Wathawurrung	Kulin	South-Eastern PN	Blake (1998 ed.)
Mathi-Mathi/Letyi-Letyi/ Wati-Wati	Kulin	South-Eastern PN	Blake et al. (2011), Morey (p.c.)
Yorta Yorta	Yorta Yorta	South-Eastern PN	Bowe & Morey (1999), Morey (p.c.)
Bunganditj	Bunganditj	South-Eastern PN	Blake (2003, p.c.)
Ngarrindjeri	Lower Murray	South-Eastern PN	Bannister (2004), Yallop (1975)

Table 1 (continued)

Language name	Genetic status		References
	Pama-Nyungan (PN)		
	Lower-level subgroup	*Bowern & Atkinson (2012)*	
Arabana/ Wangkangurru	Karnic	Central PN	Hercus (1994)
Pitta-Pitta	Karnic	Central PN	Blake (1979b, p.c.)
Diyari	Karnic	Central PN	Austin (1981, 2011)
Yandruwandha (Innamincka)	Karnic	Central PN	Breen (2004a, b)
Paakantyi	Paakantyi	Central PN	Hercus (1982)
Atynyamathanha	Thura-Yura	Central PN	Schebeck (1974)
Wirangu	Thura-Yura	Central PN	Hercus (1999)
Alyawarra	Arandic	Central PN	Yallop (1977)
Arrernte (Mparntwe)	Arandic	Central PN	Wilkins (1989)
Warumungu	Ngumpin-Yapa	Western PN	Simpson (1998, 2002), Simpson & Heath (ms), Capell (1953)
Warlpiri	Ngumpin-Yapa	Western PN	Hale (1995), Hale et al. (1995), Nash (1986), Simpson (1983), Swartz (1982)
Bilinarra	Ngumpin-Yapa	Western PN	Meakins & Nordlinger (2014, p.c.)
Jaru	Ngumpin-Yapa	Western PN	Tsunoda (1981, p.c.), Blythe (p.c.)
Walmajarri	Ngumpin-Yapa	Western PN	Hudson (1978), Hudson & Richards (1984), Richards (1979)
Nyangumarta	Marrngu	Western PN	Sharp (2004)
Karajarri	Marrngu	Western PN	McKelson (1989), Sands (1989)

Table 1 (continued)

Language name	Genetic status		References
	Pama-Nyungan (PN)		
	Lower-level subgroup	*Bowern & Atkinson (2012)*	
Yankunytjatjara	Wati	Western PN	Goddard (1985)
Wangkajunga	Wati	Western PN	Jones (2011)
Martuthunira	Ngayarta	Western PN	Dench (1994)
Yindjibarndi	Ngayarta	Western PN	Wordick (1982)
Panyjima	Ngayarta	Western PN	Dench (1991)
Tharrgari	Mantharta	Western PN	Klokeid (1969)
Wajarri	Kartu	Western PN	Douglas (1981), Marmion (1996)
Yingkarta	Kartu	Western PN	Dench (1998)
Nhanda	Nhanda	Western PN	Blevins (2001)
Nyungar	Nyungar	Western PN	Douglas (1976)
Ritharngu	Yolngu	Western PN	Heath (1980)
Dhuwal (Djapu/Djambarrpuyngu)	Yolngu	Western PN	Morphy (1983), Wilkinson (1991), Jepson (p.c.)
Djinang	Yolngu	Western PN	Waters (1989)[4]
Yanyuwa	Warluwaric	Western PN	Kirton (1971), Kirton & Charlie (1996), Bradley (1992)
	non-Pama-Nyungan		
	Family		
Kayardild	Tangkic		Evans (1995a), Round (2013, p.c.)
Lardil	Tangkic		Klokeid (1976)
Garrwa	Garrwan		Mushin (2012, p.c.)

---

4 Note that Waters' grammar also includes some information about Djinba, "[t]he Yolngu language most similar to Djinang" (Waters 1989: xv). Djinba is not part of my sample.

Table 1 (continued)

Language name	Genetic status	References
	non-Pama-Nyungan *Family*	
Marra	Marran	Heath (1981), Dickson (p.c.)
Marra	Marran	Heath (1981), Dickson (p.c.)
Alawa	Marran	Sharpe (1972)
Mangarrayi	Marran	Merlan (1989)
Wambaya	Mindi	Nordlinger (1998a, p.c.)
Jingulu	Mindi	Pensalfini (2003)
Jaminjung	Mindi	Schultze-Berndt (2000, p.c.)
Emmi	Western Daly	Ford (1998)
Marrithiyel	Western Daly	Green (1989, 1997)
Matngele	Eastern Daly	Zandvoort (1999)
Ngan'gityemerri/ Ngan'gikurunggurr	Southern Daly	Reid (1990, 1997)
Malakmalak	Northern Daly	Birk (1976), Tryon (1974), Hoffmann (p.c.)
Wadjiginy (Bachamal)	Anson Bay	Ford (1990), Tryon (1974)
Wardaman	Wardaman/ Wagiman	Merlan (1994)
Gaagudju	Gaagudju	Harvey (2002)
Limilngan	Limilngan	Harvey (2001)
Tiwi	Tiwi	Lee (1987)
Giimbiyu	Giimbiyu	Campbell (2006)
Warray	Gunwinyguan	Harvey (1986, ms)
Rembarrnga	Gunwinyguan	McKay (1975), Saulwick (2003)

Table 1 (continued)

Language name	Genetic status	References
	non-Pama-Nyungan	
	Family	
Anindilyakwa	Gunwinyguan	Leeding (1989), van Egmond (2012, p.c.), Bednall (p.c.)
Bininj Kunwok	Gunwinyguan	Evans (2003a)
Dalabon	Gunwinyguan	Cutfield (2011)
Burarra	Maningrida	Green (1987), Glasgow (1994), Carew (p.c.)
Ndjébbana	Maningrida	McKay (2000)
Mawng	Iwaidjan	Singer (2006, 2016, p.c.), Forrester (2015, p.c.)
Gooniyandi	Bunuban	McGregor (1990, p.c.)
Nyulnyul	Nyulnyulan	McGregor (2011, p.c.)
Bardi	Nyulnyulan	Bowern (2012a, p.c.)
Yawuru	Nyulnyulan	Hosokawa (1991)
Worrorra	Worrorran	Clendon (2000, 2014)
Ungarinyin	Worrorran	Rumsey (1982), Spronck (2015, p.c.)
Miriwung	Jarrakan	Kofod (1978)

Overall, the sample represents about 40% of all languages spoken at first contact, on conservative counts (like Dixon 2002: 5–7). If we take the number of languages with detailed descriptions available, the sample includes about 70% of these.[5]

---

[5] This percentage is based on the number of languages marked as having a 'grammar' in Hammarström's (2014) overview of documentation of Australian languages (i.e. not a 'grammar sketch' or 'wordlist'). 74 of the 106 languages in this category are in my sample, 32 are not. (Note that for this count I have treated different varieties of the same language as one, e.g. Djapu and Djambarrpuyngu, and excluded creoles.) The other 26 languages in my sample are less detailed grammars, often for regions where little detailed information is available, or more recent studies not yet included in Hammerström (2014).

An overview of the sample can be found in table 1, showing the genetic classification and the sources used for each language. General databases like OZBIB (Carrington & Triffitt 1999; Triffitt 2006; OZBIB) and Glottolog (Hammarström et al. 2019) can be consulted for further sources on individual languages.

Map 1 on page XVIII links every language of the sample to a location in Australia, accompanied by a numbered, alphabetical list. Map 2 below provides a geographic overview of the sample, showing the non-Pama-Nyungan languages in orange (as mentioned above, this actually covers 21 different families), and the Pama-Nyungan languages in blue.

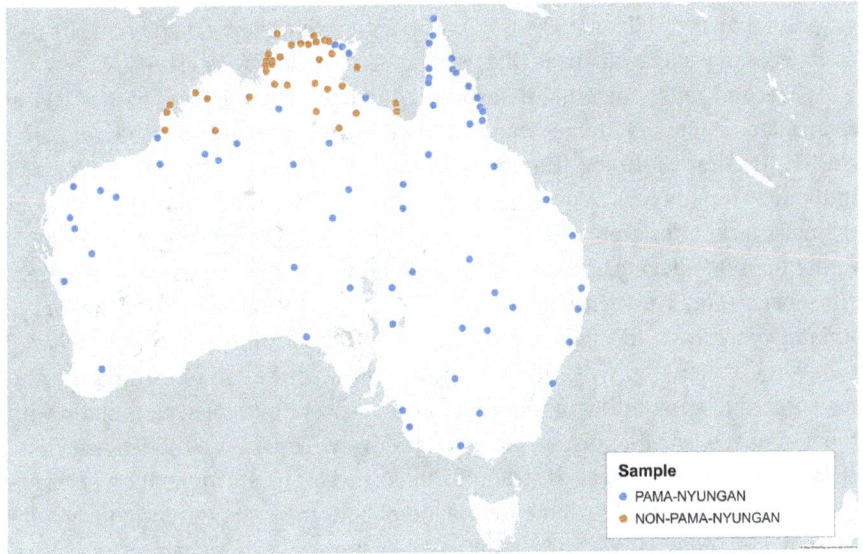

Map 2: Overview of the sample. For an online, dynamic version of this map, see: http://bit.ly/sample-pn-npn.

Some further notes about the sample are in order here. A first note concerns the treatment of language varieties. As can be seen in the table above, some of the labels used for the sample languages consist of different varieties, like Margany/Gunya or Arabana/Wangkangurru. Since these varieties are often treated together in one grammatical description, I do not usually make a distinction between them in my analyses and treat them as one language. The same goes for Dhuwal, even though in this case, the two varieties are described in separate grammars (Djapu in Morphy [1983], and Djambarrpuyngu in Wilkinson [1991]). The situation is different for Yankunytjatjara and Wangkajunga, which are treated as separate languages in this sample, even though they are both varieties of the Western Desert language. This is a well-known case of a dialect continuum, however, and Yankunytjatjara and Wangkajunga represent different dialectal groups, viz. the 'south-eastern' and the 'north-western' group respectively. These show quite a few linguistic differences (e.g. Jones 2011: 9–10, 11–22; Goddard 1985: 6–8), which warrant a treatment as separate languages for my purposes (see for instance chapter 6 and corresponding tables 10 and 11 for differences in word order and locus of case marking in the NP; or chapter 2, section 2.1 for differences in generic-specific structures). Note that other varieties of the dialect continuum are not further discussed in this study, with the exception of a few references to Pitjantjatjara (south-eastern group), which was the subject of a study with particular focus on NP constituency (Bowe 1990). Finally, Alyawarra and Mparntwe Arrernte are included in the sample as separate languages, following Wilkins (1989: 6–15), who argues that they should not be treated as varieties of a single language (the position taken earlier by Hale [1962]).

A second note concerns the orthography used for language names. Many Australian language names have several spelling variants (see Austlang [AUSTLANG] or Glottolog [Hammarström et al. 2019] for alternative names of individual languages). Where there is a choice, I use the form that is used in the most recent description of the language (e.g. I use *Bundjalung* [Sharpe 2005] rather than *Bandjalang* [Crowley 1978]) or the one that represents the most recent consensus (e.g. I use *Jaru* instead of *Djaru*, *Paakantyi* instead of *Bāgandji*, *Anindilyakwa* instead of *Enindhilyakwa*, and *Bininj Kunwok* instead of *Bininj Gun-wok*). Otherwise, I use the language names as they are best known, and have not made any orthographic adjustments, except by replacing ŋ and ɲ with the more keyboard-friendly *ng* and *ny* respectively. Thus, I use *Dyirbal* instead of *Dyirrbal*, and *Gumbaynggir* instead of *Gumbaynggirr*. The orthography of examples is equally left as it is. More information about the orthographic conventions for individual languages can be found in their respective grammars.

2.2 Data

2.2.1 Delineation

The focus of this study is on simple NPs with nominal heads, like the two NPs in (7), the first one with an adjective, demonstrative and third person pronoun modifying a head noun ('man'), and the second one with a combination of a generic ('game') and a specific noun ('kangaroo').

(7) Arrernte (Mparntwe) (Wilkins 1989: 111)
 [Artwe kngerre nhenhe re] [kere aherre] tyerre-ke.
 man big this 3SG.A game kangaroo shoot-PST.CONT
 'This big man shot a kangaroo.'

In other words, there is a whole range of structures that I do not include in my analysis. For instance, I do not include NPs with pronominal heads. Complex NPs are also excluded, like NPs with other NPs embedded in them (e.g. elements marked with an adnominal case marker),[6] as in (8), or inclusory constructions, as in (9), which consist of a non-singular pronoun and an element referring to a member of the group identified by this pronoun. For studies of these types of NPs, see, for instance, Dench & Evans (1988) and Singer (2001).

(8) Yingkarta (Dench 1979; cited in Dench & Evans 1988: 8)
 ngatha mapara-nma-rni kunta **kartu-wu japurta-parri-yu.**
 1SG.NOM bring-PST-HENCE water man-DAT beard-PROP-DAT
 'I brought water for the man with a beard.'

(9) Guugu Yimidhirr (Haviland 1979: 105; cited in Singer 2001: 35)
 Ngaliinh Dyaagi-ngun gambarr balga-y
 1DU.EXCL(NOM) <name>-ERG pitch(ABS) make-PST
 'Jack and I made the pitch' (literally: we two, including Jack [DL])

2.2.2 Data collection

The main sources of data for this study are of course the grammatical descriptions available, as listed in the right-hand column in table 1 above. This has some well-known limitations, which are typical of any typological study. The most important limitation is the indirect approach, viz. the need to rely on other people's analyses and on the information provided in the grammar. I have tried to make up for this in two ways. First, in addition to studying grammars I have also had the chance to discuss some questions with fieldworkers who have first-hand experience with some languages (see table 1 above and the Acknowledgements for more details). Second, I have always used both the description itself and any texts or other examples that accompany the description. Especially for grammars where the description of the NP is less detailed or seems to be based mostly on elicitation materials, I have browsed the texts and examples to add to the available information (though of course I have not done any detailed discourse analysis). Whenever I have done this, this is mentioned explicitly in the relevant tables that summarise my analysis of the sources. It should also be noted here that part of the examples in grammars are the result of

---

[6] This means that I exclude possessor NPs from my analysis, but include possessive pronouns (even though they often have similar distributions).

elicitation work, which yield a different type of data than narratives or other types of natural speech. In several languages, for instance, the use of longer NPs (i.e. more than two or three words) is reported to be rare in natural speech (e.g. Cutfield [2011: 56] on Dalabon; Reid [1997: 167] on Ngan'gityemerri/ Ngan'gikurunggurr), and examples of longer NPs often seem to be more artificial. In general, I have tried to use all information available in the grammars, but whenever there is an issue with the quality of the data, I try to address this explicitly.

One of the consequences of this indirect approach is that not all languages can be categorised for all of the features studied, as some grammars provide limited information – or none at all – on a specific feature. When information is based solely on examples, this of course also has its limitations: it is especially difficult to prove that something is *not* there (e.g. an alternative word order or a type of number marking). This means that counts of the type 'X languages show number marking of type X' are often only approximate. This is especially the case for the counts in Part I (the survey), for which the analysis is less detailed than in Part II.

2.2.3 Terminological and other conventions

In most of this study, I use the term 'noun phrase' (NP) in a general functional sense, and not a syntactically precise one (for the sake of easy reading and straightforward connection with the general literature), except where constituency is itself the subject of the discussion. This is the case particularly in chapter 6, where I distinguish between NPs as nominal expressions that show evidence for constituency, and NEs (nominal expressions) as the general term for nominal elements that belong together semantically, regardless of whether they show evidence for constituency. In this, I follow the terminological conventions used in Himmelmann (1997). Similarly, terms for word classes (like noun and adjective) are not to be understood as claims about word class status in individual languages, which as mentioned above is a recurrent issue for Australian languages (and is not entirely resolved for individual languages in this book). Whenever word class status itself is not the subject of discussion, relevant terms are to be understood in a broad, functional sense. For instance, the term adjective is used for property words which function as attributive modifiers in a nominal expression, regardless of whether they are specialised in that function or not in the individual language. The exception is, of course, where word class status is itself the subject of discussion, as in the sections on classifiers (chapter 2), adjectives (chapter 3) or quantifiers (chapter 4).

Finally, a short comment is required on the representation of examples and templates of NP structures in the rest of this study. Examples are given in their original orthography, but glossing is mostly unified according to the Leipzig

Glossing Rules (Comrie et al. [2015]; see Abbreviations for more details). In what follows, I occasionally also present templates for NP structures (especially in chapters 6 and 7). For this, I use the following conventions: (G) indicates that the template is provided as such in the grammar; (W) indicates that the grammar does not provide a template, but word orders are described explicitly in the grammar, and put in template format by me; (E) indicates that the template is based on examples throughout the grammar and texts (as explained in section 2.2.2, analyses based on examples and text samples should be treated with caution, especially if the number of examples is limited). A combination of these is also possible, e.g. (W+E) indicates that the template is partly based on what is specified in the grammar and partly on examples (for instance, when the order of a particular modifier is not given by the author, I have checked the examples for this). The use of brackets in NP templates indicates optionality, but because not all grammars in the sample provide information on this issue, the absence of brackets does not indicate that all elements are obligatory.

2.3 Maps

2.3.1 Using the maps

Throughout this study, I use maps to visualise the data and corresponding analyses. These maps basically include a data-point for each language of the sample, and further show how languages are categorised according to a particular feature.

The purpose of the maps is slightly different for the different parts of the study. The maps in the survey chapters (Part I) are mostly intended as a practical and efficient way to present data. In line with the set-up of these chapters, they are not meant to be exhaustive: they represent data that was available fairly directly in the grammars, without too much interference of my own analysis (see also above). The maps in Part II, by contrast, are a representation and visualisation of my own analysis, and they add significantly to the information found in the text and the corresponding tables. They are more exhaustive than the survey maps, and as such they can also be used to investigate areal and genetic patterns.

In practical terms, each map has two versions, an online and an offline one. The offline version is an image inserted in the text. The online version is the more interesting one, as it is dynamic and allows the user to zoom in and to see extra information. Hovering over a language point reveals the language name, while clicking on a language point gives more information on certain features. For example, in the case of map 2 above, the information window shows more details about the genetic status of the language in question. All maps used here can be found via this webpage: http://dlouagie.carto.com/maps. Individual (shortened) links are provided with each map as well. All maps are publicly available. The underlying material for the maps is archived in the University of Leuven's repository (retrievable via this shortened link: http://bit.ly/data-maps-Louagie2020); note that this does not represent a full database nor an analysis in itself.

2.3.2 Making the maps

The maps have been created with the online mapmaking tool Carto, inspired by Gawne & Ring (2016). In Carto, I use Open Street Map ('Positron (lite)') as my basemap.[7]

Information on the location of the languages is based on Bowern's (2011) dataset 'Centroid Coordinates for Australian languages'. For a few languages in the sample some additional choices had to be made. First, the data set consists of coordinates at the level of language varieties or dialects, while my sample is situated at the level of languages (see section 2.1). In other words, some languages of my sample have more than one set of coordinates (viz. one for each variety) in the data set. In such cases, I have used the coordinates of one variety only, so as to have one data-point per language. For example, Margany and Gunya are two dialects of the same language (Breen 1981a: 275), and are treated together in the grammatical description and in my analysis (see section 2.1). They are, however, represented by separate coordinates for each dialect in Bowern's file. I have only represented them by one set of coordinates on my maps, viz. those of Margany. Such choices do not pose a problem for the interpretation of the maps, as the aim is to provide a general visualisation of data and analyses, and multiple data-points would only create confusion. (Besides, the locations of the varieties are often very close to each other.) A second comment concerns two languages in the sample (Giimbiyu and Matngele) which do not have 'point' locations in the file, but 'area' locations (Bowern 2011: 'Polygon Coordinates for Australian languages'). This was resolved by taking the coordinates of a random point roughly in the middle of these areas. Finally, there are two languages in the sample, Rimanggudinhma and Umbuygamu, that do not seem to have coordinates available at all in the files. For these languages, I have used coordinates provided by Verstraete (p.c.), based on his fieldwork and archival work in the region.

---

[7] See https://carto.com. Open Street Map is open data (see http://www.openstreetmap.org/copyright for more details).

Part I: **Survey of NP features**

Part I of this study provides a survey of what we know about NPs and related expressions in Australian languages. The aim is to develop a consolidated account of the literature, by testing some of the ideas found in earlier work on the languages of my sample, and by linking back to the broader typological literature to show where these languages stand in relation to languages in the rest of the world. This lays the groundwork for more detailed analysis in Part II, where I take up what I consider to be the most urgent questions to come out of the survey, viz. the question of NP constituency and the status of determining elements. I hope that the survey provided here can be used as a basis for further work by typologists and fieldworkers dealing with Australian languages.

The chapters in Part I are set up along basic functional lines, covering four broad functional domains, viz. classification (chapter 2), qualification (chapter 3), quantification (chapter 4) and determination (chapter 5, section 1), as well as the overarching question of NP constituency (chapter 5, section 2). This organisation is inspired by a wide range of functionalist work on NP structure, most prominently Rijkhoff (2002), but also McGregor (1997b) and Van Valin (2005: 21–30). The same basic domains have also been singled out in general typological surveys, e.g. Corbett (1991) and Aikhenvald (2003) on classification, Riessler (2016) on qualification, Corbett (2000) on number, and Himmelmann (1997) and Lyons (1999) on determination. The question of NP constituency has its origins in the Australianist literature (e.g. Hale 1983; Blake 1983; Heath 1986), but has also been discussed in other typological studies (e.g. Rijkhoff 2002: 19–22; Krasnoukhova 2012: 167–191). In any case, the domains used here should be understood in a broad sense, as a heuristic tool for organising issues and data in this survey, and not as a theory of how NPs are structured in Australian languages.

As mentioned in the introduction, one recurrent issue in all of these domains is the tension between categories and functional structure: is there a dedicated word class for a particular function, or only a functional slot that can attract elements from various non-specialised categories?[8] In chapter 2, this tension surfaces in the syntactic analysis of generic-specific structures, where competing ideas about the status of generics as 'true classifiers' are resolved in a structural analysis (Wilkins 1989). In chapter 3, this issue plays a role in the debate on the word class status of 'adjectives', and the relative value of the various criteria used to distinguish such classes. Chapter 5, finally, discusses how a determiner role can be realised by different word classes (section 1), and how the overall flexibility of categories in different functions plays a role in the analysis of word order in the NP, and consequently also in the analysis of NP constituency (section 2).

---

8 Many thanks to Kristin Davidse for her queries and suggestions with respect to this issue.

https://doi.org/10.1515/9781501512933-002

Each chapter also contains a number of maps (see also section 2.2 in chapter 1), to give the reader an idea of the spread of particular features in the sample. In the spirit of this part of the study, the maps are intended to give a first overview based on the available data, but not to present an exhaustive analysis of certain features, or to discern areal patterns.

2 Nominal classification

Nominal classification is the domain that has been studied in most detail in the literature. In the first section, I discuss how nominal classification is defined in the typological literature, specifically which types of nominal classification can be distinguished, and I give an overview of the available Australianist literature and of the types of classification found in Australian languages. Sections 2 to 4 then study each of these types of classification in more detail, viz. noun classifiers (section 2), verbal and adjectival classifiers (section 3), and noun classes (section 4). The final sections discuss two peculiar cases, viz. systems that are in between two types of classification (section 5), and languages that have multiple classification systems at once (section 6). In the spirit of a survey chapter, this is an overview of the main tendencies in my data, but not an exhaustive analysis in any way.

1 Typology of nominal classification

Nominal classification is a cover term for systems that overtly distinguish subclasses of nouns, and mark them as such with classifying elements that co-occur with the nouns or their dependents. For instance, in Kugu Nganhcara *yampim* 'yam' is classified as a type of vegetable food by co-occurrence with *mayi* in (10), and in Ungarinyin *ari* 'man' is classified as masculine by the use of the masculine form of the modifying anaphoric pronoun in (11).

(10) Kugu Nganhcara (Smith & Johnson 2000: 432)
 ngaya thuca-nga **mayi yampim** wa'i-nhu-wu
 1SG.NOM bend.over-1SG VEG yam dig-INF-DAT
 'I'm bending over to dig up yams.'

(11) Ungarinyin (Spronck 2016: 27)
 ari jirri
 man M.ANAPH
 'man'

Several authors have argued that a more precise set of criteria is needed to define classification systems, in order to distinguish them from other structures with related functions, like compound structures (McGregor 2002: 4–22; Seifart 2010). For instance, to speak of a classification system, a substantial proportion of the nouns needs to be classified, by combination with a smaller number of classificatory elements, and only in well-defined grammatical contexts. Thus, in Ungarinyin, all nouns are classified into four or five classes, including the masculine class illustrated in (11) above, and this is indicated by patterns of agreement throughout the NP (i.e. in a clear grammatical context). By contrast, compound structures like *blueberry* and *strawberry* in English are somewhat similar in that they name different types of berries, but it is not true that a substantial proportion of the English nouns is classified in this way, or that this is tied to certain grammatical contexts (it is rather a matter of lexicon). These criteria have been put together in a definition of nominal classification by Seifart (2010: 719; in an adaptation of McGregor 2002: 16–22):

(i) "Nouns collocate in well-defined grammatical environments with classificatory elements (these may be free forms, clitics, affixes, etc., and these may also occur elsewhere).
(ii) The number of classificatory elements is larger than 1 but significantly smaller than the number of nouns.
(iii) Classificatory elements show different patterns of collocation with nouns, i.e. they impose a classification (some overlap is allowed; prototypically, there is a relatively equal division of the nominal lexicon by classificatory elements).
(iv) At least a substantial subpart of nouns are classified in this way."

(Seifart 2010: 719)[9]

Within the domain of nominal classification, much of the typological work shows a consensus on a basic distinction between noun class or gender systems on the one hand and classifier systems on the other hand (e.g. Dixon 1982a, b, c; Grinevald 2000: 55–62; Aikhenvald 2003; Corbett 2007: 253–258; Seifart 2010; though see further in this section for some more recent work that questions this distinction). Both types are functionally systems of classification as defined above, but the major difference relates to whether the system is mainly grammatical, i.e. a closed system with clear morphosyntactic implications beyond the classifying element, or more lexical, i.e. a fairly open system with few morphosyntactic implications. The two types have been linked in terms of a process of grammaticalisation (Grinevald 2000; Seifart 2010), with some cases in between (Corbett 2007: 254–255; see also section 5), although it is not clear whether this is a necessary link (see section 6). A table summarising the main differences

---

9 Concerning point (iii), it is unclear whether classification systems really divide the nominal lexicon relatively equally and whether this should be a decisive criterion; see also section 2.

between the two types can be found below, taken from Grinevald (2000: 62), based on Dixon (1982c; 1986).

Table 2: Noun class vs. classifier (Grinevald 2000: 62).

	Noun class – gender systems	Classifier systems
1.	classify *all* nouns	do not classify all nouns
2.	into a smallish number of classes	into largish number
3.	of a *closed* system	of an open system
4.	fused with other grammatical categories (Def, Nb, Case)	independent constituent
5.	can be marked on noun	not affixed to noun
6.	realised in agreement patterns	marked once
7.	N uniquely assigned to a class with no speaker variation	N possibly assigned to various classes at speaker's will
8.	no variation in register	formal/informal uses

Noun classes are typically a relatively small and closed set, and they are defined mainly in terms of their morphosyntactic implications, e.g. the patterns of agreement they trigger. An example is Jingulu (Pensalfini 2003: 160–169). Jingulu has four noun classes, masculine, feminine, neuter and vegetable, which are marked in the agreement patterns of the noun modifiers ('agreement targets' in Corbett [2007: 244]) with the head nominal ('agreement controller'). This is shown in (12), where the attributive modifier and demonstrative inflect for the masculine class in (12a) and the demonstrative for the feminine class in (12b). Noun classes are widespread in the languages of the world: apart from some Australian languages (mainly non-Pama-Nyungan), they occur, amongst others, in most Indo-European and many African languages, many Papuan languages, and some North, Central and South American languages (Aikhenvald 2003: 77–80; Corbett 2013: §2).[10]

---

10 Note that noun class systems are also known as gender systems in some grammatical traditions, especially when relatively few classes are distinguished (often based on the sex of the referent), as in French, while the term noun class is often reserved for systems with a larger number of classes, as in Bantu languages (Grinevald 2000: 57; Dixon 2002: 452; Corbett 2007: 242; Seifart 2010: 731). It seems to me that this distinction has no solid morphosyntactic basis, so I treat these systems as one. I have chosen to use the term 'noun class' as a cover term, following the Australianist tradition (see further below).

(12) Jingulu (Pensalfini 2003: 106, 177)
    a. *Wunya-nga-yi* **nginda-rni marluka balika**   *ya-ju*
       give-1SG-FUT   that(M)-FOC old.man hungry(M) 3SG-do
       jabarrka   ngunya-nga-yi.
       liver   give-1SG-FUT
       'I'll give the liver to that hungry old man.'
    b. *Yawulyu, jujurrka-ju,*   **ngina-rni nayurni** *ngarnu*
       love.song love.dance-do that(F)-ERG woman   3SG.ACC.M
       maja   rriyi.
       get   will.go
       'That woman is performing a love song and dance in order to get him.'

Unlike noun classes, classifiers usually do not have morphosyntactic implications like agreement, they are often a relatively open set, and they tend to be more flexible in their use. They can be subdivided in terms of the specific grammatical construction that requires their use, for example numeral classifiers, genitive classifiers, verbal classifiers, and – the most general type – noun classifiers (see e.g. Grinevald 2000; Seifart 2010). Only noun classifiers are common in Australian languages; verbal classifiers also occur in a few languages, and there is one instance of adjectival classifiers. I briefly exemplify noun classifiers and verbal classifiers here.

Noun classifiers are not triggered by a specific grammatical construction (as other types of classifiers are) but generally occur with nouns. They are normally free forms (Grinevald 2000: 64–65; Seifart 2010: 722). An example can be found in (13), from Kugu Nganhcara, where the two nouns in the structure are accompanied by noun classifiers (glossed in small capitals). Apart from in Australian languages, noun classifiers are found in Mesoamerican and some South American languages, and in some Western Austronesian, Oceanic, Tai-Kadai and Austroasiatic languages (Aikhenvald 2003: 96–97).

(13) Kugu Nganhcara (Smith & Johnson 2000: 386)
    yuku pinci   aara   agu   muci-ng   mata
    THING crocodile that.ABS PLACE bank-LOC climb
    'That crocodile climbed the bank.'

Verbal classifiers are morphologically part of the verb, but they classify nouns that are arguments of this verb. Verbal classifiers can take the form of an incorporated element (which can also be used as a root), as in (14) from Bininj Kunwok, or of an affix (which cannot be used as a root), as in (15) from Anindilyakwa (van Egmond 2012: 247–249; see also Grinevald 2000: 67 and

Seifart 2010: 722–723, for more details and other examples). Apart from a few Australian languages, verbal classifiers are found in some North American languages, in Lowland Amazonian languages, and in several Papuan languages (Aikhenvald 2003: 169–171).

(14) Bininj Kunwok (Evans 2003a: 328; also cited in van Egmond 2012: 248)
    a. *An-barnadja*   *ngarri-**mim**-bo+wo-ni.*
        III-owenia.vemicosa   1A-fruit-water+put-PST.IPFV
        'We used to put the fruit of *owenia vernicosa* in the water (to poison the fish).'
    b. *An-barnadja*   *(**an-mim**)*[11] *ngarri-bo+wo-ni.*
        III-o.vemicosa   III-fruit   1A-water+put-PST.IPFV
        'We used to put *owenia vernicosa* fruit in the water.'

(15) Anindilyakwa (van Egmond 2012: 251)
     *na-**lyangk**-arrnga*   *awarnda*
     N-hard.and.round-break.ATOMICPST   N.rock
     'the rock broke'

While a distinction between noun class and classifier is part of a broad typological consensus, it is not always as neat as suggested by the discussion so far (see table 2). For example, noun class systems sometimes allow variable assignment of nouns to classes, depending for instance on perspectivisation, as argued by Singer (2016) (see further in section 4.2.2). The characterisation of classifier systems is also not as simple as the table above suggests: it is unclear, for example, where the boundary is between genuine classifier systems and somewhat less systematic combinations of generic and specific nouns (as discussed in more detail in section 2.1 for the Australian sample). Finally, the fact that many languages (including some in Australia, see section 6) have multiple systems also seems to undermine the validity of this distinction somewhat (see Fedden & Corbett 2017 for argumentation). In spite of these issues, however, I think the distinction is useful as a basic typological tool, and I keep it as a way of organising the data in this chapter, in order to allow more focused discussion as well as comparison between different systems.

Turning to my sample, a total of 64 languages, or almost two thirds of the languages, have some form of nominal classification. Of these, 31 languages have noun classes, 37 have (incipient) noun classifiers, and four have verbal classifiers.

---

[11] The brackets indicate the optionality of this element (Evans 2003a: 328).

There is one language, Anindilyakwa, that can be said to have 'adjectival classifiers'. These counts are approximate, because it is not always straightforward to determine whether a language truly has a classification system, especially in the case of noun classifiers (traditionally known as generic-specific structures in the Australian literature; more on this in section 2 below). An overview map showing the languages which I analyse as having a system of nominal classification can be found below (map 3). Geographical and genetic distribution is discussed per system, in each of the corresponding sections.

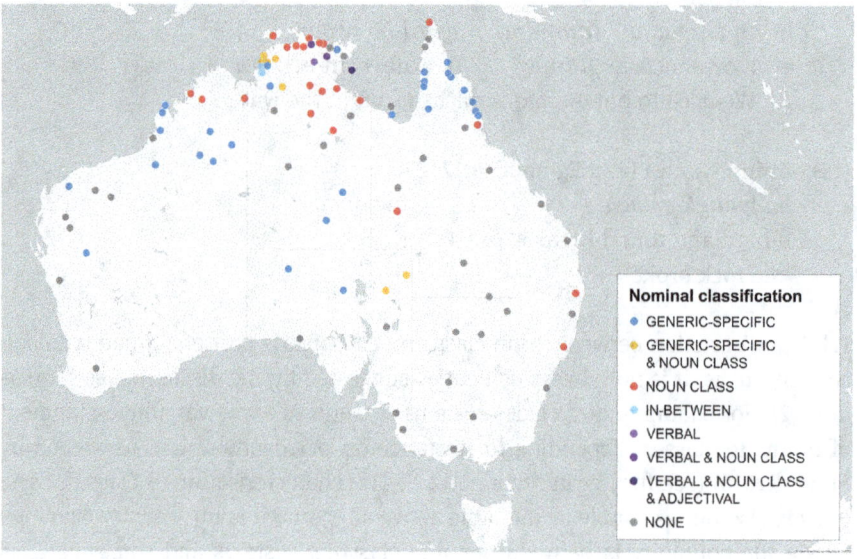

Map 3: Nominal classification: overview. For an online, dynamic version of the map, see: http://bit.ly/classification-overview.

There is quite a bit of literature on nominal classification in Australia, which is the best studied aspect of NP structure overall for Australian languages. Sands (1995) provides a good cross-linguistic study, discussing the types of classification that can be found in Australian languages, as well as proposing reconstructions for some classifier forms. Dixon (2002: 449–514) focuses on the distinction between types of classification, and devotes special attention to the distribution of the different types across the continent and the motivation for the assignment of nouns to classes. Apart from these two continent-wide surveys, there are many studies of classification in individual languages or regions, especially for noun class systems. For instance, the contributions in Harvey and Reid (1997) focus on classification in northern Australia, with studies on noun class assignment, the function of nominal classification, systems in between noun classes and classifiers, and the distinction between classifiers and generic-specific constructions. McGregor (2004: 146–150) discusses noun classes in the languages of the Kimberley, and McGregor & Rumsey (2009: 50–51) discuss noun classes in Worrorran languages. Singer (2016) presents an in-depth study of noun classes in Mawng, showing how a noun class system is not always purely grammatical in all respects. Most of these studies mainly deal with noun classes, while noun classifiers have received less attention in the general literature. However, there is one particularly influential study of noun classifiers, viz. Wilkins (2000), which is discussed in more detail below.

2 Noun classifiers and generic-specific constructions

In this section I discuss noun classifiers and related structures. In fact, the most common name used in Australian languages is simply 'generic-specific constructions'. This partly reflects tradition,[12] and partly the reluctance of some grammarians to analyse the generic noun as a genuine noun classifier, which may also relate to questions about the headedness of these structures. Before going into these questions, I give a general overview of the distribution of these structures in the sample and in Australian languages in general.

There are 37 languages in the sample that have some sort of generic-specific structures, 25 of which are Pama-Nyungan and 12 non-Pama-Nyungan.[13] I use a slightly broader definition here than the one given in section 1, as in some of these languages the structures are infrequent and not a 'substantial subset' of nouns is classified in this way. In most, if not all, languages it is also not clear that these systems impose an 'equal division' of the lexicon (as the general definition suggests in point (iii)); see also footnote 9. I include borderline cases precisely to allow discussion on the delineation of classification systems (see further in section 2.1.2). The proportions here are different from the ones posited in Sands (1995: 257), which can be explained by her stricter counts, including only

---

[12] Johnson (1988: 199) attributes this terminological choice to Dixon (1972; 1977).
[13] As explained in chapter 1, counts in this part of the book are approximate. When a particular feature (like the availability of generic-specific structures) is not described in a grammar, it is often unclear whether it is truly absent in the language or merely left undescribed. However, as nominal classification is one of the best-described domains for Australian languages, it is likely that, if it is present in an individual language, it will also have been described in the grammar.

'true' noun classifiers (although she too admits to problems of delineation [1995: 270]). Map 4 below gives an overview of the spread of generic-specific structures across Australia (this corresponds to the dark blue and orange dots in map 3 above). They are especially common in Cape York Peninsula, central Australia and north-western Australia, as well as in the Daly River area and neighbouring languages. The online version of this map provides more information on the morphosyntax of these structures in the individual languages (clicking on a language point reveals an extra information window).

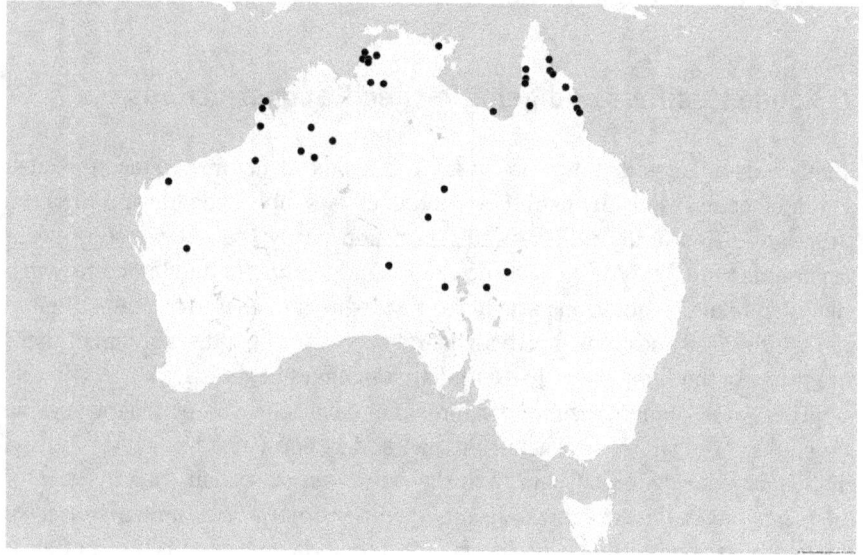

Map 4: Generic-specific structures. For an online, dynamic version of this map containing more details on morphosyntax, see: http://bit.ly/generic-specific.

In the rest of this section, I first discuss the syntax of these structures (section 2.1), starting with some general morphosyntactic features, but mainly focusing on the status of the generic elements. Following this, I give an overview of the semantics and use of these structures (section 2.2), covering the number of classifiers, principles of assignment and variability in use, and frequency and discourse functions.

2.1 Morphosyntax

Morphosyntactically, generics are usually free forms, although in a few languages they are analysed as prefixes or as part of compounds (which, incidentally, contradicts point 5 of the standard typological definition given in table 2) (see below in section 2.1.1). The order is fixed to generic-specific in most languages, as in (16) from Alyawarra. There are nine languages in which the opposite order is also possible, either regularly (e.g. Gooniyandi, McGregor [1990: 261]) or rarely (e.g. Yidiny, Dixon [1977: 247]). Variable orders may have different meanings (see further in section 2.1.2), although this is not explicitly discussed for most languages. An example of variable order is given in (17) from Wangkajunga, showing generic-specific order in (17a) and specific-generic order in (17b). Languages with variable order have a specific geographic distribution, with six out of nine concentrated in the west/north-west of Australia (the other three are Djapu, Kayardild and Yidiny). In addition, in at least six of these languages, the use of generic-specific structures seems to be relatively infrequent overall (see also section 2.1.2).

(16) Alyawarra (Yallop 1977: 119)
 arula akarliy-ika utnthiyla
 wood wild.orange-DAT search.PRS.CONT
 '(We're) looking for wild orange wood.'

(17) Wangkajunga (Jones 2011: 240)
 a. *Jipari-rni* yunga-ma, **warta jipari.**
 plant-1SG.OBJ give-PST.IPFV tree type
 'She used to give me *jipari*, the plant *jipari*.'
 b. *Ngaa-n-pa-janampa ngarri-rra wana-nin* **Warrangkarli**
 DEM-PL-*pa*-3PL.DAT lie-SER accompany-PRS plant.name
 mayi.
 plant.food
 'These lined up [along the bottom of an illustration] are '*warrangkarli*' fruits for them.'

The main syntactic issue for these structures does not concern word order, however, but two related questions that are discussed time and again in the literature: (i) Are generic nouns really classifiers, and (ii) What is the internal structure of generic-specific combinations in terms of headedness? Both of these questions relate back to the issue of category versus functional structure (is there a dedicated category of noun classifiers, or is there a generic-specific construction that can attract elements from non-specialised categories). I first give an overview of how the grammars in the sample deal with these questions, most of which seem to focus on features of the category 'classifier', and then discuss a constructional analysis by Wilkins (2000), who focuses on the construction in which the generic and specific co-occur. In my view, this approach provides an answer to many of the outstanding questions in this domain. While it was originally proposed for Arrernte and some neighbouring languages, I believe it has the potential to offer a general analysis for most languages discussed in this section. To round off, I also discuss a small number of languages where generic-specific constructions seem to behave a bit differently from the rest of the sample.

2.1.1 Headedness and syntactic analysis

The question of headedness is answered in a range of ways in the grammars of the sample. For the 37 languages that I analyse as having generic-specific structures, there are at least four different analyses (see the online version of map 4 for information on the analysis proposed for individual languages). For 4 languages it is argued that the generic is the head of the NP, for 5 others the specific is regarded as the head, for 12 languages it is argued that the generic and the specific co-head the NP (in 6 of these the structure is analysed as one word, i.e. a compound or affixed noun), and for 3 the two nouns are analysed as being in apposition (apposition within the NP for two languages, and between NPs for the third). Another 3 languages have variable analyses depending on the order of the generic and specific, and for 10 languages it is unclear, or the grammar does not make any specific claim. The analysis may of course be different for different languages, but the decisions are probably also influenced by the weight given to certain types of evidence by individual authors.

The types of evidence used in the grammars are quite diverse; sometimes they contradict each other or do not result in any clear-cut answer. Arguments in favour of positing the generic as head include, for instance:

(i) Word order: the position of the generic follows a general tendency for the ordering of heads in the language (e.g. Gaby [2017: 200] on Kuuk Thaayorre).
(ii) Independent use: the generic can be used on its own, without a specific, and this structure "do[es] not appear elliptical" (e.g. Gaby [2017: 200] on Kuuk Thaayorre; Hill [2018] on Umpila).
(iii) Semantics: the use of the generic-specific structure is more similar to the use of the generic alone, and the specific restricts the reference of the generic (e.g. Goddard [1985: 47] on Yankunytjatjara).

Arguments in favour of analysing the specific as head are:
(i) Independent use: the specific can be used on its own, without a generic (e.g. Hill [2018] on Umpila)
(ii) Semantics: the generic-specific structure as a whole functions as a specific noun would (e.g. Gaby [2017: 200] on Kuuk Thaayorre; Johnson [1988: 201] on Kugu Nganhcara)

Arguments given in favour of co-headedness (also called 'complex head') often include a combination of the ones mentioned above, such as the fact that either element can occur as sole head of the NP (e.g. Hill [2018] on Umpila), or that the generic-specific structure has a different meaning than either the specific or the generic alone (see further below). The hypothesis of co-headedness was first suggested by Simpson (1991) and further developed by Sadler & Nordlinger (2010), who propose a syntactic account in the Lexical-Functional Grammar framework, covering not only generic-specific structures but also part-whole expressions, inclusory constructions, coordination marked by juxtaposition, and other nominal-nominal expressions. Some authors go one step further and analyse a generic-specific structure as a compound; this is further discussed below (section 2.1.2, esp. footnote 16).[14]

Some of the arguments listed above may be language-specific, but for the most part, the issue of headedness really boils down to the question whether the generic is a 'true' classifier or not. Some indications for this can be found in Wilkins (2000), Grinevald (2000) and Dixon (2002: 449–450), all of whom suggest that generic-specific structures are less grammaticalised than 'classic' noun classifiers. Thus, Grinevald (2000: 65) argues that "noun classifiers appear to exist also in Australia, although in a more incipient, less grammaticalized stage (...)", and Dixon (2002: 450) argues that Australian languages originally had a "generic noun/specifier" system (i.e. where the generic noun is the head) which in some languages further developed to a "classifier/specific noun" system (i.e. where the specific noun is the head). The main argument for such distinctions seems to be obligatoriness: generic-specific

---

[14] Another criterion that may come to mind is that the head determines the grammatical features of the phrase. However, this is not easily applicable to the sample. For example, case is most often marked at the right edge of the NP or on each element (see chapter 6, section 3.2), and number marking on nouns is limited overall (see chapter 4, section 1). Noun class is not a feature in most of the languages that have generic-specific structures, and where it is, it is not clear from the grammar which element governs agreement (see example (44) from Diyari in section 6). This criterion is not further discussed here.

combinations are optional, whereas noun classifiers occur "in *each* noun phrase with a specific noun" (Wilkins 2000: 165–166, referring to Sands 1995). However, there is no language in the sample that actually meets this requirement, nor is this the case even for the presumably 'prototypical' noun classifier language Jacaltec (Mayan; see Craig 1986a: 263; Grinevald 2000: 80). In fact, strict obligatoriness seems to be a feature of further grammaticalisation towards noun classes (see also Seifart 2010). There is a relative difference between languages, though: in a language like Jacaltec, there is only a small number of nouns that occur without a classifier (Craig 1986a: 263), and classifiers are used "overwhelmingly" in definite contexts and never in non-referential NPs (Wilkins 2000: 156), whereas in a language like Arrernte, generic-specific structures can occur in any type of context, but are nevertheless quite restricted in their use for other reasons (Wilkins 2000: 157, 178). A second argument that is used to set apart generic-specific systems is that in the typical classifier system some of the elements may be specialised in a classifier function. Again, however, even in Jacaltec, most classifiers can also be used in another function, e.g. as sole head of the NP (Wilkins 2000: 160, referring to Craig 1986b: 290). A final argument, mentioned by Grinevald (2000: 80), relates to whether the set of generics/classifiers is an open or closed class (the latter is true for Jacaltec [Craig 1986a: 261]). However, as noted in table 2, a closed set of classes is really a feature of noun class systems, while classifiers typically form a (semi-)open set. So even if generic-specific structures are less grammaticalised, the arguments against analysing them as classifiers are not very strong.

There is, in fact, another way to look at these questions, with a more satisfying outcome. All of the arguments in the debate focus on features of the classifier itself; an alternative is to focus on the construction as the source of the classifying function rather than trying to find a dedicated set of classifiers, for instance. Thus, Wilkins (2000) argues for Arrernte (and in a preliminary way for Yankunytjatjara and Warlpiri) that the generic-specific structure is a 'classifying construction', where the classifier effect for the generic noun is constructional, i.e. it arises from the use of the noun in the whole construction. This would explain the independent use of generic nouns, as well as the difficulties encountered in delineating a clear set of classifiers; in this regard, Wilkins (2000: 155) even hypothesises that "any lexicalized superordinate term which has identifiable lexicalized hyponyms can indeed occur as the generic in a 'generic-specific' construction." Wilkins does not apply this analysis beyond the languages in his study, but I expect that it can be applied more broadly, given that it can deal with many of the contradictory arguments given above, and at first sight fits the information I have on the other languages of the sample.[15]

2.1.2 A different type of structure?

There is, however, at least one set of languages where Wilkins' constructional analysis may be less successful, viz. the nine languages where a generic and specific can be combined in either order (see above). It is unclear how flexible elements can fit a constructional configuration like the generic-specific one proposed by Wilkins (let alone a dedicated classifier analysis) – this is argued explicitly, for instance, by Wilkinson (1991: 481) for Djambarrpuyngu. Interestingly, moreover, in six of these languages generic-specific combinations are also said to be infrequent.

Features like variable order and infrequent use have invited alternative accounts, in which the relevant structures are not analysed as separate generic-specific constructions, but instead integrated in other constructional configurations posited for the language (where structure again plays a vital role). This is the case for four languages, viz. Gooniyandi (McGregor 1990: 260–264), Martuthunira (Dench 1994: 194–195), Nyangumarta (Sharp 2004: 311), and Nyulnyul (McGregor 2011: 406).

The configurations with which these structures are associated are of two types. The first type is found, for instance, in Gooniyandi (McGregor 1990: 260–264), where a Classifier slot is identified in the position immediately before the Entity slot in the NP (see chapter 5, section 2 for more details). The Classifier "indicates the type of thing referred to by the phrase" (McGregor 1990: 260); the examples in (18) illustrate the semantic range of Classifier-Entity NPs. In the case of a generic-specific structure, the element in the Classifier role can indicate "the generic type of which the Entity is a specific example" (as in (18a), where rain is a type of water), or "the purpose or use of the object" (as in (18b), where kangaroo is a type of (edible) meat). Conversely, in the case of a specific-generic structure, as in (18c), the element in the Classifier role "distinguish[es] the specific type of a more general Entity" (where the water lying on the ground is rain water). In other instances the

---

15 Wilkins does make a distinction between languages like Arrernte in central Australia and languages in 'north-eastern Australia' in terms of the (discourse) function of the classification system, but it is unclear whether he would also characterise the generic-specific structures in the second group of languages as classifying constructions or as genuine classifier-noun structures (2000: 162).

Classifier element classifies a person by "'race' or cultural group", as in (18d), or a thing by "its typical location in space or time" as in (18e).

(18) Gooniyandi (McGregor 1990: 261–262)
    a. *gamba yiwindi jigjigji*
       water rain it:spotted
       'Rain spotted the ground.'
    b. *maa thirroo*
       meat kangaroo
       'the edible animal kangaroo'
    c. *yiwindi gamba bagiri*
       rain water it:lies
       'Rain water is lying about.'
    d. *gardiya Colin*
       white:person <name>
       'the white man Colin'
    e. *garrwaroo warda*
       afternoon star
       'evening star, Venus'

The second type of configuration can be illustrated with McGregor's analysis of Nyulnyul (2011: 406). The Nyulnyul NP only includes a Qualifier role (immediately before the Entity), and not a separate Classifier role like in Gooniyandi. This is because the functions of "quality and category specification" are "treated as the same" in this language (McGregor 2011: 406). A Qualifier-Entity NP can thus involve both the attribution of a quality to the referent, as in (19a), and the subcategorisation of the referent, for instance in the form of a generic-specific (19b) or specific-generic structure (19c).

(19) Nyulnyul (McGregor 2011: 407, 408, 409)
    a. *maank mungkan*
       black hair
       'black hair'
    b. *bin bardangk karnbalm*
       that tree tree:type
       'that *karnbalm* tree'
    c. *kinyingk larrkird bardangk*
       DEF boab tree
       'this boab tree'

Note that Dench's analysis of Martuthunira (1994: 194–195) involves a combination of the two types illustrated above: he analyses specific-generic structures as Classifier-Entity constructions, and generic-specific structures as Entity-Qualifier constructions.

It is unclear whether the other five languages with flexible order of generic and specific (or even other languages for that matter) could also be analysed in a similar way. One way to look at this may be in terms of grammaticalisation (as hinted at by Dixon [2002: 449–451], see above in section 2.1.1). If noun classifiers are a further grammaticalisation of generic-specific constructions, then perhaps generic-specific constructions represent a further grammaticalisation (or constructionalisation) of the types of structures described in this section (which are more flexible and even less specialised). Obviously, this remains speculative in the absence of more detailed discourse-based and diachronic work on these languages.

To round off this section, I want to mention two further languages that do not fit Wilkins' analysis, but for a different reason. In Bardi, potential generic-specific structures like (20a-b) are analysed as compounds (Bowern 2012: 254), because they have a different locus of case marking than NPs (i.e. following the whole structure, rather than following the first element as in NPs), and show a distinct stress pattern.[16] Nothing more is said about generic-specific structures, so presumably they are not very frequent. In Arabana/Wangkangurru (Hercus 1994: 102–103), generics are prefixed to the head noun, evidenced by the fact that they are not fully accented, while the head noun receives full stress. However, this system is not fully developed and only a few nouns can be 'prefixed'.

---

16 Compound analyses have also been suggested for other languages, for instance Oykangand (Hamilton 1996: 5) and Rimanggudinhma (Godman 1993: 38), but apart from distinct stress patterns in the latter, the evidence is not convincing (for instance, the fact that elements that have a fixed order and cannot be separated are also characteristics of (some) types of noun phrases). Additionally, some counter-arguments for a compound analysis can be found in Johnson (1988) for Kugu Nganhcara, and in Kilham (1974) for Wik-Munkan (not in the sample). Syntactically, the deletion of the classifier is possible, which is less typical for compounds; semantically, the classifier is superordinate to the whole construction and the classified element has the same sense as the entire construction, while this does not (necessarily) hold for compounds. An in-depth study of the general issue of delimitation of compounds and other 'complex nominal heads' in Australian languages can be found in Lesage (2014). See also Harvey (1992) (and McGregor's reply on this), on a potential compound analysis of Classifier-Entity structures.

(20) Bardi (Bowern 2012: 259)
    a. *oorany-baawa; miida-baawa*
       woman-child   male-child
       'girl; male child, boy'
    b. *[Mayala gooljoo-yoon] i-ng-oorr-oo-moogar-na-na=rr*
       mayala   grass-SOURCE   3-PST-AUG-TR-make-CONT-REMPST=3A.DO
       ngirray milon
       huts   long.ago
       'Long ago, they used to make huts from spinifex grass (*mayala* grass).'

2.2 Meaning and use

The number of generics in the languages of the sample ranges from 2 or 3 to 32. An overview is given in map 5 below. It is often difficult to give the exact number of classifiers/generics in a language, for the reasons mentioned above. Nevertheless, most grammars at least give an approximation, if not an exact figure. In several languages, only a handful of generics are regularly used, and a range of others are attested less frequently. In such cases, the frequently used ones usually[17] include at least those for vegetable food and meat food/animals (see also Dixon [2002: 455] and Sands [1995: 270]).

2.2.1 Semantic range

The semantic range of the generics across the languages is broad, and seems to categorise the natural environment as well as culturally important objects. To illustrate this broad variety of generics I list some of the main types of generics found in the languages of the sample. Most languages have a generic for vegetable food, i.e. plants that are used as food source. There are also generics for different kinds of flora, like tree/wood,[18] grasses, seeds, paperbark trees and

---

17 Languages lacking both of these are languages in which generic-specific structures are infrequent (e.g. Patz [1991: 290] for Djabugay) and/or for which an alternative analysis has been proposed (e.g. Bowern [2012: 169, 259–260] for Bardi; see above). If only one of the two is lacking, then it is the plant food generic (as in Arabana/Wangkangurru, Kayardild, Lardil, Wajarri, Walmajarri and Yandruwandha). For Kayardild, Evans (1995a: 17) attributes this to the "low proportion of plant food in the diet" of Kayardild (and presumably also Lardil) speakers.
18 Apart from the 'plant food' and 'meat food' generics, the 'tree' generic seems to be the most common generic: almost all languages have one. Exceptions include languages that only have generics for vegetable food and meat food (Emmi, Martuthunira, Wardaman) and languages which are otherwise limited (e.g. with infrequent use of generic-specific structures, as Arabana/Wangkangurru).

2 Noun classifiers and generic-specific constructions — 39

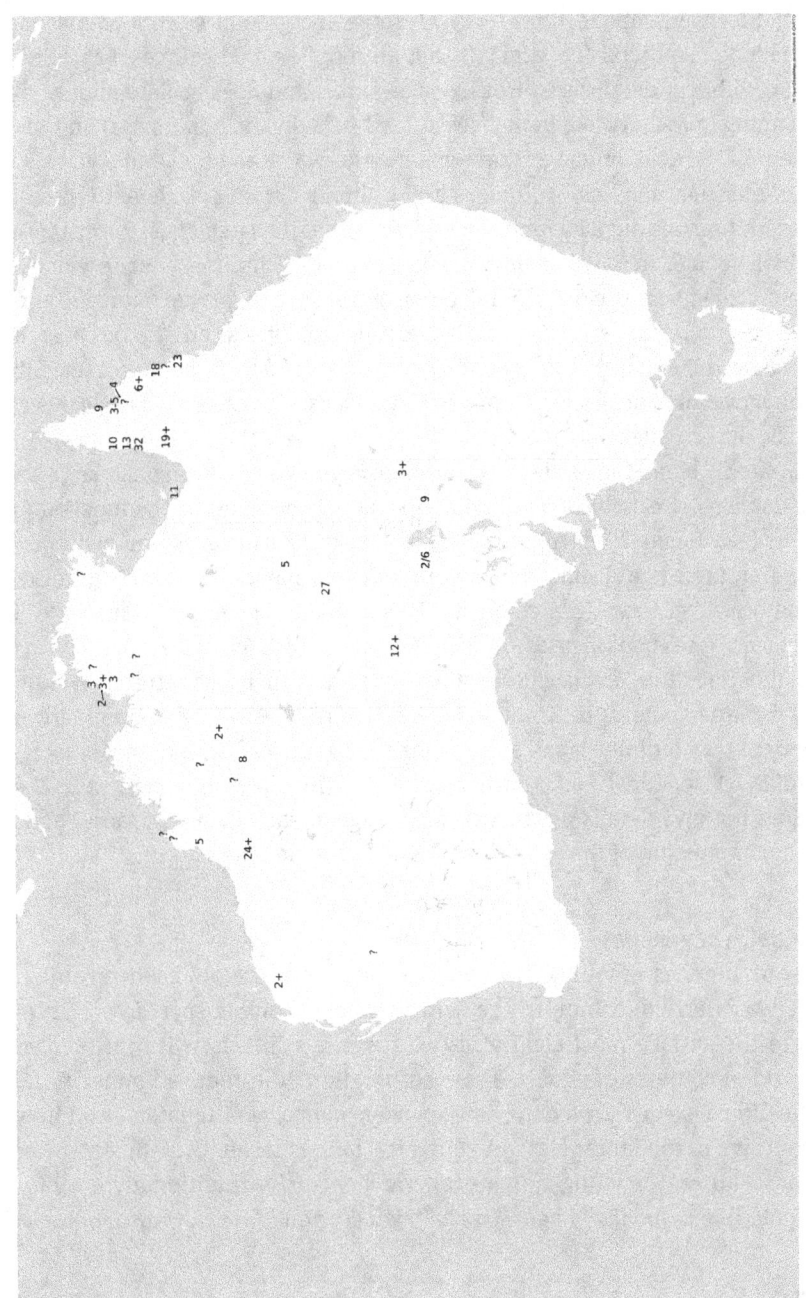

Map 5: Number of generics. For an online, dynamic version of this map, see: http://bit.ly/generics-number.

yams, and for landscape features like rock/stone and ground/earth. Generics for fauna include meat food (i.e. animals that are used as food source), fish, birds and bats, edible grubs, insects, frogs, snakes, ants, and dogs/social animals, as well as animal products like honey/sweet food (usually including bees) and termite mounds. Several languages have generics for water and fire, and some also for other elements such as wind/air, stars or thunder storms. Different types of generics for humans are also found in at least half of the languages, for instance Aboriginal people, initiated men, women, children, white men, white women and family members. Generics for language/speech and place/camp are also found in several languages. Finally, a whole range of objects can also be categorised by generics, either by the general effects or dynamics of the object (useful, harmful, moveable), or in a more narrow sense (spears, woomeras, bags, canoes, fire sticks, digging sticks).

Within this broad range, there are several suggestions to distinguish large semantic domains of classification, based on what is believed to be the function of classifiers (e.g. Denny 1976; Allan 1977). For Australian languages, the main proposal is that there is a distinction between 'inherent nature' generics (e.g. rock), 'function or use' generics (e.g. edible meat food) and 'social status' generics (e.g. initiated man) (see e.g. Wilkins 2000: 152–154; Dixon 2002: 456–457).

To illustrate how such classification systems can be structured overall, table 3 lists the generics for three languages (as discussed in the grammatical descriptions), including a small system (Emmi, 2 generics), an intermediate one (Kayardild, 11 generics) and a rather large one (Arrernte, 27 generics).[19] The table does not give details on the exact coverage of each item, but rather aims to give an impression of the existing range in a given language.

2.2.2 Choice of generics

The list of generics mentioned above gives an initial idea of their meaning, but the way they contribute to the semantics of a generic-specific structure comes to the surface most clearly in two types of contexts: with introduced items, and in contexts of choice. The incorporation of introduced items in the classification system shows both how speakers conceive of the item, and how they conceive of the larger class in which the item is located, as illustrated in (21). For instance, the Wangkajunga generic *mangarri* is traditionally used for plant food, like in *mangarri ngarlukurtu* 'bush coconut', but now also includes

---

[19] Note that Wilkins' (2000) study specifically focused on generic-specific structures, which may partially explain the very high number of generics posited for Arrernte compared to the other languages, but this is certainly not the full story.

Table 3: Range of generics in some classification systems.

Language	Generics
Emmi (Ford 1998: 100–103)	*awa* 'meat'; *miya* 'edible plant'
Kayardild (Evans 1995: 246–247)	Inherent nature: *wuranda* 'animate'; *dangkaa* 'humans'; *yarbuda* 'birds and reptiles'; *yakuriya* 'bony fish'; *wanku* 'elasmobranch fish (sharks and rays)'; *kunbulka* 'large sea animals (turtles, dugongs and cetaceans)'; *karnda* 'grasses and seaweeds'; *thungalda* 'trees' Use: *wuranda* 'food'; *yarbuda* 'harmful objects'; *thunglda* 'useful objects'
Arrernte (Wilkins 2000: 152–155)	Inherent nature: *thipe* 'flying, fleshy creatures (birds and bats)'; *yerre* 'ants'; *arne* 'ligneous plants (trees and bushes)'; *name* 'long grasses'; *ntange* 'seeds of a nut or grain-like nature'; *ure* 'fire related entities'; *kwatye* 'water related entities'; *pwerte* 'rock related entities' Function/use: *kere* 'meat creatures'; *merne* 'edible foods from plants'; *ngkwarle* 'sweet honey-like foods/drinks'; *tyape* 'edible grubs'; *ingwelpe* 'native tobacco'; *awelye* 'medicines'; *arne* 'artefact, useful thing' Social status: *artwe* 'initiated man'; *relhe* 'woman'; *ampe* 'child'; *pmere* 'place' Uncategorised:[20] *ahelhe* 'earth types (soils)'; *angkentye* 'languages'; *angkulye* 'clouds'; *apmwe* 'snakes'; *atne* 'animal guts'; *kwerralye* 'stars'; *rlke* 'winds'; *urtne* 'carrying dishes (coolamons)'

manufactured plant-based food like breakfast cereals (as in 21c) (Jones 2011: 61). See also Hoogmartens (2018) on the choice of generics used with the specific nouns for the introduced items sugar, flour and tea.

(21) a. Umpithamu (Verstraete p.c.)
   mayi   wurrkan,   mayi   nani
   VEG.FOOD dust/ashes VEG.FOOD sand
   'flour, sugar'
 b. Yandruwandha (Breen 2004b: 167)
   wathi   mutuka
   WOODEN.OBJECT motorcar
   'motorcar'

---

[20] Generics were categorised in terms of three semantic domains in Wilkins' earlier work (1989), but for theoretical reasons (as outlined in section 2.1), he did not include any more recently 'detected' generics (2000).

c. Wangkajunga (Jones 2011: 61)
mangarri   witiz
PLANT.FOOD   Weeties
'breakfast cereal'

In some languages, some nouns can occur with different generics, as is expected in a system of noun classifiers (see point 7 of the definition in table 2). Again, this gives us an interesting perspective on the way the generic contributes to the meaning of the whole structure. One option is that the use of a particular noun with a different generic entails a different reference. In such cases, we usually deal with homonymy, where the two lexemes that formally coincide each take a different generic. An example is the set of Kuuk Thaayorre structures in (22), where the word form *kermpl* can either be preceded by the 'plant food' generic *may*, or by the 'meat food' generic *minh*. In the former structure it refers to a type of fruit, while in the latter it refers to a type of bird. As it is difficult to reconcile these two senses into one underlying sense,[21] it is necessary to posit two separate lexemes, each occurring with a particular generic (Gaby 2017: 198).

(22)   Kuuk Thaayorre (Gaby 2017: 198)
    a. *may   kermpl*
       VEG.FOOD   large.white.berry
       'large white berry'
    b. *minh   kermpl*
       MEAT.FOOD   corella
       'corella'

The second option with variable generics is that one referent may be presented in different ways. A common variant is that a specific noun referring to a type of tree can occur with the 'tree' generic in reference to the tree itself, as in (23a), or with the 'vegetable food' generic in reference to the fruit of that tree, as in (23b). Another example is when (shell)fish is classified either as food or as an object that is not eaten (e.g. the shells), as in Kugu Nganhcara (Smith & Johnson 2000: 447), or similarly in Kayardild where seaweed can be classified as an object (for humans) or as food (for dugongs) (Evans 1995a: 247).

---

[21] Some parallel cases in other languages may have a metonymic basis; for instance one term may be used both for a tree and for the bird for who the fruit of the tree is the typical food (Evans 1997).

(23) Oykangand (Hamilton 1996: 4)
  a. *uk   atulwanych*
     TREE Leichardt
     'Leichardt tree'
  b. *egng atulwanych*
     FOOD   Leichardt
     'Leichardt tree fruit'

These types of variation have been studied in great detail for Arrernte by Wilkins (2000), who analyses them as highlighting "specified sets of knowledge structures" or "discourse relevant properties of the referent" (2000: 148, 200), and consequently backgrounding others. For instance, the specific noun *arlkerrke* 'meat-ant' can occur in a classifier construction with the generic *yerre* 'ant', where the hearer is expected to think about the referent as an ant (i.e. a kind of living thing that tends to live in nests in the ground, commonly bites people, etc.) or with the generic *awalye* 'traditional medicine', where the hearer is expected to think about the referent as a medicine (i.e. an object which is used to cause a person to be better etc.). *Arlkerrke* can also be construed with the generic *pmere* 'place' to mean 'place associated with the meat-ant totem'.

In some languages, nouns can occur with more than one generic at the same time. In Arrernte, the usual combination is that of a function or use generic followed by an inherent nature generic, as in (24), while Yidiny shows the reverse order, as in (25a). Another option is that a more general generic is combined with a more specific one, as in (25b) from Yidiny. In both of these languages, the use of more than one generic seems to be productive. In other languages, structures that appear to combine generics are actually syntactically different: some generic-specific constructions have become lexicalised, and can then again be used as a specific noun with a generic. This is the case for the lexicalised structure *minh patp* [MEAT hawk] 'hawk' in Kuuk Thaayorre, which when combined with the FISH classifier *ngat* comes to mean 'spotted eagle-ray' (Gaby 2017: 77, 199).

(24) Arrernte (Wilkins 2000: 154)
   kere thipe nyengke
   MEAT BIRD   zebra.finch
   'a zebra finch (edible)'

(25) Yidiny (Dixon 1977: 148)
  a. *wira   gala   biwuṛ*
     MOVEABLE.OBJECT   SPEAR fish.spear
     'fish spear'

b. *bama   buɲa   yabu:ɾ*
   PERSON WOMAN pubescent.girl
   'pubescent girl'

2.2.3 Use of generic-specific structures

In many languages in the sample, nouns are often only optionally accompanied by the appropriate generic. Thus, a language can have nouns that never occur with a generic, nouns that sometimes occur with a generic and nouns that virtually always occur with a generic (as discussed for Kuuk Thaayorre in Gaby [2017: 77, 199]). Unfortunately, variation in the (non-)use of generics, or its motivation, is not discussed in much detail for most languages of the sample. In this section, I provide a brief survey of what can be found in the literature.

Starting with frequency, the use of generic-specific structures[22] appears to be quite infrequent in the languages in the west and north-west of Australia (e.g. Martuthunira [Dench 1994: 194–195], Nyangumarta [Sharp 2004: 310], Wangkajunga [Jones 2011: 239], Yawuru [Hosokawa 1991: 79], Wardaman [Merlan 1994: 239], and Emmi [Ford 1998: 101]).[23] In north-eastern Australia, generic-specific constructions are used quite frequently in the languages on the west coast of Cape York Peninsula (e.g. Kugu Nganhcara [Smith & Johnson 2000: 420; Johnson 1988: 199], Kuuk Thaayorre [Gaby 2017: 77], Oykangand [Sommer 1970: 170; Hamilton 1996: 3]), but they are less frequent on the east coast (e.g. Umpila [Hill 2018: 155], Umpithamu [Verstraete 2010], Kuku Yalanji [Patz 2002: 120], Djabugay [Patz 1991: 290]), except perhaps for the 'plant food' and 'meat food' generics (e.g. Patz [2002: 120] on Kuku Yalanji) or in elicitation (e.g. Verstraete [2010, p.c.] on Umpithamu). Incidentally, there seems to be a positive correlation between the frequency of use for generic-specific structures and the number of generics a language has (see maps 4 and 5 above).

Turning to their use in discourse, only scattered pieces of information are available, so I can only give a list of uses as they are reported for individual languages. A common practice is that generic-specific structures are used to introduce a referent in the discourse, and reference is then continued by a generic

---

[22] A different type of frequency relates to the proportion of nouns that can enter into a generic-specific construction in a particular language. This is probably correlated with the overall frequency of use in discourse, but it is important to keep these two apart analytically.

[23] The languages in the Daly region are an exception: use of generics is frequent in Murrinh Patha (not in the sample; see Walsh [1997], Blythe [2009: 103]); Ngan'gityemerri/ Ngan'gikurunggurr and Marrithiyel have hybrid systems and are further discussed in section 5.

alone (e.g. Ford [1998: 101] for Emmi; Sommer [1970: 185–186] for Oykangand; Hill [2018: 156] for Umpila). Use in discourse also seems to depend on the semantic load of the generics in generic-specific structures. In some languages, like Yidiny, Kugu Nganhcara and Jaru, it seems that the contexts of use of a generic-specific structure and a specific alone are very similar, i.e. the generic does not seem to contribute much in terms of semantic content (e.g. Wilkins 2000: 166–169; Johnson 1988: 201; Tsunoda 1981: 94). In such languages, the use of a generic-specific structure can also be related to aesthetics or speech style. Dixon (1977: 495) for instance, argues that question-answer sequences in Yidiny usually involve an alternation between a generic and a specific, in the sense that (either) one is used in the question and the other in the reply. In other languages, like Arrernte, Yankunytjatjara and Gooniyandi, the generic does seem to have a higher semantic load, and the use of a generic-specific structure is related to how the referent is framed (Wilkins 2000: 169–177; McGregor 1990: 274). For instance, the generic 'animal food' can only be used in contexts of hunting or eating/cooking, as in (26a), but not in other contexts, as in (26b). Wilkins also notes how the classifying construction in such languages can be used for humorous effects by creating intentional mismatches (2000: 200–206).

(26) Arrernte (Wilkins 2000: 172, 173)
  a. *the   imarte arratye* **kere**   ***aherre*-ø**
     1SG.ERG then   truly   game/meat   kangaroo-ACC
     arlkwe-tye.lhe-me-le.
     eat-GO&DO-NPST.PROG-SS
     'When I got there, I ate some kangaroo meat ["had a good feed of kangaroo meat"]'
  b. ... *anwerne   ingke   anteme   alhe-ke   Ayampewerne-atheke.*
     ... 1PL.NOM   foot   now   go-PST.COMPL   Yambah-ALL-wards
     Iwerre-ke   anwerne **aherre   arunthe-ø** *are-ke.*
     way/path-DAT 1PL.ERG kangaroo many-ACC   see-PST.COMPL
     'Then we (sadly) set out on foot towards Yambah Station. On the way we saw some kangaroos.'

3 Verbal and adjectival classifiers

Verbal classifiers in Australian languages take the form of verb-incorporated generics, which are co-referential with a free-standing or 'external' specific noun.[24] An example is given in (27) from Bininj Kunwok, showing how the generic *rrulk* 'tree' is incorporated in the verb and classifies the free-standing *an-dubang* 'ironwood tree'. This is what Evans (2003a: 234–241) calls a "unification construction", because material from the verb (*rrulk*) and external material (*an-dubang*) are "unified to give full referring expressions" (Evans 2003a: 234).[25] Since verbal classification originates outside the NP in these structures, it falls outside the scope of this study, but I include a short discussion here for the sake of completeness.

(27) Bininj Kunwok (Evans 2003a: 236)
 *Ga-**rrulk**-di* ****an-dubang****.
 3-tree-stand.NPST III-ironwood
 'There's an ironwood tree there.'

Verbal classifiers are found in two to four languages of the sample: definitely in Bininj Kunwok (Evans 2003a: 236) and Anindilyakwa (van Egmond 2012: 237, 247–279), and in a less clear form in Dalabon (Cutfield 2011: 105; see also Ponsonnet [2015] on incorporation of nouns in Dalabon more generally) and Rembarrnga (Saulwick 2003: 373, 376–381). All these languages belong to the Gunwinyguan family and are situated in Arnhem Land and nearby Groote Eylandt.[26]

These structures are just as difficult to analyse syntactically as the generic-specific structures discussed above, as also noted by Sands (1995: 272): "the decision on where to draw the line between simple noun incorporation and verb-incorporated classification is hazy." In Bininj Kunwok and Anindilyakwa,

---

24 Note that this is not the same as verb classification. While a verb classification system classifies verbs, verbal classifiers classify nouns (even though they occur in the grammatical context of the verb). See McGregor (2002) on verb classification in Australian languages.
25 The idea of unification as an aspect of grammar was introduced by Bresnan (1982) under a Lexical-Functional Grammar framework, and further developed by Simpson (1983, 1991), Simpson and Bresnan (1983), and Nordlinger (1998b). Other examples of 'unification constructions' are when the number of the referent(s) of a NP is only expressed on the verb (see further in chapter 4, section 1) or when an incorporated noun can be modified by an external adjective (see chapter 3, section 2) or demonstrative. This is one way in which some Australian languages can have 'distributed' nominal expressions (see also chapters 1 and 6).
26 Sands (1995: 273) claims that Tiwi also has verbal classifiers, but according to Lee (1987: 164) "[t]hese verbal and other types of incorporated forms do not, in general, have a corresponding external form in the clause with which they are cross-referenced." Languages not in the sample that are described as having verbal classifiers are Ngalakgan, Ngandi and Nunggubuyu (see Sands 1995: 273–274; Dixon 2002: 460; Baker 2002; Saulwick 2003: 379). These also belong to the Gunwinyguan family. Warray, the remaining Gunwinyguan language of the sample, does not appear to have verbal classifiers or verb-incorporated generics (Harvey ms: 186).

the incorporated generic is analysed as a true classifier (Saulwick 2003: 371–381; Evans 2003a: 330–335; van Egmond 2012: 248), while this is argued not to be the case for Rembarrnga (see Saulwick [2003: 371–381] for a detailed discussion). The analysis for Dalabon is unclear, but it seems that only some (incorporable) generic nouns "can function as classifiers" (Ponsonnet 2015: 42).

Like independent generics (see section 2.2 above), incorporated generics can also occur without an (external) specific, in all four languages (Evans 2003a: 334; van Egmond 2012: 247; Ponsonnet 2015: 42; Saulwick 2003: 378). This is illustrated in (28) from Anindilyakwa. In Bininj Kunwok (Evans 2003a: 330), Dalabon (Ponsonnet 2015: 43) and Rembarrnga (Saulwick 2003: 331), incorporable generics can also occur in non-incorporated form; this is not the case in Anindilyakwa (van Egmond 2012: 248) (see examples (14) and (15) above).

(28) Anindilyakwa (van Egmond 2012: 247)
nv-**rrekv**-rndangmi-ji-na
3M/N-long.and.flexible-make.a.noise-CAUS-N.NPST
'he is strumming it [the guitar(N)]'

The number of generics that can be used in this construction is very high: Bininj Kunwok appears to have 60 incorporating generics (Evans 2003a: 332), and Anindilyakwa even 80 (van Egmond 2012: 250). The generics in Anindilyakwa mostly originate in incorporated body parts, which have undergone semantic extension (e.g. *ngarr-* 'ear' > 'items with rough skin', or *lhakbak-* 'leg' > 'short and upright') (van Egmond 2012: 251, 260). The same pattern is found in Bininj Kunwok, but only for a few generics (e.g. *ganj-* 'flesh, muscle' > 'meat') (Evans 2003a: 334). Interestingly, this same set of generics can also be incorporated in adjectives in Bininj Kunwok and in Anindilyakwa. In Bininj Kunwok, this is only possible when the adjective is used predicatively (Evans 2003a: 126), as in (29). In Anindilyakwa, however, the adjective-with-incorporated-generic can modify a head noun (van Egmond 2012: 237), as in (30a-d). Aikhenvald (2003: 151) claims that in such cases, the incorporated generics are numeral classifiers, but van Egmond (2012: 250, fn. 8) shows that this is not a good characterisation, as they can be incorporated in all types of adjectives (including but not limited to numerals). In this sense, we could regard this case as a rare instance of adjectival classifiers. The examples below also show how incorporated generics are combined with noun class marking, and how the choice of the incorporated generic is variable, "emphasising its different features, or providing a different perspective on a noun" (van Egmond 2012: 248).

(29) Bininj Kunwok (Evans 2003a: 453)
ba-m-bo-re-i, ba-bo-lobm-i, **an-bo-gimuk**
3PST-hither-liquid-go-PST.IPFV 3PST-liquid-run-PST.IPFV VE-liquid-big
'when the floodwaters used to come running high'

(30) Anindilyakwa (van Egmond 2012: 248)
   a. *mi-**lyakv**-babvrvngka*   *mvnhvnga*
      VE-elongated.and.solid-RDP.dry VE.burrawang
      'pile of dry burrawang nuts'
   b. *mi-**lyang**-bvlhvrra*   *mvnhvnga*
      VE-round.and.hard-unfinished VE.burrawang
      'unripe burrawang nuts, not ready to use'
   c. *m-**arrk**-inungkurakba*   *mvnhvnga*
      VE-small.and.round.and.many-old VE.burrawang
      'many old burrawang nuts'
   d. *m-**embirrk**-ambilyvma* *mvnhvnga*
      VE-round.and.flat-two VE.burrawang
      'two crushed burrawang nuts'

4 Noun classes

As already mentioned, noun class systems are different from classifier systems (or generic-specific systems) in terms of their morphosyntactic implications, more specifically the fact that they trigger agreement. The noun itself often shows no overt marking, but its modifiers and/or the pronouns cross-referencing it do show overt marking to agree in noun class (see section 1). Noun class systems are at the grammatical end of the classification continuum, often having grammaticalised from noun classifiers (e.g. Grinevald 2000: 55–58; Dixon 2002: 450; Seifart 2010: 727–728).

There are 31 languages in the sample that have noun classes, 23 non-Pama-Nyungan languages and 8 Pama-Nyungan languages.[27] Noun classes in Pama-Nyungan languages are mainly found in systems of free personal pronouns that can be used adnominally (see chapter 7, section 3.3) and thus show agreement with the noun they modify (Pitta-Pitta, Diyari, Yandruwandha, Gathang, Kala

---

[27] This is a higher percentage than the one provided in Sands for Pama-Nyungan languages (2 out of 190), but this can be explained by the fact that she excludes languages that only have a class distinction in free pronouns (Sands 1995: 257, 331).

Lagaw Ya).²⁸ This is illustrated in (31) from Kala Lagaw Ya, where the personal pronoun shows feminine agreement with the noun *apuwan* 'mother' in (31a), and masculine agreement with the personal name *Tomagani* (referring to a male character) in (31b). The other Pama-Nyungan cases are Yanyuwa, which shows agreement on all modifiers in the NP (Kirton 1971: 21), Bundjalung, where (some) adjectives agree with the head noun (not in all dialects) (Sharpe 2005: 42),²⁹ and Dyirbal, where demonstratives agree with the head noun (Dixon 1982b).³⁰

(31) Kala Lagaw Ya (Stirling 2008: 179, 182)
  a. **Nadh**   **apu-w-an**   waaku   nge   uma-n.
     3SG.F.ERG   mother-w-ERG   mat(ACC)   then   make-NFUT
     'The mother was making a mat then.'
  b. **Nuy**   **Tomagani**   gabudan   pathay.
     3SG.M.NOM   Tomagani(NOM)   slowly   cuts(NFUT)
     'Tomagani cut slowly.'

The non-Pama-Nyungan cases are more classic types of noun class systems, as illustrated for Wambaya in (32a-b), where all modifiers agree with the head noun belonging to the first and third class respectively (glossed with Roman numerals). As could be expected, the majority of non-Pama-Nyungan languages in the sample have noun classes (viz. about two thirds of the non-Pama-Nyungan languages in the sample, the same proportion as observed in Dixon [2002: 469]). There are only 10 non-Pama-Nyungan languages without noun

---

28 Note that I exclude languages that only show a gender distinction in personal pronouns and do not show agreement (cf. Corbett 2007: 242).
29 Third person singular pronouns in Bundjalung also have masculine and feminine forms, but they are not used as modifiers to nouns and thus cannot be said to show agreement. Note that nearby languages Gathang and Gumbaynggir show remnants of an earlier noun class system in the form of suffixes on, for instance, feminine nouns or nouns for trees (Eades 1979: 288–289; Lissarrague 2010: 47). Crowley (1978: 48–49) mentions that similar evidence is found in languages on the (south)east coast from Wollongong to Brisbane.
30 Sands (1995: 274–275) proposes to analyse the system in Dyirbal as demonstrative classifiers rather than noun classes. Her arguments are (i) that the class of the noun is only marked on the demonstrative and nowhere else, and (ii) that one of the classes has zero realisation, which Sands argues is the set of nouns that is unclassifiable. As to the first point, there are several languages that show agreement only in some word classes, which suggests that this argument is not a sufficient reason to dismiss a noun class analysis. The second point may be more valid. In terms of morphosyntactic features, however, e.g. obligatory agreement and number of classes (small), the Dyirbal system clearly fits in the noun class group rather than the classifier one (see table 2 above).

classes:[31] the Tangkic and Garrwan languages on the Gulf of Carpentaria, which are structural outliers in other ways, but also some languages in the southern Kimberley (Bardi, Nyulnyul, Gooniyandi and Yawuru), as well as three other languages (Jaminjung, Matngele, Dalabon).

(32) Wambaya (Nordlinger 1998a: 132, 115)
    a. *Ayani   ngi   ninaga   galalarrinyi-nka bugayini-nka*
       look.for 1SG.S(PRS) this.I.SG.DAT dog.I-DAT   big.I-DAT
       'I'm looking for the big dog.'
    b. ***Mama**   **burnaringma**   ng-a   nawu.*
       this.III.SG.ACC wild.orange.III.ACC 1SG.A-PST step.on
       'I sat on this orange.'

4.1 Morphosyntax

Morphosyntactically, noun classes are typically manifested in agreement patterns, on modifiers such as adjectives, numerals/quantifiers, possessive pronouns and demonstratives (as in (32) above), in personal pronouns (as in (31) above), in the cross-referencing prefixes on the verb, and on prefixed body part nouns or inalienably possessed nouns. Languages differ in this respect: there are several languages, for instance, where a class distinction is only seen in the free personal pronoun, and potentially on the verb. In other languages, the adjectives are the only place where agreement is marked. Several languages have a distinct class of uninflected 'adjectives', next to a class that is always marked in agreement (see chapter 3, section 1 on what this implies for adjective status). A more detailed discussion of each of these agreement targets can be found in Sands (1995). In addition to agreement, noun classes can also be marked on the noun itself. This is found in about one third of the languages and in most of these, only for part of the lexicon. Overt marking on the noun can be lexically determined, or semantically transparent. An example of the latter is when noun class marking distinguishes several different meanings of a stem. This is illustrated in (33) from Bininj Kunwok, where the prefixes on the head noun mark distinct but related meanings (Evans 2003a:

---

[31] Ford (1998: 97) argues that Emmi does not have noun classes. However, some pronominal suffixes on the verb show a male-female distinction, as do deictics (which can be used adnominally) (Ford 1998: 125). Two other non-Pama-Nyungan languages of the sample not mentioned here are Ngan'gityemerri/Ngan'gikurunggurr and Marrithiyel, which are discussed in section 5.

5, 124–125; see also below in sections 4.2 and 6). There is one case where overt class marking on the noun has a more specific function, viz. when it can also be absent. In Wubuy, for instance, the presence of overt class marking on the noun is associated with a 'topic' function, while its absence is associated with a 'non-topic' function (see Baker [2008] for a detailed study, also covering Ngalakgan and Marra).[32]

(33) Bininj Kunwok (Evans 2003a: 5, 186; own glossing)
   a. *na ngordo*
      I leprosy
      'male leper, cripple'
   b. *al ngordo*
      II leprosy
      'female leper, cripple'
   c. *gun ngordo*
      IV leprosy
      'leprosy'

Noun class markers obviously mark class membership, but they can also mark other features, including case and/or number. Number and class in particular are often connected in some way (also typologically, cf. e.g. Corbett 1991: 189–203; Corbett 2014: 98–99; Tsegaye et al. 2014: 191–214). In Alawa, for instance, the masculine and feminine noun class markers alternate with the non-singular number prefix (Sharpe 1972: 64), which can be analysed either as a restriction of class marking to singular forms, or alternatively as a system containing three classes (see below for more discussion). Similarly, in languages where the third person pronoun has a class distinction, it is usually only found in singular forms (e.g. Diyari [Austin 2011: 64]). In other languages, the human classes have separate minimal and dual forms but there is only one augmented form (e.g. Anindilyakwa [van Egmond 2012: 95–96]), or there is a separate 'collective' marker for non-human referents (e.g. Anindilyakwa [van Egmond 2012: 95–96]).

---

32 Sands (1995: 259–260) argues that another specific function of overt class marking on the head of the nominal expression is to mark argument roles (i.e. case). However, it seems to me that an analysis which takes case marking as the main function of overt marking of noun classes on the head is difficult to maintain, for example because portmanteau marking of class and case is found not only on the head of the nominal expression but also in agreement.

4.2 Meaning and use

The number of noun classes in the languages of the sample ranges from 2 to 7 in the singular (cf. also Sands 1995: 258). Additionally, in some languages, number markers, either general dual/plural markers or semantically specific markers like male and female dual forms, alternate with the class markers. In these cases, the number markers seem to behave like class markers, but in some instances there is also some evidence to keep them as a separate grammatical category (in other words, class distinctions are limited to singular forms). An example is Ungarinyin, which has a masculine class, a feminine class, two distinct neuter classes, as well as a neuter collective/human plural class (Rumsey 1982: 37–41; Spronck 2015: 26–27). The collective/plural class could in principle either be analysed as a separate noun class or as a pure number prefix which alternates with class prefixes. Spronck (2015: 26–27, p.c.) argues that the main reason for analysing it as a fifth noun class is that the collective/plural prefix alternates with the (singular) class prefixes and occurs in the same environments (i.e. on the same agreement targets). In addition, NPs marked with this prefix are non-countable when referring to non-human entities, and "unlike other plurals cannot trigger dual or paucal agreement on the verb" (Spronck 2015: 26–27, referring to Rumsey [1982: 39]).[33] In map 6 below, I provide the number of singular/minimal classes in the sample, followed by the number of non-singular classes if appropriate (e.g. Ungarinyin: 4+1). This number is always the maximal number of classes displayed by a language (e.g. when a language shows neutralisation in some word classes, this is not represented on the map). It only includes third person classes, not other person/number markers which in some languages can also alternate with class markers (even if these also show a class distinction, like Anindilyakwa, which distinguishes for instance 1DU.M from 1DU.F [van Egmond 2012: 96]).

---

33 Conversely, a reason to treat them as a separate grammatical category (i.e. number) may be that nouns from any of the four singular classes can occur with the plural prefix, while this type of regular switch is not possible across the singular classes (Spronck p.c.). Finally, there is a set of nouns that only occur with the collective/plural prefix, which can either be argued to constitute evidence for a noun class analysis, or can simply be seen as pluralia tantum when advocating a number-analysis (Spronck p.c.).

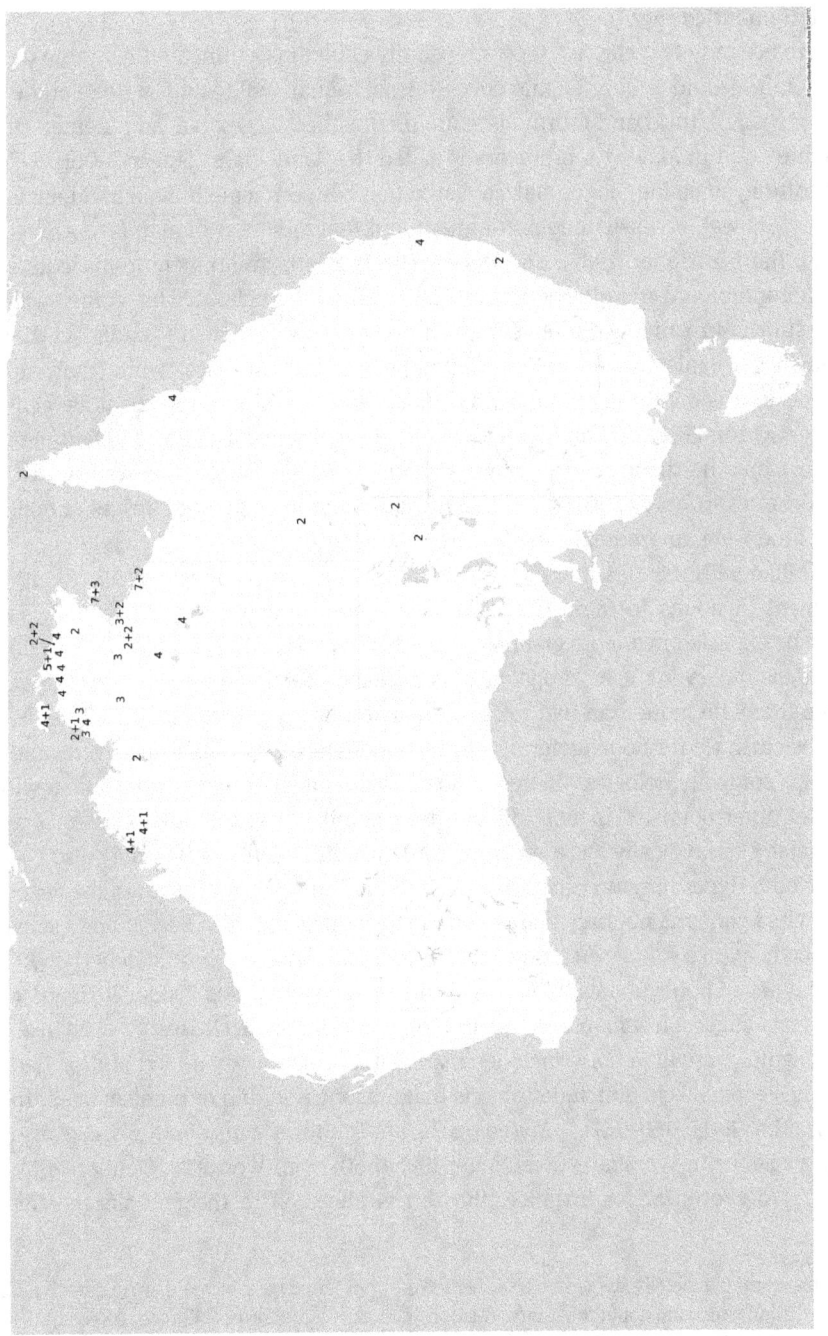

Map 6: Number of noun classes. For an online, dynamic version, see: http://bit.ly/nc-number.

4.2.1 Semantic range

If there are only two classes, they are usually called masculine and feminine (or non-feminine and feminine), and cover at least human male and female referents respectively. A third and fourth class are often called 'vegetable' and 'neuter' or 'residue', and in Mawng a fifth class is called the 'land' class (Singer 2006: 164). In addition, some languages make a distinction between male human and female human, as well as masculine non-human and feminine non-human (see Alpher [1987], Bani & Alpher [1987], and Harvey [1997] on the assignment to masculine and feminine, and the question which is the unmarked class). This is the case, for instance, in Yanyuwa; interestingly, however, only the female genderlect distinguishes a male human and a masculine non-human class, while they are merged in a general masculine class (human and non-human) in the male genderlect (Kirton 1988). In Limilngan, there are no separate masculine and feminine classes, but the distinction is between humans and animates (as well as two other classes) (Harvey 2001: 45).[34] Yanyuwa, finally, distinguishes a class of non-meat food from an arboreal class (Kirton 1971: 28–29).

Unlike with the classifier constructions described in sections 2 and 3, the assignment of nouns to these classes is overall less semantically transparent, as could be expected in a more grammaticalised system. However, Corbett (2007: 258) maintains that even the most opaque systems have a semantic core to their classes. When there are more than two classes, the masculine and feminine can either be used exclusively for nouns referring to male and female humans respectively (and perhaps some mythological figures or domestic animals) or they can include a variety of other nouns. It is more difficult to generalise over the other classes. The vegetable class typically has a semantic core including plants, but usually also has many other types of noun assigned to it. In Bininj Kunwok, for instance, the vegetable class contains not only plants and their products, but also sexual and excretory body parts, song, ceremony and custom, fire, (vegetable and other) food, some types of honey, boats, planes and cars, and so on (Evans 2003a: 202). Some grammars suggest a semantic core based on shape for some classes. For instance, the Jingulu masculine class includes inanimates which are rounded and/or flat, and the vegetable class includes objects that are long and thin or pointed, or sharp (Pensalfini 2003: 160–161).[35] Mythological and cultural considerations can also play a role, as in Wambaya (Nordlinger 1998a: 60) or in Worrorra (Clendon 2014: 70–72). In Worrorra, for instance, the sun is allocated to the feminine gender

---

34 This is more generally the case in Northern Worrorran languages, including Wunambal and Gunin/Kwini, which are not in the sample (McGregor 2008: 191; McGregor & Rumsey 2009: 50).
35 Note that this is typologically somewhat unexpected: round shape is usually associated with a feminine class and straight shape with a masculine class (e.g. Aikhenvald 2003: 276–278).

because the operation of the sun involves a "mother sun who (...) give[s] birth to daughter suns, each of whom in turn travels through the sky and dies at the end of each day" (Clendon 2014: 71); the moon is allocated to masculine gender (Clendon 2014: examples). Incidentally, this pattern (sun F and moon M) is found in a number of languages (e.g. Bininj Kunwok [Evans 2003a: 204], Burarra [Green 1987: 15], Dyirbal [Dixon 1980: 274], Gaagudju [Harvey 2002: 391, 396], Giimbiyu [Campbell 2006: 41], Jingulu [Pensalfini 2003: 161], Mawng [Singer 2006: 164], Ungarinyin [Rumsey 1982: 38], Wambaya [Nordlinger 1998a: 62]; see also Dixon [2002: 492]), though not in all (in Marra, for instance, sun is neuter [Heath 1981: 74]). Another potentially relevant principle is that entities which are exceptional members of their class also have exceptional class assignment (e.g. Dyirbal [Dixon 1972: 308–311]; Mawng [Singer 2006: 165]). For example, in Mawng snakes belong to the masculine class, except for *wulminkaykay* 'file snake', the only snake that is a traditional food source, which belongs to the feminine class (Singer 2006: 165). Phonological features do not seem to play a role in the majority of languages, although Harvey (2002: 149–150) argues that phonological similarity can provide a basis for assignment to a particular class in Gaagudju (similarly in Anindilyakwa for loanwords [van Egmond 2012: 99], in Jingulu [Pensalfini 2003: 160], in Limilngan [Harvey 2001: 45], and in Worrorra for English loanwords [Love 1934: 20; McGregor p.c.]). The underlying principles of class assignment are often also demonstrated in the way in which loan words are integrated in the system. In Tiwi (Lee 1987: 81), for instance, loan words are classified based on the same principles as traditional ones: *pirijirayita* 'refrigerator' is classified as feminine because it is 'large, round and ample', while *tayipuli* 'table' is classified as masculine because it has legs.

4.2.2 Variable class assignment

As with classifiers, many languages show at least some instances of variable assignment to classes, though perhaps not as frequently. In grammatical descriptions, this is often called 'disagreement', as only the class markers on the agreement targets change while the form of the head noun remains unchanged. Variable assignment is perhaps more unexpected for a more strongly grammaticalised system like noun classes, and the question is in how far this affects the supposedly 'grammatical' status of these systems. There are two main motivations for variable agreement, one relating to natural gender, and another relating to perspectivisation (similar to the variation described for classifiers, see section 2.2.2). In addition, there are also two types of structures that look like variable assignment, but are in fact quite different phenomena.

The first type of variability is agreement according to the natural gender of the referent. Some languages have nouns that do not have an inherent class, but can control masculine or feminine agreement (i.e. "nouns of common gender" [Corbett 2007: 251]). This is the case, for instance, in the Ungarinyin structures in (34) (Rumsey 1982: 38). In other cases, the noun does have an inherent or grammatical class, but this can be overruled by natural class. This is possible, for instance, in Wambaya (Nordlinger 1998a: 70–71), where the noun *wuwunji* 'honey, sugarbag' is inherently a class I noun (an animate class), but can trigger agreement as class IV, based on the natural inanimacy of the referent, as in (35a). In (35b) this is 'corrected' in repeated, monitored speech.

(34) Ungarinyin (Rumsey 1982: 38)
    a. *yila   djiri*
       child M.ANAPH
       'little boy'
    b. *yila   njindi*
       child F.ANAPH
       'little girl'

(35) Wambaya (Nordlinger 1998a: 70–71)
    a. *Aliyulu ng-a   bulyungu   wawunji.*
       find   1SG.A-PST little.IV(ACC) sugarbag.I(ACC)
       'I found a little sugarbag.'
    b. *Aliyulu ng-a   bulyingi   wawunji.*
       find   1SG.A-PST little.I(ACC) sugarbag.I(ACC)
       'I found a little sugarbag.'

A second motivation for variable assignment is a different representation based on the discourse context. This is, in fact, not unlike the variability we observed for generic-specific constructions, where different generics profile different aspects of the referent in different discourse contexts (see section 2.2.2). For instance, animals can receive masculine or feminine class marking when represented as Dreamtime beings in Anindilyakwa (van Egmond 2012: 98), Mangarrayi (Merlan 1989: 51) and Ungarinyin (Rumsey 1982: 37). Other examples are found in three further languages of the sample. In Mawng (see Singer [2006, 2016] for detailed accounts), class marking can alternate when an entity undergoes a transformation to serve a human purpose, e.g. when iron (masculine) is used to make a shelter (shelters and houses regularly belonging to the edible noun class). It can also alternate when a Dreamtime being becomes a permanent landscape feature. Other alternations in Mawng are argued to be instances of homonymy (see below), but they may in fact also fall under this type. These are, for instance, alternations based on trees and their products (as in (39c-d) below), or the alternation seen for *kurrula* 'sea, seawater', which controls masculine agreement in (36a) for reference to "the sea as a body of water or 'force of nature'", and land agreement in (36b) for reference to the actual liquid (Singer 2006: 171). Similarly, in Giimbiyu, *wukkuk* 'water' can be classified in the vegetable class when seen as a feature of the landscape or in the neuter class when seen as something to drink (Campbell 2006: 42). Finally, in Limilngan, humans can be classified in class II instead of the regular class I, to indicate that the referent is comparatively more powerful (see Harvey [2001: 48] for more details).

(36) Mawng (Singer 2006: 171)
 a. *"Inyi ku-ti-ø wurlupurlup nu-latparlangkat ja kurrula."*
    NEG.IMP 2PL-STAND-NPST swim M-strong M sea
    "Don't swim the sea's rough (lit: strong)."
 b. *"Tuka ta kurrula. Inyi kurrun-ta-ø."*
    DEM:PROX.LL LL saltwater NEG 2PL>3LL-drink-NPST
    "This is seawater. Don't drink it."

Such 'perspectivising' uses of noun classes are rarer than in classifier systems (the examples above are the full list in the sample),[36] in line with the fact that noun classes are more grammaticalised systems. However, the fact that they do occur shows that a clear-cut distinction between noun class and noun classifier cannot be maintained (see section 1).

There is another set of alternations in the sample that look similar, but is analysed slightly differently in the literature, because it is not entirely clear that one single lexeme is involved. Examples (33) above and (37) below from Bininj Kunwok illustrate how one noun stem can occur with different prefixes, in both cases lexicalised, but with related meanings (e.g. in a relation of metonymy), as argued by Evans (2003a: 183–184, 186–188). Similarly, example (38), from Anindilyakwa, shows the same noun stem meaning 'mouth' in the neutral class and 'cave' in the vegetable class. Van Egmond (2012: 98) argues that these are separate lexemes, though with related meaning, because there is no flexibility in class assignment synchronically. Finally, the examples in (39) from Mawng are slightly different in that the form of the nouns is the same, but they control

---

36 It also, and perhaps more regularly, occurs in Ngalakgan (Baker 2002), which is not in the sample. Baker (2002) focuses on the noun class marker on the verb, which disagrees with the noun it cross-references based on the context: e.g. is the object we are talking about seen as a 'type of spear shaft' or a 'type of tree'?

different class agreement. Singer (2006: 168–169) regards these as homonyms. In fact, the borderline between cases like these and variable agreement as discussed above is not always clear: for instance, if the senses are clearly related, as in (39c-d), alternations could also be analysed as one referent being treated from different perspectives (the tree in itself vs. the belt made from that tree). The key question is probably whether the different senses are related in a synchronically transparent way and whether there is any indication of lexicalisation.

(37) Bininj Kunwok (Evans 2003a: 5; own glossing based on other examples)
    a. *kun mim*
       IV   fruit
       'eye'
    b. *man mim*
       III   fruit
       'fruit'

(38) Anindilyakwa (van Egmond 2012: 98)
    a. *edhvrra* 'mouth' (N)
    b. *medhvrra* 'cave' (VE)

(39) Mawng (Singer 2006: 168–169)
    a. *minyngu*
       'dirt and sweat on the body' (VE)
    b. *minyngu*
       'ceremony' (M)
    c. *marriwi*
       'tree species used to make string' (VE)
    d. *marriwi*
       'string belt' (M)

To round off this discussion of variable assignment, I discuss one last phenomenon that looks like it, but should in fact be analysed in terms of class neutralisation, with an unmarked class that can replace regular agreement. This phenomenon is also known as 'superclassing' in the Australianist literature, whereby "an unmarked agreement class (the superclass) may replace the inherent class of the referent noun that would normally appear on the modifier" (Sands 1995: 264). This is found in at least 7 languages of the sample: Bininj Kunwok (see below), Gaagudju (Harvey 2002: 153–157), Jingulu (Pensalfini 2003: 166–169), Limilngan (Harvey 2001: 46–49), Wambaya (Nordlinger 1998a: 71–72), Warray (Harvey ms: 33–34) and Worrorra (Clendon 2014: 90–94;

especially in possessives).[37] Superclassing is usually organised in terms of one human/animate superclass (masculine) and one non-human/inanimate superclass (depending on the language, vegetable or neuter), with potentially even one single super-superclass (masculine). For instance, in Bininj Kunwok, the masculine and vegetable class are the unmarked animate and inanimate classes respectively, while the female and neutral classes are marked. Overall, the inanimate class is more marked than the animate class (Evans 2003a: 200). This can be seen in neutralisations like in (40a), where the plural context results in masculine agreement, instead of the expected feminine agreement (Evans 2003a: 212–216). This can also be observed in differences between dialects (Evans 2003a: 182): Kunwinjku has the maximum of four classes, but Mayali only has three, where the most marked class (neutral) has disappeared and now shows vegetable agreement; compare (40b) from Kunwinjku with (40c) from Mayali. Kune has even lost its noun class system altogether and all nouns control masculine 'agreement' (which means that the gloss M in the example is etymological and only valid with respect to the dialects which do distinguish noun classes), as shown in (40d).

(40) Bininj Kunwok (Evans 2003a: 214, 182; own glossing for b-d)
  a. *Na-meke dah-daluk birri-gih-gimuk.*
     M-that   RDP-woman   3A.PST-RDP-big
     'Those women are big.'
  b. *kun-warrde kun-mak*
     IV-rock   N-good
     'good rock' (Kunwinjku)
  c. *gun-warrde an-mak*
     IV-rock   VE-good
     'good rock' (Mayali)
  d. *kun-warrde na-mak*
     IV-rock   M-good
     'good rock' (Kune)

---

37 Another candidate is Mangarrayi (Merlan 1989: 110–111). In this language, the demonstrative paradigm is defective in the neuter paradigm, i.e. there is only one neuter form which can be used for nominative and accusative, and not for other cases. When there is no neuter form available, the masculine is used. Interestingly, the masculine form is also sometimes used in nominative and accusative (even though a neuter form is available). This neutralisation seems to be less extensive than in the other languages.

4.2.3 Use of noun class systems

We can round off this section with some comments on how and why noun class systems are used. Unlike with noun classifiers (or generics, see section 2 for discussion in the Australian context), the use of noun classes is grammatically determined and thus normally obligatory (but see section 4.1 for an exception). As a grammatical system, its function has mainly been associated with 'reference tracking' (e.g. Corbett 1991; Heath 1983), but Merlan et al. (1997) see a much broader function, which includes both the instantiation and the maintenance of reference (labelled together as "reference management"). Singer (2016: 81; 83–102) adds to this the function of verb sense disambiguation in Mawng: noun class agreement helps in selecting the relevant sense of the verb.[38] For instance, the verb –*la* 'consume' typically takes land gender object agreement when the sense 'drink' is intended, even if the object noun itself typically has another gender. In (41), for example, the speaker is asked to describe a vampire drinking blood and first gives the response in (41a), with the verb showing vegetable gender marking, in agreement with the gender of the object ('blood'), but then immediately corrects it with the agreement prefix on the verb in the land gender which is felt to be more natural (41b) (Singer 2016: 83). Apart from these general functions, noun class systems may also have more specific discourse functions. In Warray, (dis)agreement with female nouns is argued to be correlated with new (agreement) vs. given information (disagreement), although Harvey admits that this claim needs further substantiation and no contrastive examples are given (1986: 55).

(41) Mawng (Singer 2016: 83)
    a. *Maningul kamani-la-ø.*
       blood(VE) PRS.3M>3VE-consume-NPST
       'He drinks blood.'
    b. *Not*   *kamani-la-ø!*   *K-ani-la-ø.*
       (English) PRS.3M>3VE-consume-NPST PRS-3M>3LL-consume-NPST
       'Not "He consumes it (VE)" but "He drinks it (LL)".'

5 In between classifier and noun class systems

There are two languages in the sample whose systems of classification are in between the two poles of noun class and noun classifiers: Ngan'gityemerri and Marrithiyel, from the Southern Daly and Western Daly families respectively,

---

38 Some of these agreement patterns have even become lexicalised (Singer 2016: 103–172).

genetically unrelated but part of the Daly River Sprachbund (Evans 2003b: 13). Both cases have been discussed extensively in the literature (Reid 1997; Green 1997), and especially Ngan'gityemerri has been cited as evidence of the grammaticalisation pathway towards noun classes in several typological surveys (e.g. Aikhenvald 2003: 92–93; Corbett 2007: 254–255; Seifart 2010: 727–728).

The classification systems in Ngan'gityemerri (Reid 1997) and Marrithiyel (Green 1997) show features of both noun classifiers (or generics, see section 2) and noun classes. As with classifier systems, there is quite a large number of generics (15 and 13 respectively), (some) generics have free forms (alone or in addition to bound forms), the use of freeform generics is optional, generics can occur by themselves (anaphorically or in reference to a general category), class assignment is semantically quite transparent, and not all nouns are assigned to a class (although most are). As with noun class systems, however, some generics have bound forms (alone or in addition to free forms), there is agreement in the NP (both for free forms and for bound forms,[39] albeit optionally), and elliptical NPs have to include a generic/class marker to be grammatical (as illustrated in (42) for Marrithiyel). The examples from Ngan'gityemerri in (43a-c) illustrate the availability (and co-occurrence) of free and bound forms. Variable assignment is possible, both for free forms, as in (43d), and for bound forms, as in (43e-f). The variation in (43e-f) can be explained in the following way: the head noun denotes a tree which has no useful parts apart from its fruit and is thus assigned to the 'vegetable' class, with its modifiers normally showing 'vegetable' agreement, as in (43e) where reference is actually made to the fruit, and not the tree. However, when explicit reference is made to the whole tree rather than its fruit, the modifiers 'disagree' with the head noun and receive 'tree' agreement, as in (43f). In other words, the variation seems to involve different construals of the referent.

(42) Marrithiyel (Green 1997: 244–245)
    a. *watjen sjikim ginidin-a*
        dog   black 2SG.S:REAL:see-PST
        'Did you see the black dog?'
    b. *a-sjikim ginidin-a*   c. **sjikim ginidin-a*
        LA-black 2SG.S:REAL:see-PST   black 2SG.S:REAL:see-PST
        'Did you see the black creature?'

---

39 If there is a choice between free forms and bound forms, the bound forms are used for agreement.

(43) Ngan'gityemerri (Reid 1997: 177, 175, 174, 178, 201)
    a. *(tyin)　　　gan'gun　　　　(tyin)　　kinyi*
       WOOMERA fish.spear.woomera WOOMERA this
      gugarra　　red.ochre
      nganam-garri-fulirr-ngirim
      1SG.S:AUX-leg-rub-1SG.S:sit
      'I am rubbing ochre into the length of this fish spear-type woomera.'
    b. *(miyi) mi-meli　　　wurrbun-ba-ket*
      VEG　　VE-purple.plum　3PL.S.lash-arm-cut
      'They are picking purple plums.'
    c. *wa=tyerrmusye (wa=)mirrisyarra perrety-meny*
      M=old.man　　M=blind　　　　　die-3SG.S:do
      'That old blind man has died.'
    d. *syiri　　yawurr; kini　　　yawurr*
      STRIKER stick　　DIGGING.STICK stick
      'stick for fighting'; 'stick for digging'
    e. *mi-menem　　　mi=biny werrmim-ba-ket*
      VE-billygoat.plum VE=ripe 3PL.S:AUX-arm-cut
      'They are picking ripe billygoat plums.'
    f. *mi-menem　　　　yerr=kinyi yerr=syari yubu-ket-ø*
      VE-billygoat.plum TREE=this TREE=dry 2SG.S:AUX-cut-IMP
      'Chop down this withered billygoat plum tree!'

The 'in between' status of these two languages has been analysed as the result of an evolution from a noun classifier system to a noun class system, with agreement as a first step in the grammaticalisation process (see e.g. Dixon 1982c; Reid 1997; Seifart 2010). These languages also provide another illustration why the distinction between noun class and noun classifiers may not be not as clear-cut as presented in table 2. In fact, Green (1997) argues that an alternative approach to this problem is simply to state that agreement is not necessarily a feature of noun class systems, but only typically.

6 Multiple classification systems

To round off this chapter, I briefly comment on those languages in the sample that have more than one classification system. I should first note that there are several languages for which the descriptions posit several concurrent systems, but which I analyse in a different way. For instance, van Egmond in her description of Anindilyakwa (2012: 94–100, 108–111) distinguishes 'gender' (for human referents) from 'noun class' (for non-human referents). The two sets of markers are in complementary distribution, however, so it is unclear to me why it is necessary to posit separate classification systems (except that the human classes distinguish number and the non-human ones do not, see above). Harvey in his grammar of Gaagudju (2002: 127–128) distinguishes between 'gender' (four classes, marked on adjective, demonstrative and absolutive verb prefixes, and commonly with non-human reference) and 'noun class' (two classes, marked on numerals, ergative verb prefixes, free pronouns, indirect object clitics and number clitics, and rarely having non-human reference). Since there is a regular mapping between the two paradigms (Class I = Masculine gender, Classes II, III, IV = Feminine gender), and a neat correlation with word class and/or case, the smaller paradigm can in fact be analysed as a neutralisation of the four 'genders' in certain word classes or cases (see also Sands 1995: 248–249). Finally, Evans in his analysis of Bininj Kunwok (2003a: 181–184), uses 'noun class' for a set of derivational prefixes that are part of nouns (i.e. part of the lexicon), while 'gender' is used for inflectional agreement prefixes on the modifiers of the noun (i.e. the type of nominal classification studied here).

Apart from such apparent cases, there are 10 languages in the sample that genuinely have more than one classification system: seven have both generic-specific structures and noun classes, and three have both verbal classifiers and noun classes (one of which also has adjectival classifiers).

Two languages of the first group, Diyari and Yandruwandha, are situated in central Australia. Diyari has regular, quite well-developed generic-specific structures with 9 generics; Yandruwandha has a set of 5 generics, which are, however, only used "with a minority of nouns" (Breen 2004a: 54). In addition, both also have a feminine – non-feminine distinction in the personal pronouns, which can be used as modifiers to nouns and thus show the noun class of the noun (see also in chapter 7, section 3.3). Class assignment is quite simple: only animates whose reference is "distinctly female" (Austin 2011: 64) belong to the feminine noun class and all others to the non-feminine noun class. The interaction of the two systems is illustrated in (44), which shows a generic-specific structure (*pirta pathara*) and a third person pronominal modifier marked for non-feminine agreement (Austin 2011: 98, examples; it is not mentioned which of the two nouns controls the agreement and could thus be considered the head; in independent use both trigger non-feminine agreement).

(44) Diyari (Austin 2011: 98)
ngathi **nhinha** **pirta pathara** *dandra-rda purri-yi*
1SG.ERG 3SGNF.ACC tree box.tree.ACC hit-PTCP AUX-PRS
'I chop the box tree'

The other five languages with both noun classifiers and noun classes are all found in one region in the north of Australia, viz. the three Daly languages Emmi, Malakmalak and Wadjiginy, and nearby Wardaman and Warray. They all have a small number of generics, and for three languages (Emmi, Wardaman and Warray), the use of generic-specific structures seems to be infrequent. The noun classes show limited agreement, and in Warray they are said to be 'semi-lexicalised' (e.g. some adjectives receive a fixed class prefix, regardless of the noun they modify). The interaction of these systems is illustrated in (45) from Malakmalak. Example (45a) shows how the generic *mi* for non-meat food is used in a generic-specific structure, while the adjective *munanki* shows agreement for vegetable noun class. In (45b), the generic *tɛ* for meat food occurs in a generic-specific structure; masculine agreement is only seen outside the NP in this example, viz. on the auxiliary *yunguny*. Malakmalak has a set of 3 to 5 generics that are used in a similar way; use of such structures is not rare (Birk 1976: 97–98; Hoffmann p.c.). In addition, it has a limited noun class system: agreement occurs only on bound pronouns and on the small, closed class of adjectives (Birk 1976: 98–104).

(45) Malakmalak (Birk 1976: 102, 49)
    a. mi   munytyalk   munanki
       CLF lily   young (SG.VEG)
       'young lily'
    b. tɛ   yingi   kark   yunguny
       CLF crocodile come.up 3SG.M(S).CONJUG2(PROGR)
       'The saltwater crocodile was coming up.'

For the languages with both verbal classifiers and noun classes, we can distinguish between Bininj Kunwok and Anindilyakwa on the one hand, and Rembarrnga on the other hand. Rembarrnga has both a limited noun class system, with only a female – non-female distinction in free pronouns in agreement with a head noun, and a limited system of incorporated generics. The other two languages have both a well-developed noun class system and a well-developed verbal classifier system (see section 3). In addition, Anindilyakwa has a system of adjectival classifiers (as already discussed in section 3, see example (30) which illustrates how modifying adjectives show class agreement with the head noun and can at the same time have classifying generics incorporated).

In most of the languages where two systems co-occur, it seems that at least one of them is rather limited, in terms of the size of the system or its use. The other system can be better-developed (as in Diyari), or both systems can be somewhat limited (as in Emmi, Malakmalak, Wadjiginy, Warray and Rembarrnga).

Bininj Kunwok and Anindilyakwa are the exceptions to this generalisation: as just mentioned, they have both well-developed systems of noun classes and of verbal classifiers.

The existence of languages with multiple nominal classification systems raises questions concerning the grammaticalisation pathway from noun classifier to noun class. If the two co-occur, does this mean that just part of the classifier system has undergone grammaticalisation into noun class while another part has not, or has one classifier system grammaticalised into noun class while a second classifier system emerged in a later stage? Would the systems eventually merge in one noun class system? These questions can only be answered in diachronic studies, which are beyond the scope of this book.

7 Conclusion

This chapter has provided a survey of nominal classification, which is without any doubt the most intensively studied aspect of NP structure for Australian languages. I have tried to synthesise the available literature, and have situated Australian languages in a general typology of nominal classification. The data from the sample are largely in line with the literature: generic-specific structures and noun classes are well-attested, and verbal and adjectival classifiers are rare. The survey also highlighted a few issues that remain unresolved. For instance, the syntactic analysis of generic-specific structures remains a subject of discussion. There is some debate on which element is the head of the structure, and whether the generics in these structures are 'true' noun classifiers (even though, as argued above, the status of these noun classifiers is equally unclear, which makes it difficult to use them as a standard of comparison). I have suggested that Wilkins' proposal (2000) to take the construction (rather than the individual generic) as the basic classifying unit is the most interesting lead for future analysis in many languages. Another point that surfaced concerns the distinction between noun classes and noun classifiers, which is not always as clear-cut as suggested in some of the typological literature (as also argued by Fedden & Corbett 2017). For instance, class variation for perspectivisation is not only found with generics, but also in systems with noun classes (see, in particular, the work of Singer [2016]), though to a lesser extent and in fewer languages. A second relevant argument, well-known from the literature, concerns languages that show features of both classifiers and noun classes, and are thus clearly in-between the two, like the two Daly languages Ngan'gityemerri and Marrithiyel.

3 Qualification

The second survey chapter discusses the domain of qualification, which is reasonably well-analysed in the Australian literature, but not to the same extent as classification. Qualifiers can be defined functionally as modifiers in the NP which describe a property of the referent, like *tall* in the English structure in (46).

(46) English
   the tall man

In English, an element like *tall* belongs to a word class that is specialised in this function, viz. adjectives, and it can qualify the head of the NP directly, as shown in (46). Not all languages, however, have a specialised word class for qualification or allow direct qualification of the head noun. These two issues, viz. word class and syntactic realisation, are interrelated, and at the same time they are the most prominent questions in the literature on the typology of qualification. They will be discussed in sections 1 and 2 respectively.

1 Adjectives as a word class

The question of identifying a word class of adjectives has been tackled in many different ways in the literature, using various combinations of criteria, relating to meaning ('adjectives denote properties'), morphology ('adjectives have distinct morphological potential') and syntax ('adjectives can serve as modifiers in referential phrases') (e.g. Dixon [1982d, 2004, 2010], Hengeveld et al. [2004], Schachter & Shopen [2007] amongst many others; see also Haspelmath [2012] for an overview of the literature). For some languages there is a clear consensus on the existence (or not) of a separate adjective class, whereas for others there is serious debate (many Australian languages belong to the last category, as shown in this section).

There are three basic typological options in this respect (following the analysis of Hengeveld et al. [2004: 530–541] and Hengeveld & Rijkhoff [2005: 407]; see van Lier & Rijkhoff [2013] for an excellent overview of this approach and others). The first two both involve languages with rigid classes, in which each lexeme is associated with one specific function. The first option is then that a language has a differentiated class of adjectives, which is associated only with the function of attribution (this can be an open class or a closed one); in this case, the language normally also at least has differentiated classes of verbs and nouns (following the hierarchy proposed in Hengeveld et al. [2004]). The second option is that a language has rigid classes of verbs and nouns, but no distinct class of adjectives. If there is no adjective class, this means that elements from other classes, with other basic functions, will take over the adjectival function using special constructions, e.g. a relative clause in languages that only have a rigid class of verbs. The final option does not include rigid word classes, but flexible ones. With flexible classes, lexemes are not specialised in one single syntactic function, but are flexible between functions (or, in other words, they are category-neutral [van Lier & Rijkhoff 2013]). For example, the typical attributive function of modification is one of the functions of a broader word class that has other functions as well, e.g. there is a class of 'nominals' (or 'non-verbs' in Hengeveld's terminology, as opposed to the class of verbs) that can serve directly, i.e. without any morphological or other changes, as the head and as the modifier of a referential phrase. Both Hengeveld & Rijkhoff (2005: 414) and McGregor (2013: 243–245) characterise flexible items as semantically vague, but the meaning components attributed to these items differ. Hengeveld & Rijkhoff, on the one hand, attribute a larger set of meaning components to each lexeme, where their use in one function highlights the meaning components relevant to that function (inspired by Wilkins' [2000] analysis of classification constructions [see chapter 2, section 2]). McGregor, on the other hand, argues that only meaning which is recurrent in all uses is coded meaning (i.e. there is no highlighting of meaning components; additional meaning is derived compositionally from the grammatical relations and unit the lexeme is in).

For Australian languages, there has been much debate on whether they have rigid adjective classes (i.e. the first type discussed above) or rather flexible nominal classes (i.e. the last type discussed above). In two major surveys about twenty years apart, for instance, Dixon argues both for and against the idea that Australian languages have a distinct adjective class: Dixon (1980: 274) states that they "have a rich open class of adjectives with some hundreds of members," while Dixon (2002: 67) argues that "[n]ouns and adjectives generally show the same morphological and syntactic possibilities, so that it can be difficult to give criteria for recognising them as distinct classes." Another classic reference is Hale (1982: 219), who only distinguishes verbs from nominals, without a noun-adjective distinction, in Warlpiri. Because of this attention in the general Australianist literature and following Hale (1982), most grammatical descriptions in the sample explicitly discuss the question whether a particular language has distinct classes of nouns and adjectives or one encompassing class of 'nominals'. The arguments in favour of or against a separate adjective class are diverse, and the conclusions can diverge, even if very similar criteria are used.

There are four types of criteria that grammars rely on: conceptual, functional, morphological, and syntactic. I list these briefly below; more detailed discussion of each separate criterion follows in the next few sections.
(i) Conceptual basis: Nouns generally denote things, while adjectives denote properties.
(ii) Function: Nouns normally function as referential heads, while adjectives normally function as attributive modifiers. If adjectives appear to function as heads, this is only in elliptical contexts. If nouns function as modifiers, this is restricted to particular contexts.
(iii) Morphological processes:
   a. Nouns and adjectives have different morphological potential, e.g. they undergo different derivational processes.
   b. The same lexeme has different forms when functioning as a noun or as an adjective (i.e. one can be derived from the other).
(iv) (Morpho)syntax:
   a. There is a difference in word order for nouns and adjectives.
   b. Nouns normally belong to only one noun class, while adjectives are marked for the class of the noun they modify (and can thus be marked for any class).
   c. Adjectives can be modified by degree modifiers, while nouns cannot.

Before going into the specifics of each criterion, it may be useful to look at how the criteria are combined in particular languages and what can be concluded from such combinations. I will first discuss how grammatical descriptions deal with this question, before presenting a slightly different perspective, focusing on how the tension between category and structure can be dealt with.

To illustrate how grammars deal with these questions, I have organised data for 10 languages in the sample in a table (table 4), showing which criteria are relevant and what is concluded from them in the grammatical descriptions. The descriptions in the header of the table refer to the criteria listed above.

As the table shows, the three main options concerning the question of word classes in the sample are (a) a separate adjective class, (b) no separate adjective class but rather one 'nominal' class, (c) one 'nominal' class in which several subclasses, like nouns and adjectives, can be distinguished. In terms of the general typology outlined above, Australian languages either have a rigid class of adjectives, or a flexible class that covers both adjectival and nominal functions; the other options in the general typology are not attested.⁴⁰ The relevant classes are usually open, as they are in all of the languages in this table, but there are a handful of languages in the sample that have closed classes, viz. Malakmalak (Birk 1976: 27; Hoffmann p.c.), Nyangumarta (Sharp 2004: 84), Tiwi (Lee 1987: 88), Gaagudju (only for two of the three subclasses of adjectives, Harvey 2002: 129), and possibly⁴¹ Mathi-Mathi (Blake et al. 2011: 78), Paakantyi (Hercus 1982: 53) and Dharumbal (Terrill 2002: 37). Note that many languages also distinguish further subclasses of nouns/nominals, like kin terms and body parts (see e.g. Ponsonnet [2015] for an account of Dalabon); this is not further discussed in this book, although these types of classes may also influence how the NP is construed (see chapter 8 for some suggestions).

Even if the overall profile of Australian languages is clear, however, it is far from straightforward to see what evidence leads to what conclusion about word classes in this domain. As can be seen in the table, evidence is used in different ways in the literature, and the decision often boils down to the weight one gives to each of the criteria and to where one draws the line (if you wish to draw a line at all; see also Haspelmath [2012]). For instance, for both Anguthimri and Arrernte it is argued that there are separate noun and adjective classes, but for Anguthimri this is done on the basis of word order differences and differences in conceptual basis only (Crowley 1981: 162), whereas Arrernte also shows morphological differences between nouns and adjectives (Wilkins 1989: 104–105). Conversely, in Yawuru, it is argued there is no separate adjective class, in spite of some morphological and functional differences (Hosokawa 1991: 20–21). In general, many authors decide on a 'compromise' solution in which nouns and adjectives are seen as subclasses of the nominal word class, since there are some differences between them but not enough to posit separate classes (e.g. Meakins & Nordlinger [2014: 80–82] on Bilinarra; Patz [2002: 42] on Kuku Yalanji; Green [1989: 44] on Marrithiyel). Often, there are also other subclasses in the same nominal word class, like demonstratives or pronouns (e.g. Wadjiginy [Ford 1990: 71]; Duungidjawu [Kite & Wurm 2004: 23]; Jaminjung

---

40 Note that Australian languages also generally allow nominals to be used predicatively. This is, however, not a sufficient reason to abandon a distinction between verbs and nominals, because verbs cannot normally be used referentially (see for instance McGregor [2013] on this issue in Gooniyandi). As this book focuses on NPs, I do not further investigate the predicative use of nominals.

41 Adjectives are "few in number" (Blake et al. [2011: 78] on Mathi-Mathi; Hercus [1982: 53] on Paakantyi), but it is unclear whether they are truly a closed class, or that just not many examples of adjectives have been attested. Similarly for Dharumbal, "[t]here are three clear adjectives in the data" (Terrill 2002: 37).

Table 4: N vs. A in 10 languages of the sample.

Language	Conceptual basis	Function	Morph. potential	Differences in Form	Word order	Classification	Degree mod.	Conclusion in the grammar
Anguthimri	yes	?	no	no	yes	n/a	?	separate A class (Crowley 1981: 162)
Arrernte	yes	yes	yes	some	yes	?	yes	separate A class (Wilkins 1989: 104)
Bardi	yes	yes	yes	no	yes	?	yes	distinction between N and A, but not very robust (Bowern 2012: 158)
Garrwa	?	unclear	no	no	no	n/a	?	no separate A class (Mushin 2012: 44)
Gumbaynggir	yes	no	no	no	no	n/a	?	no separate A class (Eades 1979: 271)
Kuuk Thaayorre	yes	no	no	some	yes	yes	yes	'nomen' class includes A, N and quantifiers (Gaby 2017: 75)
Walmajarri	?	no	yes	yes	no	?	?	unclear

Yankunytjatjara	yes	no	?	yes	?	nominal class includes N, A, dem, pron and definite marker; distinction between N and A not always clear-cut (Goddard 1985: 17)[42]
Yawuru	yes	yes	some	no	n/a	?	formally one class of 'common nominals' (incl. N, A, indef pron) (Hosokawa 1991: 20–21)
Yir Yoront	yes	no	some	yes	?	yes	'noun' class includes substantives and adjectives (Alpher 1973: 50)

[42] Note that Bowe (1990: 8) posits a separate adjective class in Pitjantjatjara (the Western Desert variety closest to Yankunytjatjara) on syntactic grounds.

[Schultze-Berndt 2000: 45]). When there are only conceptual differences, some authors decide that there is one word class (e.g. Eades 1979: 271–272 on Gumbaynggir), while others regard this as sufficient evidence for separate subclasses (e.g. Haviland [1979: 45–46] on Guugu Yimidhirr).

Despite the neat list of criteria above (i-iv), I do not think that they all have the same status. Even though conceptual criteria (i) are often mentioned in grammars, I consider them to be less decisive than other criteria (or even entirely indecisive, see below). The other criteria can be slightly re-organised in two groups instead of three: on the one hand, criteria which concern the form of the lexical elements by themselves, and on the other hand, criteria which are construction-based, i.e. which concern the distribution of elements in structures. The first group includes purely morphological criteria (iii), while the second group includes both functional (ii) and morphosyntactic (iv) criteria. It is exactly the tension between these two groups of criteria that explains the difficulties encountered in debates concerning word class. Is any of the two groups more decisive than the other?

In order to answer this question, in sections 1.1 to 1.3 I first analyse the different individual criteria listed above (i-iv), as discussed in the grammars of the sample, and summarise the specific arguments and conclusions based on the presence or absence of these criteria. In section 1.4, I round off with my own conclusions about the question of adjectives, showing that all three options (separate adjective class, undifferentiated nominal class, and adjectival subclass of nominals) are available in the sample, depending on the relation between morphological and constructional evidence.

1.1 Conceptual criteria

Conceptual basis is probably the most vague and least decisive criterion in the set, but it is used in the grammars of the sample in a number of ways. Perhaps the most interesting application of this criterion is found in the grammars of Bardi (Bowern 2012: 265) and Yir Yoront (Alpher 1991: 25), where the distinction between nouns and adjectives is linked to the choice of question words. In Bardi, for instance, the answer to a question *nyirra* 'how' or *jana* 'which' is in the form of an adjective, while the answer to a question *anggi* 'what' is in the form of a noun (Bowern 2012: 265). In other grammars, conceptual basis is used in a more general way: there are 47 languages (see map 7) where the grammar mentions a general semantic distinction between nouns, which typically express entities, and adjectives, which typically express properties or qualities (the other grammars simply do not mention this criterion at all, or they posit one nominal class despite conceptual differences). Obviously, it is not possible to make such distinctions in a systematic way, as also argued in Dixon (1982d), who shows how features that are cross-linguistically associated with adjectives are not necessarily all found in the adjective class of one particular language. Several grammars in the sample make related observations. For example, in Diyari, the adjective class covers, amongst others, the semantic domains of value ('good'), dimension ('big'), and physical properties ('ripe'), whereas other domains like human propensity ('fear'), which could be expected to fall in the same category, are expressed by nouns (Austin 2011: 40–41). Similarly, in Gaagudju: "The adjective class does not conform that well to the corresponding semantically defined classes. The adjective class includes a number of stems which are not prototypically adjectives, and conversely a considerable number of prototypically adjectival stems are not members of the formal adjective class in Gaagudju" (Harvey 2002: 130). Conversely, authors who argue for one nominal class, include both entity-denoting and property-denoting elements. For instance, Hale (1983: 84) subsumes pronouns, names, substantives, attributives and quantifiers, mental and psychological statives, and locatives and directionals in the nominal class. Because conceptual differences are very general and not clear-cut, this criterion by itself in most grammars is considered insufficient to discern a separate class of adjectives, a position that I agree with.

1.2 Morphological criteria

Morphological differences are often seen as one of the major reasons to argue for a separate adjective class, or, in the absence of any, against it. However, once again, there is a tension between different criteria: are only small differences enough to consider nouns and adjectives separate classes, or conversely, can classes be distinguished even in the absence of morphological correlates? These questions have been answered differently in different grammars of the sample. For instance, Dyirbal is argued to have separate noun and adjective classes based on differences in nominal classification (see section 1.3), even if there are no morphological differences (Dixon 1972: 61), while Kayardild is argued not to have separate noun and adjective classes, as they have "identical inflectional and derivational possibilities" (Evans 1995a: 85). As argued above, this tension can be resolved by sorting out the results from the different criteria and looking at them separately.

In the sample, two thirds of the languages (67 to be exact) show no morphological distinction between adjectives and nouns (or no information is provided on this in the grammar), implying that they do not have a separate morphologically defined class of adjectives. For most of the other languages, i.e. those with morphological differences, such differences are rather limited, and they come to the surface only in part of the lexicon, in specific circumstances. There are two types of morphological criteria that occur: one is that nouns and adjectives have different morphological potential, the other is that nouns can be derived to form adjectives, or the other way around. I discuss these in turn; see also map 7 for more details on individual languages.

First, when nouns and adjectives have different morphological potential, this is good evidence for positing separate word classes. A first example of differences in morphological potential is when only adjectives, and not nouns, can be used with inchoative or causative affixes to form a verb. This is found in 7 languages. An example is Anindilyakwa, where "the inchoative and causative verbalising stem formatives are almost always suffixed to an adjective" with one or two exceptions where they are suffixed to nouns (Leeding 1989: 144). Similarly in Wambaya (Nordlinger 1998a: 47–48), the suffix *–mi*, which derives a verb meaning 'cause to be X, make X', is only found with adjectives, as in (47a), and not with nouns, as in (47b).[43]

(47) Wambaya (Nordlinger 1998a: 48)
    a. *gurijbi guriny-mi*
       'good'   'make good, make better'
    b. *juwa *juwa-mi*
       'man'   'make into a man'

A second example concerns differences in the process of reduplication for nouns and adjectives. This is found in at least 14 languages (see also below on the use of reduplication to derive adjectives from nouns). In fact, this is not a purely morphological feature because most differences lie in the semantic value of reduplication and not in its form. Typical effects of reduplication for nouns are plurality, diminution, repetition, and derivation of a new noun (or adjective, cf. below), while reduplication of adjectives typically has an intensifying or attenuative effect, or derives adverbs. For instance, in Emmi (Ford 1998: 99), a reduplicated noun marks plurality, as in (48a), while a reduplicated adjective is intensified, as in (48b). Another example is Diyari (Austin 2011: 62), where reduplicated nouns are diminutive, as in (49a), while reduplicated adjectives are intensified, as in (49b). In one language, viz. Arabana/Wangkangurru, there are also purely morphological factors: nouns reduplicated for a diminutive effect allow a maximal reduplication of two syllables,

---

[43] Nordlinger (1998a: 47–48) argues that these different derivational possibilities are due to semantic differences rather than a word class distinction. However, given that verbalisation is not even possible in a context that would license the right semantics (e.g. Dreamtime stories [Nordlinger 1998a: 48, fn. 5]), it really looks like a morphological difference.

while adjectives derived by reduplicating nouns ('having a great quantity of X') and reduplicated adjectives have a fully reduplicated form, even if the original is longer than two syllables (Hercus 1994: 96–99).

(48) Emmi (Ford 1998: 140)
    a. *perre*   *perreperre*
       'grub'   'grubs'
    b. *dukandji* *dukduk*
       'big'   'very big'

(49) Diyari (Austin 2011: 62)
    a. *kinthala* *kinthakinthala*
       'dog'   'doggy, puppy, little dog'
    b. *parti* *partiparti*
       'silly'   'mad, crazy'

The other examples of different morphological potential in the sample are a mixed bunch. For instance, some derivational affixes are only attached to nouns, and not to adjectives (e.g. Kuku Yalanji [Patz 2002: 44–45]; Walmajarri [Richards 1979: 103]). In Arabana/Wangkangurru, adjectives can derive adverbs while most nouns cannot (Hercus 1994: 60), and in Bilinarra, adjectives can be derived from coverbs while nouns cannot (Meakins & Nordlinger 2014: 81). In Biri, case marking appears on the head of the NP and all types of modifiers (demonstratives, numerals, quantifiers), except adjectives (Terrill 1998: 14).[44] Adjectives have an oblique stem in Warray, while nouns do not, and they take different inchoative suffixes (Harvey 1986: 70, 74). In Gaagudju, adjectives inflect for all persons and they usually inflect for number, while nouns do not inflect for person and are only exceptionally marked for number (Harvey 2002: 129). In Kuku Yalanji, finally, comparative and intensity markers *jarra-* 'rather, more' and *-baja(ku)* 'very' can only occur on adjectives and quantifiers and not on nouns (Patz 2002: 44).

The second type of morphological difference does not involve divergent morphological potential for the two categories; instead, there are languages where an item from one category can be derived to form an item from the other. In other words, the same lexeme can have different forms when used as a noun or as an

---

44 Note that the possessive pronoun also seems to be unmarked for case (Terrill 1998: examples).

adjective. This is found in 16 languages of the sample; in all of them, however, only a small part of the lexicon seems to be involved in the process. In several languages it is possible to form an adjective by reduplicating the noun, as shown in the examples in (50). In the other languages, affixes are used to derive adjectives from nouns, as for instance in (51a), or conversely, to derive nouns from adjectives, as in (51b).[45] It is unclear if this really provides good evidence for separate categories. The need for derivation does suggest that there is not one flexible class of nominals which can be used as head or modifier without morphological adaptation, but even if this argument is accepted, only a small number of elements is involved, which implies that the evidence remains really minor.

(50) a. Warray (Harvey ms: 27)
    muya   *-muya-muya*
    'tucker'   'greedy for tucker'
   b. Yuwaalaraay (Giacon 2017: 11)
    buya   *buyabuya*
    'bone'   'thin, boney'

(51) a. Yir Yoront (Alpher 1973: 374)
    ṯuma (stem)   *ṯumuy*
    'fire'   'hot'
   b. Anindilyakwa (Leeding 1989: 183)
    aningapwa   *ni-ngkw{i}-aningapwi*
    good   3>3M-NMLZ-good
    'good'   'show-off'

Differences in classification possibilities (i.e. noun class assignment or use of generic nouns) are discussed in the following section, as this is not a purely morphological criterion but also involves syntax.

1.3 Constructional evidence: Functional and morphosyntactic criteria

The criteria discussed in this section distinguish constructionally defined classes, i.e. based on whether different elements are distributed differently in the same structure. Classes can be distinguished if they behave differently, for instance if only one of the two classes can fill a particular position in a structure. This is the

---

[45] But see van Egmond (2012: 125) for a critical analysis of Leeding's (1989: 194–199) analysis of the nominaliser and adjectiviser prefixes.

case for 60 languages in the sample. I first discuss the functional criterion, which is interesting but difficult to generalise since in most grammars it is not discussed in detail. The rest of the section then discusses morphosyntactic criteria, which are equally interesting and more often mentioned in grammars.

The functional criterion can generally be described as follows: nouns function as head of the NP, while adjectives function as attributive modifiers, and usually not the other way around. There are a few issues, however, which make this question less clear-cut than it might seem.

One issue is that much depends on the analysis of structures where the 'adjective' is the only element of an NP: is the adjective considered to be the head of an NP, or is it considered to be the modifier of an ellipsed head noun? The former analysis (as posited by Eades [1979: 272] for Gumbaynggir, and Nordlinger [1998a: 47] for Wambaya, for instance) could be an argument against separate word class status for nouns and adjectives, as they can both function as the head of a referential phrase. The latter analysis (as argued by Bowern [2012: 158] for Bardi, Smith & Johnson [2000: 387] for Kugu Nganhcara, and Green [1989: 44] for Marrithiyel, for instance) could be an argument in favour of separate word class status, as nouns and adjectives do have different functions.

Another issue is where to draw the line for 'nouns' acting as modifiers in the referential phrase: in some languages, nouns cannot act as modifiers at all (e.g. Alyawarra [Yallop 1977: 116] and Burarra [Carew ms on object nouns]), but in others they can (e.g. in Wambaya, though unusually [Nordlinger 1998a: 48]). Can only the first group of languages be seen as having separate noun and adjective classes, or also the second? Unfortunately, for most languages, it is not mentioned whether nouns can function as modifiers, and if so, if there are any limitations or restrictions. Most examples I have encountered in the grammars seem to involve human stage-of-life terms, as in (52), or terms for 'man' or 'woman', as in (53b) below, which at least suggests that there may be some restriction. If there really are restrictions on the type and number of modifying nouns (but not of adjectives for instance), the existence of modifying nouns should not necessarily be taken as evidence against separate noun and adjective categories (cf. Dixon 2010: 84–85). A related point, observed for one language in the sample, is that NPs with elided heads can only have adjective modifiers that stand alone, as in (53a), while this is not possible with noun modifiers, as in (53b) in Bardi (Bowern 2012: 158).

(52) Mathi-Mathi (Blake et al. 2011: 112)
painggu murunhi
child young.woman
'a little girl'

(53) Bardi (Bowern 2012: 158)
   a. *moorrooloo baawa* 'little child' > *moorrooloo* 'the little one'
   b. *aamba baawa*   'male child'*> *aamba*   (intended) 'the male one'

Other functional criteria that are cited in favour of a distinct class of adjectives are that it is obligatory to have a noun in the NP but not an adjective (e.g. Uradhi [Crowley 1983: 334]), or that adjectives are more likely to be used as predicates than nouns (e.g. Wardaman [Merlan 1994: 58]).

Turning now to morphosyntactic criteria, the first feature that is often mentioned in the grammars concerns word order. There are 30 languages for which nouns and adjectives occur in a strict order. For 11 of these, the grammar uses this as an argument to distinguish the categories. For instance, in Arrernte, adjectives always follow nouns in NPs (Wilkins 1989: 104). In a few cases, one form can have both an adjective sense and a noun sense, e.g. *iperte* 'hole' (noun) or 'deep' (adjective); when used together in the NP, speakers always identify the first occurrence as the head noun and the second as adjective, as in (54) (Wilkins 1989: 104). Other examples are Anguthimri (Crowley 1981: 162), Emmi (Ford 1998: 138), and Kugu Nganhcara (Smith & Johnson 2000: 386). For a further 19 languages, ordering principles are mentioned (or they can be derived from examples) but they are not used as evidence for the question of word class (e.g. Uradhi [Crowley 1983: 371]). A slightly different implementation of this criterion is found for Bardi: when an adjective acts as modifier, the order of head and modifier is flexible, but if a noun acts as modifier, the order is fixed to modifier-head (Bowern 2012: 264).

(54) Arrernte (Wilkins 1989: 104)
   iperte iperte
   hole   deep
   'deep hole'

In Bininj Kunwok, adjectives can be distinguished in compound formation, where they are always the second element, as in (55), and never the first (Evans 2003a: 127).[46]

---

[46] Another way to identify adjectives in Kune (one of the Bininj Kunwok variants) is that their prefix *na-* is dropped when used in compounds. This prefix is a remnant of nominal classification, the formal marking of masculine gender, which is generalised to all nouns in this language variety, and is normally attached to adjectives to agree with the head noun of the NP (Evans 2003a: 126) (see also chapter 2, section 4.2.2).

(55) Bininj Kunwok (Evans 2003a: 127)
 Yi-geb-gimuk.
 2-nose-big
 'You have a big nose' or 'Your nose is big.'

A second morphosyntactic criterion involves nominal classification, which is used as distinguishing feature for 24 languages. Nouns normally occur in only one noun class or with one generic noun (with some flexibility allowed,[47] cf. chapter 2), whereas adjectives can occur in all classes or with all generics, since they simply agree with the head noun (see also Dixon 2002: 67–68; Dixon 2010: 85–86). For instance, Nordlinger argues for Wambaya: "while nouns inherently belong to only one gender (...), an adjective has no inherent gender; but potentially can be marked for any of the four genders in agreement with the noun that it modifies (...)" (1998a: 47). A variant of this criterion is mentioned for two languages: an explicit noun class marker is found on adjectives, but not on nouns (Gaagudju [Harvey 2002: 128, 151]; Bundjalung [Sharpe 2005: 23]). As already mentioned in chapter 2 (section 4.1), class marking on nouns is rare in any case, but if it is really absent on one set of elements and present on the other, this is a good argument to recognise different word classes.

Essentially the same type of argument, but in a different form, is found for Kuku Yalanji and Dhuwal, which have two different sets of case marking ('neutral' vs. 'potent' in the former, and 'human' vs. 'non-human' in the latter). Many nouns inherently take one type of case marker,[48] while any modifying adjectives agree with their head noun in the type of case marker they take (Patz 2002: 125; Wilkinson 1991: 114).

A third morphosyntactic criterion relates to degree modification; this is mentioned as a distinguishing criterion for nine languages, and occurs in three forms. First, it is observed in some grammars that adjectives can be modified by degree adverbs or intensifying particles or the like, while nouns cannot. For instance, in Bardi, *giija* 'very' can only modify adjectives, but not nouns, as in (56) (Bowern 2012: 265). The same is true for six more languages (Dhuwal [Wilkinson 1991: 146, 682–684], Kuuk Thaayorre [Gaby 2017: 203], Mathi-Mathi

---

[47] The fact that some nouns may belong to more than one noun class (for instance in the case of superclassing) is exactly why Nordlinger (2014: 238) argues this is not always a solid criterion for distinguishing nouns from adjectives. Conversely, for Ungarinyin it is said that not all semantic adjectives agree with the head noun in class marking, which again suggests that this is not necessarily a solid criterion for distinguishing nouns from adjectives (Spronck 2015: 18).
[48] However, there are some nouns that can show either type of case marking, depending on construal, which weakens this argument as evidence for separate word class status.

/Wati-Wati [Blake et al. 2011: 191], Umpila [Hill p.c.], Wajarri [Douglas 1981: 244], and Yir Yoront [Alpher 1991: 23]). This is good evidence for distinct categories, since one class can be used in a certain structure (in this case, with a degree modifier) and the other cannot.[49]

(56) Bardi (Bowern 2012: 265)
    a. *boordiji giija*
        big   very
        'very big'
    b. **iila giija*
        dog   very
        'very dog'

Secondly, in some languages the same degree modifier can be used to modify nouns and adjectives, but with a different semantic result. In Yir Yoront, when *morr* follows a noun, it means 'real, actual', as in (57a), whereas if it follows an adjective, it means 'very', as in (57b) (Alpher 1991: 23). Similarly in Arrernte, *nthurre* following a noun means 'a real X', following an adjective 'very X', as in (58a-b) (Wilkins 1989: 105). A final phenomenon related to degree modification is that nouns and adjectives can both be intensified, but with different elements. In Diyari, there are different intensifiers for nouns (*pirna*) and adjectives (*marla*) (Austin 2011: 40).

(57) Yir Yoront (Alpher 1991: 23)
    a. *warrchuwrr morr*
        woman   real, actual
        'a real woman (not one in a dream)'
    b. *wil morr*
        bitter very
        'very bitter'

(58) Arrernte (Wilkins 1989: 105)
    a. *artwe nthurre*
        man   INTENS
        'a real man [one who has been initiated]'

---

49 There are also authors (e.g. Wilkinson [1991: 682–683]) who attribute this difference to semantic differences (e.g. entity-denoting nominals are not gradable and can therefore not be modified by degree modifiers), and suggest that it cannot be used as evidence for distinct categories (cf. also section 1.1).

b. *kngerre nthurre*
   big   INTENS
   'very big'

There is a range of other syntactic criteria, mentioned for just one or two languages in the sample, which I briefly mention here. In Alawa, (some) adjectives can be used to modify verbs, while nouns never can (Sharpe 1972: 60). In Bundjalung and Mangarrayi, adjectives can take complements, while nouns cannot (Sharpe 2005: 23, referring to Crowley 1978: 29–30; Merlan 1989: 27–28). Finally, in Jingulu, nouns and adjectives can both function as predicates, but their arguments (in bold in the examples) differ in the case marking they take: ergative for the former, as in (59a), and absolutive (unmarked) for the latter, as in (59b) (Pensalfini 2003: 57–58).

(59) Jingulu (Pensalfini 2003: 57)
   a. **Jama-rni-rni** *jawularri-nama.*
      that-ERG-FOC   young.man-time
      'He's still a young man.'
   b. **Miringmi** *bardakurru-mi.*
      gum   good-VE
      'Gum is good.'

1.4 Conclusion

Having discussed each of the criteria in more detail, let us now return to what can be concluded on the basis of how they are combined. As discussed above, conceptual differences are considered less decisive and are thus not further taken into account here. The other criteria can be organised in two groups: criteria based on the morphological form of the lexeme, and criteria based on how lexemes behave in structures. Table 5 below gives an overview of how the evidence is distributed across the sample; four groups of languages can be distinguished.

The two groups where both types of evidence align are easiest to interpret. First, the 31 languages which have neither morphological nor constructional evidence for a distinction between nouns and adjectives can clearly be concluded to have only one 'nominal' class whose members can function both as referential head and as modifier to a referential head (i.e. it is a flexible category).

Second, there is a group of 24 languages that show both morphological and constructional evidence for a separate adjective class. In other words, these languages have both a class of nouns and a class of adjectives. An important note

Table 5: Evidence for a separate adjective class.

	Morphological evidence	No morphological evidence	Total
Constructional evidence	24	36	60
No constructional evidence	9	31	40
Total	33	67	100

here is that, if a language has both a morphologically defined class of adjectives and a constructionally defined class of adjectives, it is not clear whether these classes necessarily overlap or match completely. As discussed above, morphological evidence is often quite limited and only covers a small part of the lexicon, while syntactic evidence like word order is more general and includes a larger category. A pronounced example is Kuuk Thaayorre, where nouns and adjectives can generally be distinguished on constructional grounds (differences in word order, nominal classification and degree modification), whereas morphological evidence only applies to two lexemes, which have different forms when functioning as noun or as adjective (Gaby 2017: 203).

The other two groups are more problematic in the sense that they only show one type of evidence and not the other, which perhaps explains the reluctance of many grammarians to truly argue for separate classes. A small group of 9 languages only has morphological evidence and no constructional evidence. Morphological evidence in itself is, I think, sufficient to posit a separate adjective class (especially if, for some languages, the minus on the constructional side can be attributed to a lack of available information rather than to negative evidence). However, we also need to take into account that morphological evidence is overall quite limited (see section 1.2), which reduces the strength of the argument for separate noun and adjective classes in these cases. Thus, only when morphological evidence is strong do we have sufficient grounds to posit separate classes.

The final group consists of 36 languages which show constructional evidence but not morphological evidence. These languages have distributional classes of nouns and adjectives: they are distinct classes because certain positions in structures are reserved for one class and other positions for the other, but this is not reflected in a morphological distinction. Another way to analyse this is to treat nouns and adjectives as (constructionally defined) subclasses of a larger (morphological) nominal class.

Map 7 below shows the distribution of the four categories across the continent. The online version gives additional information on the criteria used for individual languages and the conclusions drawn in the grammar. There are no clear areal or genetic trends in the data.

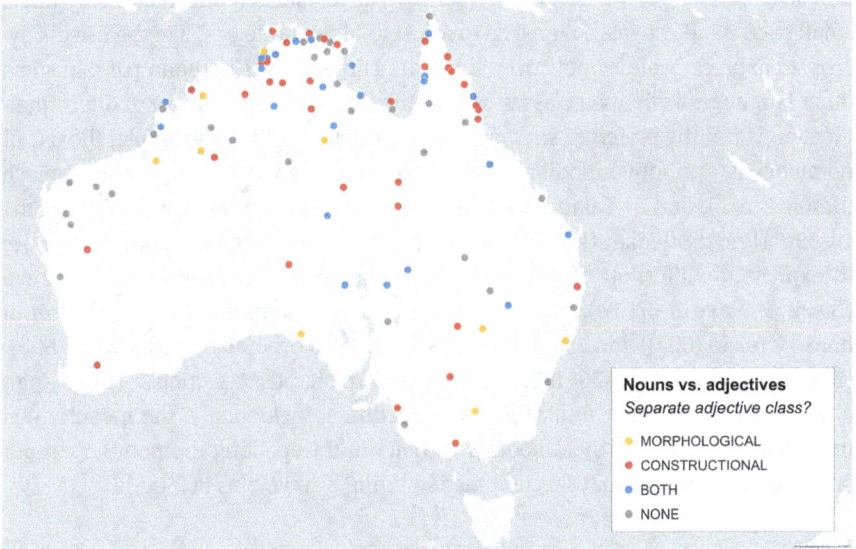

Map 7: Nouns vs. adjectives. For the online, dynamic version of this map, including more information on the criteria, see: http://bit.ly/N-A-classes.

2 Syntactic realisation

2.1 Direct qualification

Apart from word classes, a second issue in the typology of qualification is how it is realised syntactically. The answer to this question partly depends on the type of word class system a language has. A language which has a separate adjective class (i.e. specialised in serving as a modifier in a referential phrase) by definition allows direct qualification. A language without a separate class of adjectives that is otherwise flexible in its word classes also allows direct qualification, but there is no set of lexemes that is specialised in this function. A language without a separate class of adjectives that is otherwise rigid in terms of its word classes, does not have lexemes that can be used for direct modification of the referential head, and thus needs other methods for qualification (e.g. through relativisation of predicates).

In line with the basic Australian repertoire of rigid adjectives and/or flexible nominal, all languages of the sample allow direct qualification, although some authors argue for appositional structures instead of 'integrated' NP structures (see chapter 5, section 2, and chapter 6, where this is discussed in more detail). Apart from that, adjectives or nominals can modify head nouns directly. However, in some languages, this option is used infrequently. For instance, Malakmalak only has a small class of adjectives, so it needs to resort to other strategies, like the use of coverbs, to express qualities not covered by these adjectives (Hoffmann p.c.). In some other languages with open classes of adjectives or nominals, the use of direct qualification is not the preferred strategy either: in Ungarinyin, for example, the use of nominals as attributive modifiers is avoided and rarely occurs in natural speech (Spronck p.c.), and in Yalarnnga, "there are very few attributive adjectives in the corpus" (Breen & Blake 2007: 54). Such languages often also prefer other strategies to express qualification of nouns, such as secondary predication in Yalarnnga (Breen & Blake 2007: 54), or in Bininj Kunwok compounding for a closed set of nouns[50] (as in (60a)) and external modification of incorporated nouns (as in (60b)) (Evans 2003a: 172–173, 176–180, 235–237; see also chapter 2, section 3, and chapter 4, section 1.1.3 on other unification constructions). Incidentally, the incorporated noun may be modified by a modifying compound (repeating the noun), i.e. both 'alternative' strategies may be combined in Bininj Kunwok (as in (60c)).

(60) Bininj Kunwok (Evans 2003a: 178, 235, 236)
   a. *man-ngorl-kimuk*
      VE-cloud-big
      'big clouds'
   b. **An-biya** *garri-****yerrng****-ma-ng, bu garri-worrhm-i, an-dehne*
      VE-different 12A-wood-get-NPST REL 12A-light-NPST VE-this
      an-geb-warre.
      VE-flame-bad
      'We'll get some different wood when we make the fire, this (kind of) wood produces a poor flame.'

---

50 In some dialects, compounding is even the only option to express modification of one of these nouns (Evans 2003a: 177). Similar noun-adjective compounds are also found in other Gunwinyguan languages; see Baker & Nordlinger (2008) for a discussion of these structures in the LFG framework, who argue that the nouns in these constructions are generic nouns (or classifiers). This links back to the verbal and adjectival classifiers I discussed in chapter 2, section 3, where a similar structure is argued to be a generic/classifier incorporated in an adjective. It is unclear whether this concerns the same phenomenon or not, and if so, where the differences lie.

c. *Ngaye Nicholas ngani-ngime-ng ngani-**rurrk**-na-ng*
me <name> 1UA-enter-PST.PFV 1UA-shelter-see-PST.PFV
ngan-rurrk-makkaigen
VE-shelter-beautiful
'Nicholas and I went in and had a look at the beautiful (new amenities) building.'

Returning now to direct qualification in the NP, while most languages allow direct qualification for adjectives (or nominals), they are not necessarily restricted to this function within the NP, and conversely, other types of elements may also take up this function (in line with the general flexibility of the relation between categories and functional roles observed across many Australian languages). An example of the first phenomenon is that adjectives can also be used in a quantifying function, most clearly when numerals are part of the adjective class, but also, for instance, when size adjectives are used as quantifiers (see chapter 4, section 2.2 for an example). The opposite pattern is nicely illustrated in (61) from Gooniyandi, where number words or possessive pronouns can be used as qualifiers (which have a distinct distribution; qualifiers follow the head and other modifiers precede the head) (McGregor 1990: 264–267). The relation between word class and function is discussed in more detail in chapters 6 and 7.

(61) Gooniyandi (McGregor 1990: 265, 266)
    a. *yoowooloo garndiwa*
        man   many
        'many people'
    b. *tharra ngarragi*
        dog   my
        'my dog'

2.2 Complexity of qualifying structures

If direct qualification is allowed, related questions concern the complexity and internal structure of qualifying structures: does an NP allow multiple adjectives, and can adjectives themselves be modified, e.g. by degree modification? Some languages easily allow multiple adjectives, as shown for English in (62), where two descriptive adjectives qualify the head noun, and an intensifier *very* modifies the first descriptive adjective. For others, however, it has been suggested that complex qualifying structures are restricted (cf. infra for examples). Where multiple adjectives are permitted, their ordering has only been studied in detail for very few languages (e.g. English, see Bache 1978; Dixon 1982d: 24; Quirk et al. 1985: 437; Adamson 2000; Wulff 2003); cross-linguistically there is much less work on this question (but see Flanagan 2014).

(62) English (Ghesquière 2009: 314)
very beautiful little flowers

In the sample, several grammars mention that more than one adjective can modify the nominal head simultaneously, and that adjectives can themselves be modified.[51] First, the use of multiple adjectives (or modifying nominals) in one NP is allowed in at least 20 languages, as shown in some examples in (63), although for several languages it is noted that this is marked and rare in natural speech (e.g. Kuuk Thaayorre [Gaby 2017: 206]; Mangarrayi [Merlan 1989: 51]; Yindjibarndi [Wordick 1982: 141]). Usually, there is no information on ordering restrictions, but Douglas (1981: 240) notes for Wajarri that multiple adjectives tend to occur in the order colour-size-state. In addition, the same adjective can sometimes be repeated for emphasis, for instance in Muruwari (64) (Oates 1988: 87).

(63) a. Kayardild (Round 2013: 136–137)
 mudinkiya jungarrbaya bardanguya kurday
 tied.together.INS big.INS large.INS coolamon.INS
 'in the great big, bound coolamon'
 b. Mawng (Singer 2006: 95)
 "Ma-pa, annga-ma-nyi [mata ma-lijap mata ma-rntulyak
 o.k.-EMPH 2SG>3VE-get-IRR VE VE-small VE VE-long
 mata warlk]."
 VE stick
 "Go and get a small long stick."
 c. Nhanda (Blevins 2001: 129)
 indaacu-lu uthu-nggu wur'ada-lu aja-yi-nha
 big-ERG dog-ERG black-ERG bite-PST.PFV-1SG
 'The big black dog bit me.'

(64) Muruwari (Oates 1988: 87)
 kiʀa yurrun kiʀa
 wide track wide
 'a wide track'

---

[51] Beyond the domain of qualification, such features may also tell us something about the complexity of the NP structures and the question of NP constituency (see chapter 6, section 2.2.3).

The opposite pattern, viz. strict restrictions on multiple adjectives in the NP, is also found in the sample. In such cases, other structures (like afterthought or discontinuity, see chapter 6, section 4) have to be used to express attributes or qualities instead. For example, in Umpila (Hill 2018: 140–144), only one adjective is allowed in the NP, and when several modifiers are used, they need to be split over separate NPs, as in (65). Other languages with similar restrictions are Paakantyi (Hercus 1982: 99), Rembarrnga (McKay 1975: 70), and Yuwaalaraay (Giacon 2017: 367).

(65) Umpila (Hill 2018: 142, pc)
    a. *?kampinu-lu tha'i-na pu'ala yilamu mukana*
        man-ERG   hit-NFUT drum old   big
       'the man hit the big old drum'
    b. *kampinu-lu tha'i-na pu'ala yilamu /mukana*
        man-ERG   hit-NFUT drum old   big

38 grammars in the sample mention that it is possible to modify the adjectival modifier, either by morphological or by syntactic means. Morphologically, degree modification can be expressed by reduplication, or by the addition of an affix. Reduplication for intensification is found in 13 languages (but not productively in all of them), as illustrated in (66) for Mangarrayi (Merlan 1989: 166). The use of an affix is found in 16 languages (but is again quite limited in some of these), as illustrated in (67) for Walmajarri (Richards 1979: 112). These affixes are not always specialised in adjectives, but can sometimes also be used with other word classes, like nouns or adverbs (e.g. *–idjiyang* 'very' can be used with adjectival nominals (68a) and with adverbs (68b) in Miriwung [Kofod 1978: 157]). The syntactic expression of degree modification uses a free-standing degree modifier, resulting in a complex adjectival phrase (see also section 1.3 above). This is found in 15 languages, and is illustrated in (69) from Kuuk Thaayorre, showing two of the three degree adverbs the language has, with *minc* following the adjective it modifies and *waarr* preceding it (Gaby 2006: 613; Gaby 2017: 204).

(66) Mangarrayi (Merlan 1989: 166)
    guḻañi guḻuḻañi
    'long' 'very long'

(67) Walmajarri (Richards 1979: 112)
    wulyu wulyu-jinyangu
    'good' 'very good'

(68) Miriwung (Kofod 1978: 157–158)
　　a. *ngundenging　ngundengi-(i)djiyang*
　　　 'good'　　　　'very good'
　　b. *geluwirr　geluwirridjiya*
　　　 'up there'　'right up there'

(69) Kuuk Thaayorre (Gaby 2006: 613)
　　inhul　　**ngamal minc**,　*meer.pungk*　　**waarr ngamal**
　　this.one　large　　really　eyebrow(NOM)　very　large
　　'this [crocodile] was really large, [it had] enormous eyebrows'

Finally, note that, as conclusions on the status of the word classes are often unclear for individual languages, I will use the term 'adjective' in a broad sense in the rest of this study, to refer to NP modifiers which describe a property of the referent lexically. In other words, use of the term 'adjective' beyond this section is not to be understood as a statement on word class status in individual languages.

3 Conclusion

This chapter has provided a survey of the domain of qualification in the NP, which is reasonably well-studied in Australian languages, but has more open questions than the domain of classification discussed in chapter 2. The focus of the existing literature mostly lies on the issue of word classes, i.e. whether there is a specialised adjective class or rather one broader 'nominal' class. The literature and the grammars use a great variety of criteria to distinguish nouns and adjectives: in this chapter, I consistently tried to distinguish between morphological evidence on the one hand and constructional evidence on the other hand, which results in a clearer picture of what is going on. Almost two thirds of languages in the sample show structural evidence for a separate adjective class (and approximately 40% of this group additionally show morphological evidence), while about one third of the sample can be said to have a flexible class of nominals, showing no morphological or structural evidence at all. Apart from word class status, another issue is how word class is linked to function. Adjectives do not always function as qualifiers, but can also function as quantifiers. Conversely, other elements than adjectives can also have a qualifying function in the NP. The relation between word class and functional role is, in fact, a more general issue in the analysis of NPs. This will be discussed in more detail in chapter 7, focusing on the functional role of determination.

4 Quantification

This chapter discusses the domain of quantification, which is reasonably well-studied, but again not to the same extent as classification. Quantification can be broadly defined as the way the number of referents is expressed in the NP. This can be done in roughly two ways (e.g. Gil 2015: 710). The first is by means of the grammatical category of number, which is generally associated with more general semantic distinctions (e.g. 'one' as opposed to 'more than one') and is often realised morphologically with bound forms. An example is the suffix –s attached to the head noun in English, which marks plurality, as in (70). The second way is by means of a lexical category expressing quantity, which is generally associated with more specific semantic distinctions (e.g. 'five', 'few', 'most') and often relies on syntactic patterning with freestanding forms. Examples are English quantifiers like *many* and *few*, and numerals like *two*, as in (70). This distinction between number markers and quantifiers is not always clear-cut, as for instance number marking can also be expressed by freestanding forms in some languages (Dryer 2013a; Corbett 2000: 133–15; see also section 1.1.1 on Djapu), but I use it as a basic distinction here to go through the literature and data.

(70) English
    two book-s
    two book-PL
    'two books'

The two sections in this chapter give an overview of how number and quantity are expressed in Australian languages. As this study is concerned with NPs, I focus on how number is expressed in the NP (morphologically or by a numeral/quantifier). I only provide a few brief comments on how it can be expressed in the rest of the clause.

1 Number marking

The major typological questions in the literature on number marking relate to its distribution in the clause, its obligatoriness, and the nature of the distinctions within number paradigms. The first two questions are discussed together in section 1.1; the last one is discussed in section 1.2.

1.1 Distribution and obligatoriness of number marking

Number marking can be found in several places in the clause: it can be marked on the head element of a referring expression (nominal as in (71a), or pronominal as in (71b)), on its modifiers (as in (71c)), freely in the NP (as in (71d)), and beyond the NP, e.g. on the verb (as in (71e)).

(71) a. Arabana (Hercus 1994: 154)
      Mankarra-pula wiRi kuti-kuti-nta.
      girl-DU   hair pull-pull-REFL
      'The two girls are pulling each other's hair.'
  b. Yalarnnga (Breen and Blake 2007: 26)
      Nhangu-yungu pula wala-nyaa-ma? Mirnmirri-yungu.
      what-AVERS   3DU hit-RECP-PRS   woman-AVERS
      'What are they fighting over?' – 'Over a woman.'
  c. Ungarinyin (Spronck 2015: 27)
      ari   birri
      man PL.ANAPH
      'men'
  d. Dhuwal: Djapu (Morphy 1983: 103)
      yolngu   walal
      person.ABS PL.ABS
      'people'
  e. Mawng (Singer 2006: 102)
      Arrarrkpi a-wani-ngan.
      man   3PL-stay-PST.PFV
      'Men stayed there.'

Cross-linguistically, it is more common to have number marking on pronouns and on verbs, while it is less likely to occur on other parts of speech such as nouns (Bickel & Nichols 2007: 227–228). In nouns, moreover, it is more likely to appear on kinship terms and nouns denoting humans than on nouns denoting inanimates (Haspelmath 2013). This is captured in the well-known Animacy Hierarchy, presented in (72) (Corbett 2000: 55–66; Haspelmath 2013; see also Silverstein [1976] for uses in the domain of case marking and agreement).

(72) *Likelihood of number marking: Animacy Hierarchy*
     speaker > addressee > 3rd person > kinship terms > other humans > "higher" animals > "lower" animals > discrete inanimates > non-discrete inanimates

Languages also vary with respect to the obligatoriness of number marking (see Haspelmath [2013] for cross-linguistic tendencies). This can equally be captured in terms of the hierarchy in (72): if a particular element marks number optionally, elements lower on the hierarchy will never mark number obligatorily (Corbett 2000: 70–75, 87).

In the sample, almost all languages have some form of number marking in the NP (six only have number marking outside the NP, and for four languages there is no information available). There is great variation, however, in the range of elements for which number marking is possible, the obligatoriness of its use, and the patterns of agreement that are available. The largest group of 74 languages can show number marking both on the head noun (limited to a few nouns for 19 languages) and in agreement (including all types of modifiers and/or beyond the NP). In 6 languages, number can only be marked on the head (for 3 of these, this is limited to a handful of nouns). In 11 languages, number is only available in agreement markers in the NP (in a pronoun or demonstrative modifying the nominal head),[52] and in 10 of these also beyond the NP (e.g. in bound cross-referencing pronouns). An overview can be found in the map below, based on the available information. All types of number marking outside the NP are represented in one category on the map in order to simplify the visualisation, but a distinction between marking on the verb (cross-referencing pronominal forms and specific number affixes), marking on pronominal forms (e.g. enclitic in second position, or free and appositional to the NP) and other types of number marking can be seen in the online, dynamic version of the map by clicking on the language points. It is hard to generalise about the geographical or genetic distribution of number marking: for example, number marking on the head of the NP occurs in languages across the continent (although it is limited in most languages, see section 1.1.1 below), as does number marking outside of the NP (e.g. on the verb).

1.1.1 Number marking on the head noun

Number marking on the head noun is found in several forms. Affixation is by far the most common process,[53] mainly in the form of number suffixes (in line with a cross-linguistic preference for suffixing in this domain [see Himmelmann 2014a

---

[52] Note that it is not always clear whether a pronoun is truly a modifier, or is to be analysed as appositional to the NP. This is further discussed in chapter 7 (section 2.4).
[53] Number clitics are found in a few languages (e.g. Gaagudju [Harvey 2002: 130–131, 268–280, 290–293]; Gooniyandi [McGregor 1990: 188]; Jaminjung [Schultze-Berndt 2000: 50]), but it is difficult to put them in either the head marking section or the dependent marking section, because they are phrasal in nature. See also section 1.1.2 for some comments on phrasal marking of number.

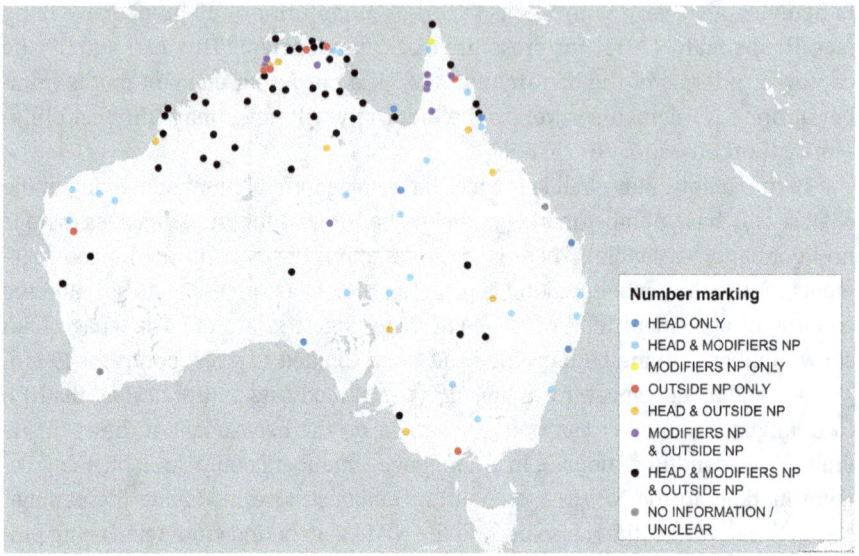

Map 8: Number marking. For an online, dynamic version of this map, see: http://bit.ly/numbermarking-overview.

and references there]). Number prefixes are relatively rare, found only in seven languages of the sample (all non-Pama-Nyungan,[54] except for Yanyuwa), and often alternating with class markers (see chapter 2, section 4.2; in Anindilyakwa there is also a separate prefix slot for the trial marker [van Egmond 2012: 82]). Reduplication and suppletion are relatively minor ways of marking plural number in the sample. Reduplication is found in many languages (see also chapter 3, sections 1.2 and 2.2 on other types of reduplication), but it is almost never a productive means of marking plurality. Most typically, it is found for only a few terms; it is my impression from the sample that these usually include some person terms like 'children', 'old people', 'women', as shown in (73), kin terms, subsection terms or clan names, as shown in (74), as well as geographical features like 'rocks' or 'mountains', as shown in (75) (e.g. Bininj Kunwok [Evans 2003a: 168]; Bunganditj [Blake 2003: 30–31]; Marra [Heath 1981: 77]; Wambaya [Nordlinger 1998a: 106–107]; Yalarnnga [Breen & Blake 2007: 52]; and many more). There are only a handful of languages where reduplication seems to be a

---

[54] The other non-Pama-Nyungan languages in the sample with (some) number marking on the head just use one or more of the other morphological means (suffixes, reduplication, suppletion or clitics).

more productive means for marking plurality, in the sense that a wider range of nouns in covered; these include, for instance, Dyirbal (Dixon 1972: 241) and Kuku Yalanji (Patz 2002: 55). There also is some variation in the number-related semantics of reduplication, which sometimes has an additional effect of vagueness, generality, collectivity or distributiveness instead of mere plurality (e.g. in Gooniyandi, McGregor 1990: 237–238).[55]

(73) Jaru (Tsunoda 1981: 234)
 maluga - *maluga-maluga*
 'an old man' or 'old men'   'many old men'

(74) Worrorra (Clendon 2014: 96)
 abiya - *abaabiya*
 'elder brother'   'elder brothers'[56]

(75) Bunganditj (Blake 2003: 31)
 pupitj – *pupitj-pupitj*
 'hill'   'a range of hills'

Suppletion is only found in a handful of languages, and is always restricted to a few terms, usually person terms ('children', 'women', 'men') or some kinship terms. In Djambarrpuyngu (Wilkinson 1991: 126), for instance, *djamarrkuḻi* 'children' is the plural form of *yothu* 'child'. Finally, there is one language which has free number markers with the head noun, Dhuwal (Morphy 1983: 47; Wilkinson 1991: 213). These number markers immediately follow the head noun, as illustrated in (76), and, as argued in chapter 7 (section 3.3), they can in fact be analysed as grammaticalised third person pronouns.

(76) Dhuwal (Wilkinson 1991: 213)
 yaka yan   ŋunhi   ŋanapurru-wuy   galiwin'ku-wuy   [yolŋu **walal**]
 NEG EMPH TEXD   1PL-EMPH   place.name-ASS person PL(3PL)
 'Not only us Galiwin'ku people'

---

55 In such cases, reduplication occurs in a broader set of nouns, for instance groups of animals like 'fish' or 'dogs', or non-paucal or uncountable collectives like 'dust' or 'pimples' (e.g. Yawuru [Hosokawa 1991: 584]; Ritharngu [Heath 1980: 33]).
56 It is not clear whether this refers to more than one elder brother (as suggested by the translation in the grammar), or has a dyadic meaning (as suggested by McGregor p.c.), or either. As this process of reduplication is also found on other nouns (like 'dog' or 'child'), it would seem that the first option is the most plausible one.

In many languages of the sample, number marking on the head noun is limited, in two ways. One limitation is that in most languages, not all nouns can receive number marking. In general, the likelihood for nouns to take number marking in Australian languages follows the hierarchy as described above in (72): for instance, number marking in many languages is limited to nouns referring to humans (e.g. Tiwi [Lee 1987: 80–81]; Yandruwandha with a few exceptions [Breen 2004a: 113]). There are also 22 languages which only allow number marking on a very small set of nouns. An example is Bardi, which has a 'group' suffix occurring on five human terms (as shown in (77)), in addition to a few irregular plural forms (Bowern 2012: 174–176).

(77) Bardi (Bowern 2012: 174)
      nyoongoorl   -   *nyoongoorl-jin*
      old.person   old.person-GROUP
      'old person'   'group of old people'

The other way in which number marking is limited is that in many languages number marking is optional, i.e. a noun that is not marked for number can refer to one or more referents. It can be optional for all nouns, or optional for some and obligatory for others. If number marking is obligatory only for some nouns, these tend to refer to humans (as could be expected from the Animacy Hierarchy), as in Ritharngu: "With human nouns (...) the Du and Pl suffixes are almost obligatory when semantically appropriate" (Heath 1980: 33). Obligatoriness of number marking can also depend on the number category that is expressed by the marker, in the sense that dual marking is reported to be more obligatory than plural marking in several languages (e.g. in Ritharngu [Heath 1980: 33], Wambaya [Nordlinger 1998a: 73] and Yalarnnga [Blake p.c.]).[57]

1.1.2 Number marking beyond the head noun

Beyond the head noun, number marking can be found on modifiers within the NP, or beyond the NP, for instance on the verb or in co-referential pronouns. Within the NP, number can be available for all types of modifiers, or for only one type. Both options are about equally frequent in the sample, but in cases where only one type of modifier is marked, this is by far more frequent for demonstratives and/or adnominal personal pronouns than for descriptive modifiers. In Arrernte, for instance, the adnominal personal pronoun is the only

---

[57] Dual marking also occurs with more types of referents than plural does in some of these languages (e.g. Arabana/Wangkangurru [Hercus 1994: 65]).

element in the NP which is marked for number, as shown in (78) (see further Wilkins 1989: 108, 129).

(78) Arrernte (Wilkins 1989: 129)
 artwe itne no ahel-irre-ke   artwe mperlkere ikwere
 man   3PL.S no angry-INCH-PST.COMPL man   white   3SG.DAT
 'The men didn't become aggressive towards the white man.'

In languages where all types of modifiers can be marked, some languages show phrasal marking (e.g. with number marked on whichever element comes in the right position), while others allow agreement throughout the whole NP (e.g. Martuthunira [Dench 1994: 203–204]). There are also some languages with a choice between phrasal and word marking, as shown in (79a-c) for the language group Dharrawal/ Dharumba/ Dhurga/ Djirringanj (Besold 2012: 289–290). (See further in chapter 6, sections 2.1.1 and 3.2, on the distinction between phrasal and word marking of categories more generally.)

(79) Dharrawal (a-b)/ Dhurga (c) (Besold 2012: 290)
 a. bambu-lali djilawaran-bula buru-lali
    big-DU   grey-DU   kangaroo-DU
    'two big grey kangaroos'
 b. **bundawari-wulali yuwinj-dju** bulma-ya-wula mirigang
    tall-DU   man-ERG[58]   hit-PST-3DU   dog
    'two tall men beat the dog'
 c. **yuwinj biraga garniina-mbaraga** bayi-na   waranj njiinj
    man   big   bad-PL   beat-NPST child this/here
    'the bad men are beating the child'

Number marking outside the NP can occur on the verb or elsewhere in the clause. On the verb, number marking mostly takes the form of pronominal affixes (typically prefixes in non-Pama-Nyungan languages). Several languages also have other number or quantifying markers which can be attached to verbs. Example (80) from Bardi shows both cross-referencing prefixes and a quantificational enclitic =nidi 'group' marking the number of the intransitive subject. Elsewhere in the clause, number can be found in personal pronouns that are

---

58 The absence of the number marker on the head noun could also be attributed to the presence of a case marker in this example: case and number marking seem to be in complementary distribution in this language group (Besold 2012: 289). This remains a hypothesis, however, as the data available for analysis is very limited.

co-referential with the NP, either bound, as in (81) from Ngiyambaa (where the pronoun is co-referential with *bura:y* 'child'), or free, as in (82) from Kuuk Thaayorre (where the pronoun is co-referential with *parr_r* 'child').

(80) Bardi (Bowern 2012: 398)
*Barnanggarra=gij i-rr-al-gal=**nidi** bigibigi ngoorrngool-ondarr.*
now=VERY 3-AUG-be-RECPST=QUANT pigs mangrove-L.ALL
'Just now all the pigs were in the mangroves.'

(81) Ngiyambaa (Donaldson 1980: 128)
*miri-gu=**naŋ-gal** bura:y gadhiyi*
dog-ERG=3ABS-PL child.ABS bite.PST
'The dog bit the children.'

(82) Kuuk Thaayorre (Gaby 2017: 215)
*parr_r inh yan **peln** school-thak*
child(NOM) DEM:SP.PROX go:NPST 3PL(NOM) school-DAT
'these children (nowadays) go to school'

Number marking beyond the head noun is also often optional, as shown in (83a-b), but not always. For instance, agreement is obligatory when number prefixes are part of the noun class paradigm (see chapter 2, section 4.1). Number agreement also often follows the Animacy Hierarchy, in the sense that inanimate nouns, for instance, often control singular cross-referencing on the verb. An example is Warray (Harvey 1986: 86), where animate nouns are often cross-referenced with a plural prefix on the verb (84a), while inanimate nouns never are (84b) (3SG is unmarked on the verb).

(83) Nhanda (Blevins 2001: 53, 58)
 a. *kurlayhi-**nu** marniwirri-**nu** inda-ba-nhaa gali-nggalu*
   river.gum-PL red-PL big-INCH-NPST gully-PATH
   'The river red gums along the gully are getting big.'
 b. *ngayi nha-'i **indaacu** wuthada uthu-thada*
   1SG see-PST big two dog-DU
   'I saw two big dogs'

(84) Warray (Harvey 1986: 86)
 a. animate referent
   *wanjlak angilak pat-**put**-nay-na-y*
   right now 1SG.S.NCOMPL-1SG.S>3PL.OBJ-RDP-see-REAL

a-kupam-u   pontalpontal
CL-lots-OBL   magpie
'Right now I can see lots of magpies.'
b. inanimate referent
yumpal   keranglul   kenganawu   ka-kulu-tj-i   pekmara
tree   two   over.there   NCOMPL-stand-AUX-IRR   between
ka-ni-ni
NCOMPL-RDP-sit
'She is sitting down between those two trees standing over there.'

Finally, number marking also shows links with other functional domains. As mentioned above, it is more likely to occur in adnominal personal pronouns and demonstratives than in other modifiers such as adjectives. In other words, in some cases number is only marked in a modifying pronoun or demonstrative, as in (85) below (and (78) above). Interestingly, both personal pronouns and demonstratives are good candidates for functioning as determiners, which suggests there may be a link between number and determination. Corbett (2000: 278–280) similarly suggests a link between number and definiteness, one of the functions commonly associated with determination. Other signs of this link are found in the use of numerals and quantifiers in determiner positions (see further in section 2.1). The link between number and determination is discussed in more detail in chapter 7 (section 3.6).

(85) Kugu Nganhcara (Smith & Johnson 2000: 392)
ku'a-m   thaaranam   pukpe   uyu   agu+ukewi-yin
dog-ABL   3PL.ABL   child   many   be.born-3PL.PRS
'Dogs have a lot of young.'

1.1.3 Relation with classes of nouns

Apart from the expression of quantity itself, the typological literature has also identified a number of implications of quantification for the semantic analysis of nouns. According to Rijkhoff (2002: 50, also 29–59), the different ways in which nouns interact with number categories and quantifiers across languages reveal subtly different features of meaning that define different types of nouns. Based on these differences, Rijkhoff distinguishes between four categories of nouns. The first difference relates to the presence of plural marking: some languages have obligatory plural marking for nouns (as the English *book*, see (70) above), while others lack plural marking for nouns, at least when combined with a numeral, or even in all contexts (as illustrated for Kayardild in (86)). This different behaviour with respect to number marking is indicative of a semantic difference. Since the first category of nouns can be directly numerated with number marking, they can be said to have a semantic feature of discreteness; they are thus called singular object nouns. By contrast, the absence of number marking on the second category suggests that these nouns do not denote individuals but rather "a set of individuals", which can contain one or more members (Rijkhoff 2002: 46–47); these are called set nouns.

(86) Kayardild (Evans 1995a: 235; cited in Rijkhoff 2002: 40)
 kiyarrng-ka yarbud-a ngarnal
 two-NOM meat-NOM white.cockatoo.NOM
 'two white cockatoos'

The other two categories are distinguished based on a second morphosyntactic feature, viz. constructions with numerals. In some languages, nouns do not just lack number marking, but they cannot even occur in a direct construction with numerals (in contrast to the first two categories). Instead, they need a classifier to combine with the numeral. This indicates that these nouns do not denote discrete entities and thus need an 'individualiser' (in the form of a classifier) to be numerated (cf. also e.g. Seifart 2010: 722). The type of classifier that is needed distinguishes sort nouns from general nouns (see Rijkhoff 2002: 47–49 for more details).

Note that languages can have nouns of several types. For instance, English has both count nouns (i.e. singular object nouns), like *book*, which can be pluralised and occur with numerals, as in *two books*, and mass nouns, like *rice*, which cannot be pluralised and cannot occur with numerals, but need a mensural classifier, as in *a cup of rice*.

In terms of this analysis, Australian languages generally have set nouns (i.e. number marking on nouns is absent or optional), and some languages may in addition have a small number of singular object nouns (i.e. when number marking on the noun is obligatory). This is partly in line with Rijkhoff's suggestion (2002: 42–44) that languages that do not have a distinct class of nouns but a flexible class of nominals (see chapter 3) also generally do not have number marking on these nominals, or at least not obligatorily (and would thus have set nouns, sort nouns or general nouns). However, there are at least some counterexamples in the sample; Garrwa, for instance, has a flexible class of nominals (see chapter 3; Mushin 2012: 44–45), but also singular object nouns (with human referents; Mushin 2012: 78). In some languages, number is marked on the whole NP and not on the noun (see footnote 53 and section 1.1.2), which makes it difficult to assign them to one of the categories, as it is unclear whether number can be analysed as a feature of the noun in these language.

1.2 Distinctions within number paradigms

If there is a distinction in number, paradigms cross-linguistically distinguish at least between singular and plural (or non-singular);[59] additionally, they can distinguish dual (two referents), trial (three referents), paucal (a few referents) or 'greater plural' (an excessive number or referents) (e.g. Corbett 2000: 19–38; Bickel & Nichols 2007: 227). Such distinctions are sometimes analysed in terms of a Number Hierarchy (predicting possible number systems: singular > plural > dual > trial), but there are several problems with this (see Corbett [2000: 38–50] for an extensive discussion). The number of distinctions need not be the same for all elements that mark number. For instance, it may be the case that pronouns involve a three-way distinction, while nouns in the same language only make a two-way distinction (Corbett 2000: 120–124). Other markers also occur, expressing for instance associativity ('X and the group associated with X'; see Bickel & Nichols 2007: 228), collectivity (marking a group of referents as a unit) or distribution (marking the members of a group as separate entities) (see Corbett 2000: 83–84, 101–111, 118 for an overview).

In the sample, the categories distinguished in paradigms of number markers are most frequently dual and plural (or unit augmented and augmented in Gaagudju [Harvey 2002: 268–280]), but some languages also have affixes expressing trial or paucal, and three languages have specifically singular suffixes (viz. Ngarrindjeri [Bannister 2004: 20–21],[60] Ngiyambaa [Donaldson 1980: 99–101], Paakantyi [Hercus 1982: 81]). The plural sometimes has a collective ('group') meaning rather than merely 'more than one', as in Paakantyi [Hercus 1982: 82–83], illustrated in (87). As mentioned in above (section 1.1.1), similar effects are also sometimes found for reduplicated nouns. There can also be a separate 'distributed plural' form, "describ[ing] a group of things taken together but considered individually" (Dench 1994: 96), as in Martuthunira, illustrated in (88). In a few languages, there are separate affixes for different animacy categories. Jingulu, for instance, has a dual and

---

59 Alternatively, some systems distinguish minimal vs. augmented (and sometimes unit augmented).
60 There is some disagreement about whether this is truly a singular suffix or rather part of the stem (Bannister 2004: 20–21).

plural suffix specifically for animate referents[61] and a 'general' dual and plural suffix for any type of referent (including animate) (Pensalfini 2003: 171).

(87) Paakantyi (Hercus 1982: 82–83)
    a. *daḻda-**lugu***
       kangaroo-PL
       'a mob of kangaroos'
    b. *yara-yara -ul' -**ug'** -ayi*
       things   -SG[62] -PL -1SG.POSS
       'the whole of my possessions'

(88) Martuthunira (Dench 1994: 96)
    *Kanyara-**warntura** nyina-lha pintirrijila, wartawirrinpi-rra*
    person-DISTR   be-PST   scattered wait-CTEMP
    ngurra-ngka   pirriyarta-la.
    camp-LOC   own.camp-LOC
    'People were scattered about, waiting each in their own camp.'

Kin terms have separate number suffixes in 12 languages of the sample.[63] For example, in Kuku Yalanji, there is a 'kinship plural' suffix for kin terms, shown in (89), as opposed to productive reduplication for marking plurality in other nouns (Patz 2002: 55–56). Another few languages have suffixes which are tied to size, as in Ngiyambaa (Donaldson 1980: 99–101), which has a set of three singular and three plural suffixes, each including 'diminutive' (small, not because immature), 'immature' (small, because immature) and 'augmentative'

---

61 Intuitively, this could be linked to a noun class system; however, noun class and number are expressed in separate suffix slots on nominals, i.e. when both are marked, the gender suffix precedes the number suffix (Pensalfini 2003: 159).
62 The singular here is used affectively (Hercus 1982: 83).
63 Additionally, Guugu Yimidhirr has a collective plural suffix *–garr* which can be used on any noun, but has a different meaning when used on kin terms, viz. it is specifically used for several people that stand "in the same relation to a single other" (e.g. wives of the same man) (Haviland 1979: 55). Several Australian languages also have another formative specialised in kin terms, viz. the kin dyad (often marked by an affix, but also by a juxtaposed free form or by suppletion in a few languages). If it is an affix, it is attached to one kin term (e.g. 'grandfather') and results in reference to two people in a reciprocal kin relation (e.g. 'grandfather and grandson'). This type of affix is found in 27 languages of the sample, and usually shows a preference for attachment to either the junior or the senior term; in three more languages the comitative affixed to a kin term results in a kin dyad construction. See also Evans (2006) on this construction.

(big) forms. In addition to basic number categories, several languages also have affixes with 'quantifying' meanings, for instance 'all', 'a lot of', 'only', or 'one of many' (see section 2 below on quantification).

(89) Kuku Yalanji (Patz 2002: 56)
 *Jana-nda manyarr-**karra**-ngka yalama-ny: "Dunga-y kuyu*
 3PL-LOC:PT wife-KPL-ERG:PT(A) say-PST go-IMP fish.ABS(OBJ)
 mani-nka!"
 get-PURP
 'The wives said to them: "Go to get some fish!"'

2 Quantifiers

Quantifiers (including numerals) are lexical elements that express quantity, usually quite specifically. These elements may occur within the NP, like *akngirra* 'many' in (90), or outside of it, like *geegirr* 'all' in (91), which forms a phrasal compound construction with the verb (Harvey 1992: 284–285).

(90) Alyawarra (Yallop 1977: 77)
 amulya akngirra *plain-ila atuna*
 lizard many.NOM plain-LOC kill.PST.CONT
 '(we) killed a lot of lizards on the plain'

(91) Gaagudju (Harvey 1992: 285)
 *djirriingi njinggooduwa yaa-bu=mba **geegirr***
 man woman 3I-went=AUG all
 'The men and women have all gone.'

Studies on quantifiers often focus on one language (e.g. individual language chapters in Keenan & Paperno [2012] and Paperno & Keenan [2017], one of which is Bowler [2017] on Warlpiri; see also Evans [1995b] on Mayali, and Bittner & Hale [1995] on Warlpiri), and there are relatively few typological or cross-linguistic studies (but see, for instance, Matthewson [2008]). A recent study of quantifiers in Australian languages is Kapitonov & Bowler (forthc.).

One interesting issue to come out of the literature concerns the link between quantification and determination and/or definiteness. This was already referred to in section 1.1 above in relation to number marking. An example of this link in relation to quantifiers is their use in positions which are typical of determiners, for instance the cross-linguistically common use of the numeral 'one' as indefiniteness marker (e.g. Dryer 2013c). In addition, Hale (1975) does not only analyse 'one' as indefinite determiner in Warlpiri, but also 'two', 'several' and 'many'. There are also more subtle effects, like relative quantifiers (such as *most*) that invoke a reference mass (to which the intended referent is compared) which is identifiable (Davidse 2004; see also several papers in Bach et al. [1995]; Gil [2015]; see further in chapter 7, section 3).

The rest of this section discusses the distribution of numerals and quantifiers and the architecture of the relevant systems. The main focus is on quantifiers within NPs, following the set-up of this book, but other types of quantifiers are touched upon when relevant for the discussion.

2.1 Distribution of numerals and quantifiers

In the NP, numerals and other quantifiers can either have the same distribution as attributive modifiers (as shown in the NP template for Yingkarta in (92a)), or they occur in their own position (as shown in the NP template for Umpithamu in (92b)). For some languages, however, there is evidence that they can also pattern like determining elements, which confirms the link between quantifiers and determiners suggested in the literature (see chapter 7 for more detailed discussion). In (92c) from Gooniyandi, for instance, the numeral 'one' is used as a determiner. The fact that quantifiers can occur in different functional roles (across and within the languages of the sample) is another example of the flexible relation between categories and structure in the nominal domain in Australian languages. Actually, it seems that quantifiers are overall particularly prone to this type of flexibility, perhaps more so than other categories.

(92) a. Yingkarta (Dench 1998: 50–51)
NP template (G):[64]
(Determiner) (Modifier) Head
with Modifier: quantifiers and adjectival nominals
b. Umpithamu (Verstraete 2010: 11)
NP template (G):
Classification – Head – Modification – Number – Identification
with Number: numerals

---

[64] See chapter 1, section 2.2.3 for conventions on templates: (G) refers to a template which was provided as such in the grammar.

c. Gooniyandi (McGregor 1990: 374)
Yoowarni-ngga / **yoowarni-ngga gardiya /** *cherrabun bore /*
one-ERG one-ERG white.person <place name>
warangji / gamba bambimnga-wirrangi *boorloomani-yoo /*
he:sat water he:pumped:it-for:them bullocks-DAT
'There was a white man at Cherrabun Bore pumping water for the cattle.'

Tying in with this NP-internal flexibility, a second interesting syntactic feature of numerals and quantifiers is that they often seem to be more syntactically 'free' than other modifiers. In discontinuous NPs, for instance, they can more easily be 'split off' from the rest of the NP, as in (93) from Kayardild. This is discussed in more detail in chapter 6 (esp. section 4).

(93) Kayardild (Evans 1995a: 250)
ngada **kiyarrng-ku** *kala-thu* **wumburung-ku** *mirra-wu*
1SG.NOM two-MPROP cut-POT spear-MPROP good-MPROP
'I want to cut out two good boomerangs.'

In terms of syntactic complexity, for four languages in the sample the grammars also mention the possibility of a 'quantifier phrase', i.e. where the quantifier itself is modified, as in (94a-b). This is the case for Arabana/Wangkangurru (Hercus 1994: 65), Arrernte (Wilkins 1989: 110), Djambarrpuyngu (Wilkinson 1991: 682–685) and Gooniyandi (McGregor 1990: 259–260).

(94) a. Arrernte (Wilkins 1989: 110)
kngwelye atningke ingkirreke
dog many all
'All of the many dogs'
b. Arabana/Wangkangurru (Hercus 1994: 65; own glossing)
kardipirla nhuka katyiwiRi
star(s) many big
'a great number of stars'

Outside the NP, numerals/quantifiers can occur in several forms. Some quantifiers are syntactically preverbs, which can have semantic scope over the noun, as in (95) from Warlpiri (Bowler [2017: 974–975], only for absolutive arguments); see also (91) above. Other quantifiers can only be used adverbially (with predicates) or predicatively (with nouns), as in (96) from Bardi (Bowern

2012: 269). See also Alpher (2001), who argues that adverbially used quantifiers to express distributivity are wide-spread in Australian languages.

(95) Warlpiri (Bowler 2017: 975)
Karnta=lu **muku** *yanu Nyirrpi-kirra.*
woman=3PL.S all/completely go.PST Nyirrpi-ALL
'All the women went to Nyirrpi.'

(96) Bardi (Bowern 2012: 269)
Balgarraniny gorna aarli, **ngarri** *jirra laya*
small-toothed.cod good fish too.much 3AUG.POSS fat
agal **ngarri** *jirra baangga.*
and too.much 3AUG.POSS flesh
'Small-toothed cod (Epinephelus microdon) is good to eat; it has lots of fat and flesh.' (lit: much is its fat and much is its flesh)

Australian languages can also use numerals and quantifiers as depictive secondary predicates, where they do not "merely specify the numerosity of the referent set (...), but [do] so in relation to the referent event" (McGregor 2005: 174). An example is given in (97), where the numeral 'one' says something about the referent ('I') in relation to the action ('eat'). The focus of McGregor's (2005) discussion is the syntactic analysis of these structures: it is often difficult to decide whether these quantifying elements are separate from the NP and thus genuine secondary predicates, or whether they are modifiers in the NP (or split NPs) and thus expressions that merely allow an interpretation as secondary predicates but are not separate constructions in themselves.

(97) Gooniyandi (McGregor 2005: 179)
igi marriyali ngirnda nyamani girli gand
no wife's:mother this big same can't
nganyi-ngga yoowarni-ngga ngabbila
1SG-ERG one-ERG I:will:eat:it
'No, mother-in-law, it's too big. I can't eat it alone.'

2.2 Architecture of numeral and quantifier systems

Australian languages generally have a relatively small set of numerals and quantifiers. Numerals are discussed in detail in Bowern & Zentz (2012), who show that the set of numerals is usually restricted (the upper limit is '3' or '4' in about three quarters of the languages of their sample), and that it shows limited internal complexity. About half of the languages can combine smaller numerals into larger ones, and such systems almost always use '2' as base, although it is often unclear if this base is additive or multiplicative (Bowern & Zentz: 54–55). For example, '4' in Gurindji (not in my sample) is formed by juxtaposing two instances of the form '2', as in (98). For broader typological context, including a discussion of cross-linguistic differences in the numeral base, see for example Greenberg (1978), Hammarström (2010) and Comrie (2013).

(98) Gurindji (Bowern & Zentz 2012: 139)
    a. *kutyarra*
       'two'
    b. *kutyarra kutyarra*
       two   two
       'four'

Quantifiers are discussed in Kapitonov & Bowler (forthc.), with a focus on the occurrence of items with different quantifier semantics in a sample of 125 languages. The counts in their study are more accurate than my own, as they did a more extensive study; in the rest of this paragraph I refer to findings from both samples. Note that, since grammatical descriptions rarely give more than just a list of elements with a quantifying meaning, and usually do not discuss the system in detail, it is often hard to generalise over the data. Overall, it seems that most languages of my sample have one or more high- to mid-range quantifiers (esp. 'many', 'much', 'a lot of'); similarly, Kapitonov & Bowler find a quantifier for 'many/much' in 109/125 languages. Other frequent types include a general interrogative 'how many', a low-range quantifier 'a few' and a universal quantifier 'all/every/each'; all of these occur in about a quarter of my sample and in roughly half of Kapitonov & Bowler's sample (which, as mentioned earlier, is the more accurate count). Note that sometimes the meaning 'a few' can also be expressed by the numeral 'three' (according to Kapitonov & Bowler [forthc.: 10], this is the case for a quarter of the languages that have this type of quantifier), and that sometimes there is one quantifier which means both 'all' and 'many' (Kapitonov & Bowler forthc.: 7; Bittner & Hale 1995: 13–17). Also frequent in my sample is the quantifier 'some/other', although it is often unclear from the grammar whether this is an existential or relative quantifier; see also Kapitonov & Bowler (forthc.: 11–13). The quantifier 'none/nothing' occurs in 51/125 languages in Kapitonov & Bowler (forthc.: 13), who included NP negation in their analysis. There are also a few less frequent elements like a collective 'group/mob of', 'the rest of', 'enough', 'half' and 'more' in my sample. For a handful of languages, it is observed that size adjectives or nominals like 'big' or 'small' can be used as quantifiers (e.g. Anindilyakwa [van Egmond 2012: 126], Umpila [Hill 2018: 141]; see also Kapitonov & Bowler [forthc.: 5–6]). This is illustrated for Gooniyandi in (99), where the nominal 'big' is used as a quantifier with the head nominal 'water' in non-count use (note that the same head nominal also has the potential to be used as count nominal, with other quantifiers, as in 'one (glass of) water' [McGregor 1990: 260]).[65]

(99) Gooniyandi (McGregor 1990: 260)
nyamani gamba
big   water
'a lot of water'

The example of Gooniyandi ties in with another issue from the literature, viz. the distinction between mass and count quantifiers, where the former "constitute expressions which denote an undifferentiated homogeneous mass" (like *much* in English), while the latter "constitute expressions which refer to one or more countable units of characteristic size and shape" (like English *many*) (Gil 2015: 707). The feature of countability generally appears to be a relatively unimportant category in Australian languages, which ties in with the fact that they mostly have set nouns rather than singular object nouns (cf. section 1.1.3). However, some languages distinguish between count and non-count quantifiers. In such cases, the distinction is made at the level of the quantifiers and not at the level of the nouns (see, for instance, the discussion above in relation to example (99) from Gooniyandi; Patz [2002: 66] on Kuku Yalanji). In Bilinarra, for example, there is one quantifier *jarrwa* 'many' for count nouns and two quantifiers *jarrwalud* and *janggarni* 'much' for non-count nouns (Meakins & Nordlinger 2014: 195). Similarly, Anindilyakwa has two quantifiers for count nouns and two for non-count nouns (van Egmond 2012: 126). As mentioned above in section 1.2, several languages also have 'quantifying' affixes which attach to nouns.

---

[65] A similar alternation between count and non-count use of nouns also occurs in English, e.g. *a cup of sugar* (non-count) vs. *two sugars* (count).

3 Conclusion

This chapter has provided a survey of the domain of quantification in the NP. Most grammars mention the basic options for number marking, but there is no overall picture of Australian languages available (though see Dixon [2002: 77] for some general comments, and McGregor [2004: 153–154] on Kimberley languages). In my sample, almost all languages have some number marking in the NP, mostly in the form of suffixes on the head noun and/or on its modifiers. Nonetheless, number marking is limited overall, because it is largely optional, and it often only occurs with a small set of nouns.

Similarly, most grammars provide a list of quantifiers, but it is often unclear how they are used syntactically. There is some literature on the architecture of numeral systems (Bowern & Zentz 2012) and on the availability of quantifiers with different semantics (Kapitonov & Bowler forthc.). In my sample, languages generally seem to have rather small systems of numerals/quantifiers, and most do not make a distinction between mass and count quantification. In terms of distribution, both number markers and quantifiers show a link with determination; this is further discussed in chapter 7.

5 Determination and NP constituency

The final survey chapter discusses the two domains that are least well-studied in the literature, viz. determination (section 1), and NP constituency (section 2). As already mentioned, these domains remain under-studied for different reasons: determination is simply not discussed very often in the general literature on Australian languages, while the question of NP constituency is mentioned very frequently, but still lacks a broad empirical basis. This chapter gives an overview of some of the issues relevant to the two domains, and summarises the Australianist literature that is available. The following chapters in Part II, then, follow up this chapter to investigate these issues in more detail.

1 Determination

The term 'determiner' is often used as a cover term for word classes like articles and demonstratives, which serve to mark the referent as (non)identifiable (Dryer 2007a: 161; Dryer 2013d: §3). More technically, the prototypical determiner can be defined by a combination of a structural and a functional criterion: (i) it occurs in a specific position in the NP, often at its edges, and (ii) it has a specialised determining function, i.e. it indicates the identifiability status of the referent (e.g. Dryer 2007a: 161; Lyons 1999: 2–7, 20; Himmelmann 1997: 11; McGregor 2004: 125; Davidse 2004; Willemse 2005: 7). An example is the definite article in English, which marks that the speaker presents the referent as identifiable,[66] is specialised in a left-edge determiner slot (or zone, see further below), as shown in (100a-b), and is obligatory for definite NPs, unless there is another determiner such as a demonstrative, as shown in (100c-d).

(100) English
    a. *the heavy book*
    b. * *the*
    c. * *heavy book*
    d. *that heavy book*

---

66 Note that definiteness and identifiability do not entirely overlap, in the sense that definiteness is a more narrow term than identifiability. This is argued by Lyons (1999: 253–281), who defines definiteness as a grammatical, rather than a semantic/pragmatic category of 'identifiability'; it prototypically expresses identifiability, but there are also other, non-prototypical uses (like inclusiveness).

For languages like English, the combination of these two criteria results in a relatively clear-cut category of determiners, which covers one specialised word class (articles), as well as a range of word classes that can also be used in other functions (like demonstratives, quantifiers or adjectives, see further below). However, there are many languages across the world that do not seem to have such an obvious determiner category in their grammar. While all languages will have some devices dealing with identifiability, they are often not obligatory or even frequent, and they do not necessarily coalesce in a structural position within the NP.

Australian languages seem to be an example of this, as they generally lack typical determiner features like specialised word classes, obligatory use and competition in a particular position (e.g. Lyons 1999: 49; Blake 2001: 424; Dixon 2002: 66–67; Stirling & Baker 2007; Baker 2008; Stirling 2008). In Yir Yoront, for instance, an NP need not include an element which marks the identifiability status of the referent, as shown in (101a-b). When it does include such elements, moreover, they are not in complementary distribution, as shown in (101c), where an adnominal personal pronoun and a demonstrative together modify the head noun.

(101) Yir Yoront (Alpher 1973: 281, 299, 306)
    a. *wârtyuwər*
        woman
        'a woman/ the woman'
    b. *púnal   kåwən   mîrlîn.*
        sun-ERG water dry-TR:PST
        'The sun dried the water up.'
    c. *pâm +áwr̞ +ôlo mîṉa.*
        man that he meat.DAT
        'That man is (e.g. went) for meat.'

Patterns of co-occurrence as in (101c) are often interpreted as evidence against a determiner category (see Himmelmann 1997: 131–132; Dryer 2007a: 161; Dryer 2013c, d: §3 for cross-linguistic context). Indeed, it has sometimes been suggested that only one element at a time can occupy this position, and that complementary distribution is a requirement for determinerhood. From this perspective, articles and demonstratives can both be regarded as instances of a general determiner category in English because they are in complementary distribution in a single slot, as shown in (102), while in a language like Yir Yoront the personal pronoun and demonstrative cannot, because they can co-occur (as in 101c) (see Dryer 2007a: 161; see also e.g. Van de Velde 2009: 253–256 for a discussion).[67]

(102) English
   * *the that book*

There is an alternative view in the typological literature, however, which recognises the co-occurrence of identifiability markers as a cross-linguistically common pattern, also known as 'overdetermination' (Himmelmann 2001, Plank 2003; see also e.g. Börjars [1998] and Julien [2005] on this phenomenon in Scandinavian languages). In this view, a determiner position can be filled by multiple elements at the same time, which together fulfil the general function of determination. In this scenario, the personal pronoun and the demonstrative in (101c) can both be analysed as determiners. More recently, similar analyses have also been proposed for prototypical determiner languages like English. Specifically, the recent literature argues in favour of a 'determiner zone', consisting of three elements that can be combined: a predeterminer, a primary determiner and a secondary determiner (e.g. Bache 2000, Breban & Davidse 2003, Breban 2010, Ghesquière 2009). In this analysis, the secondary determiner position can, for instance, be filled by adjectives like *other* in (103), which provide "additional information about the referential status of the instance(s) denoted by the NP" (Breban 2010: 158–159) by linking it to another NP (*this witch*). Together, the determiner elements form "a close-knit functional unit" (Ghesquière 2009: 315), where the pre- and secondary determiners further specify the identifiability status of the referents. This analysis is based on positional, formal, functional and diachronic evidence (see further in the references mentioned above), and I will try to apply it to Australian languages in chapter 7.

(103) English (Breban 2010: 158)
   His uncle had said <u>this witch</u> had stood there looking at him and then made some medicine with his hands. His uncle had thought he might be calling to **the other witches** to come out of their cave and help.

---

[67] Another example of the dominance of prototypical determiner languages in theorising concerns the argument found in some theories that the determiner category is really the head of the nominal expression; accordingly, they propose a determiner phrase (DP) as the basic syntactic unit instead of the NP (see Lyons 1999: 290–305 for a general discussion). This issue cannot be sufficiently investigated on the basis of the sample, but for at least one language, there is evidence that points towards a DP as syntactic unit, viz. Umpithamu (see footnote 112 in chapter 7).

Another relevant issue is that, even if a slot can be established, there is a great deal of cross-linguistic variation in which elements can go in that slot. Articles and demonstratives are the prime suspects, obviously, but there are many other candidates, like personal and possessive pronouns, or quantifying elements, whose status varies on a language-by-language basis (Himmelmann 1997: 131). Elements that are determiners in one language (because they occur in a determiner position) are not necessarily determiners in another (e.g. Himmelmann 1997: 132). One example of a category that can often be used both as determiners and as other type of modifiers is possessives. Lyons (1999: 24, 130–134), for instance, distinguishes between 'determiner-genitive' (DG) and 'adjectival-genitive' (AG) languages, depending on the function possessives have in a particular language. A language can be both DG and AG: Spanish, for instance, has both *mi casa* 'my house' (determiner) and *la casa mía* 'my house' (adjectival) (Lyons 1999: 133; see also Plank 1992). English and Swedish also allow both uses, with non-determiner possessives having a 'classifying' function in English (Willemse 2007),[68] and functions such as measuring or swearing in Swedish (Koptjevskaja-Tamm 2003). This distinction is illustrated in the English structures in (104). In (104a), the possessive *friend's* has a determiner function, because it marks the identifiability of the referent (by specifying whose house is meant). In (104b), the possessive *widow's* has a classifying function: it does not serve to identify a particular pension, but instead "contributes to the description of a (sub)type: what is being designated is the type of pension" (Willemse 2007: 538). This illustrates how even in 'classic' determiner languages, there is no necessary one-to-one mapping of word class and functional role. This is important in the light of Australian data: the idea that one type of modifier can have both determiner and other uses is investigated further in chapter 7.

(104) English (Indo-European; Willemse 2007: 538)
 a. *Matilda was supposed to be sleeping at **a friend's house** but decided to sneak home and play a joke on her family.*
 b. *At present the parties to a divorce usually have insufficient financial resources for an ex-wife even to be reasonably compensated for loss of **a widow's pension**.*

---

68 This is what McGregor (1997b) calls 'subclassification'. See also chapter 2, section 2.1.2 on the Classifier slot in Gooniyandi.

A final feature of determiner slots that has often been noted in the literature is their position: they are often found at the edges.[69] Rijkhoff (2002: 313, see also 218–223) explains this phenomenon in terms of a Principle of Scope, which states that "modifiers tend to occur next to the part of the expression that they have in their scope." As markers of identifiability, determiners have the broadest scope of all nominal categories: classification, qualification and quantification all contribute to the description of the referent, and determiners locate this in discourse. Rijkhoff (2002: 229–331) even argues for a further distinction between two categories of determiners, one of which is within the scope of the other (and accordingly occurs closer to the head). 'Localising' modifiers, like demonstratives and possessives, "specify the location of the referent in the world of discourse" (Rijkhoff 2002: 231). 'Discourse' modifiers, like articles and comparative modifiers (*the former, (the) same* ...), specify whether the referent is identifiable or not, and can additionally "relate to the location where the referent was mentioned before in the actual conversation" (Rijkhoff 2002: 231). Discourse modifiers have localising modifiers in their scope, and thus occur at the very edge. Edge position of determiners will be discussed in chapter 7 for Australian languages.

The ideas and questions on determination discussed above have received relatively little attention in the Australianist literature. This may relate to the fact that many Australian languages do not have prototypical determiners, as defined by features like obligatoriness and complementary distribution, which work for languages for English but not for languages like Yir Yoront, as illustrated in (101). In the general Australian literature, there are only a handful of studies that deal with determination. One is Blake (2001), who investigates the use of (personal and demonstrative) pronouns as determiners in Australian languages. On the basis of structures like (105), where a third person pronoun (in this example suffixed with a deictic marker) modifies the head noun, he argues that where

---

69 In some languages, determiners are not at the edges, because another slot can be identified outside the determiner slot. Languages like English or Dutch have 'peripheral modifiers' which occur before determiners (Payne & Huddleston 2002: 436–439, 452; Van de Velde 2009: 256), like *zelfs* 'even' in (i). There is some discussion, however, whether these elements should be analysed as pre-determiners (i.e. part of the determiner zone) or as a separate functional layer in the NP (Van de Velde 2009: 293–297).

(i) Dutch (Van de Velde 2009: 294)
  zelfs de hogere klassen
  even the higher classes
  'even the higher classes'

pronouns occur, they even constitute the head of the NP. The specific issue of personal pronouns used as determiners is further taken up by Louagie & Verstraete (2015), who show that this particular construction is relatively widespread in Australia, and that in some cases determining pronouns show signs of incipient grammaticalisation.

(105) Pitta-Pitta (Blake 2001: 416)
 Nhu-wa-ka karna yurta-ka.
 he-NOM-HERE man swim-PST
 'The man swam.'

Stirling & Baker (2007) and Baker (2008) focus on the semantics of determiners: they use syntactic and discourse-based evidence to argue that Australian languages have a class of 'topic determiners', whose general function is that of "managing topics" (Stirling & Baker 2007: 5, 7). These topic determiners are largely optional and thus allow "speaker management of hearer attention" (Stirling & Baker 2007: 7–8). An example is the recognitional determiner *nawu* in Gun-djeihmi (one of the Bininj Kunwok varieties), which is used for "first mentions or first re-mentions of participants that should be readily identifiable once linguistic identification is made through naming" (Evans 2003a: 297; cited in Stirling & Baker 2007: 3).[70] This is illustrated in (106), where the birds introduced earlier in the text with bare nouns are reintroduced at the end of the story with the recognitional determiner.

(106) Gun-djeihmi (Evans 2003a: 298; cited in Stirling & Baker 2007: 3)
 Djirndi na-wu na-mege goddoukgoddouk na-wu...
 quail M-REL M-that bar.shouldered.dove M-REL
 'That quail and that bar-shouldered dove...'

In individual grammars, determiners are mostly treated at the level of individual elements. Many grammars give a good picture of the semantics and morphology of demonstratives, for example, but a syntactic analysis, for instance investigating the presence or absence of a determiner slot or zone, is often not provided. Several grammars do point out that the marking of definiteness is not obligatory and that bare nouns are unspecified for definiteness or specificity (e.g. Meakins & Nordlinger [2014: 3] on Bilinarra; Cutfield [2011: 44] on Dalabon; Tsunoda [1981: 2]

---

70 The *nawu* demonstrative set has another function next to the recognitional one, viz. as relative pronoun. The gloss REL (relativiser) is used in both cases.

on Jaru; Pensalfini [2003: 201] on Jingulu). Grammars that do present a more detailed syntactic analysis are usually those that generally pay more attention to information structure and discourse, and often also present a detailed analysis of NP structure (like McGregor [1990] on Gooniyandi, Hill [2018] on Umpila/Kuuku Ya'u, or Spronck [2015] on Ungarinyin). Also, for the few Australian languages that do have a specialised determiner word class (like Marra or Pitta-Pitta), this has invited a more detailed analysis (e.g. Baker 2008; Blake 2001 resp.).

The relative lack of attention to determination in the Australian literature is the reason why I take up the issue of determiners in Part II of this study. Chapter 7 provides a more detailed study of determiners in the languages of the sample, focusing mainly on the question of syntactic status – the presence of determiner slots – and the types of elements that can go in these slots.

2 NP constituency

The question of noun phrase constituency has been quite prominent in the typological literature, driven in part by data from specific language families and areas (including Australia), and in part by the theoretical notion of non-configurationality (originally proposed by Hale [1981; 1983]; see also Nash [1986: 148–162] for a good overview of the literature leading up to this proposal and immediately following it). In its most basic sense, the issue boils down to the question whether nominal elements that belong together semantically also form a unit syntactically (i.e. an NP). Some of the classic criteria for unithood include the behaviour of nominal elements under conditions of movement and substitution, the potential for markers to attach at the edges of units, fixed linear order of elements within a nominal expression, and morphological agreement (e.g. noun class) (see Krasnoukhova [2012: 167–168] for a short discussion of several of these criteria). Thus, for instance, the elements *the*, *big* and *dogs* in the English structure in (107a) form a syntactic unit because they can only switch positions as one single unit and not separately, as shown in (107b), and because they can be replaced by one single element, like the personal pronoun in (107c). The Trumai structure in (108b) can be said to form a syntactic unit because it shows a fixed order of elements (following the general NP template given in (108a)), and because both the special morpheme *(i)yi* and the case marker attach to the right edge of the entire structure (Krasnoukhova 2012: 170). Conversely, the Nunggubuyu structures in (109) are not regarded as one single unit because the nominal elements can be split by other elements, as in (109a), and because they show flexible word order internally, as in (109b-c) (Heath 1984: 499–500; Heath 1986).

(107) English (Pavey 2010: 50–51)
    a. ***The big dogs*** *chased the cat in the street.*
    b. *It was **the big dogs** that chased the cat in the street.*
    c. ***They*** *chased the cat in the street.*

(108) Trumai (Trumai; Guirardello 1999: 29; cited in Krasnoukhova 2012: 170)
    a. NP template: dem / num – possessor – N – property word
    b. *[**ka'natl   dinoxo yi**]=**ki** chï(in)   ha fa*
       DEM:DIST.F girl   yi=DAT FOC/TENS 1SG beat
       'I beat that girl.'

(109) Nunggubuyu (Heath 1984: 502, 499, 500)
    a. ***nu:'bagiyun^g*** *ni:'maji,* ***na-wulmur-in^{y}un^g***
       that.SG.M   he:stole   SG.M-bachelor-HUM.SG
       'That one committed theft, the bachelor.'
    b. *wurunan^y, yuwa:gu*   ***wara:-'rawindi wara-mananun^g*** *big-mob*
       they:saw there(distant) PL-many   PL-women   many
       'Many women saw (found) honey over there'
    c. ***n^{g}ara-mula-maji: n^{g}ara:-'rawindi*** *namban^{g}iwan^{g}ana*
       SG.F-mosquito-if   SG.F-many   they.bite.us
       'if lots of mosquitoes bite us'

Problematic nominal structures like in Nunggubuyu have played a prominent role in the theoretical literature, as one of the defining characteristics of the broader theoretical notion of non-configurationality. Non-configurationality was originally defined in terms of a cluster of characteristics, such as free word order, discontinuous nominal expressions and null anaphora (Hale 1983); languages exhibiting these characteristics were argued to have no NPs or VPs at all (e.g. Blake 1983, Heath 1986). For instance, Kalkatungu was regarded as non-configurational because there is grammatically free word order in the clause, because elements of a nominal expression can occur in any order, and because they can occur discontinuously (Blake 1983). This is illustrated in (110), which shows how elements in the nominal expression can occur in different orders, as shown in (110a, c, d, f), and can often also be split off from the rest of the NP, as shown in (110b, c, e).

(110) Kalkatungu (Blake 1983: 145)
    a. ***cipa-yi   tuku-yu yaun-tu*** *yaɲi*   *icayi*
       this-ERG dog-ERG big-ERG white.man bite
       'This big dog bit/bites the white man.'

b. *cipa-yi ṭuku-yu yaṇi icayi yaun-tu*
c. *ṭuku-yu cipa-yi icayi yaṇi yaun-tu*
d. *yaun-tu cipa-yi ṭuku-yu icayi yaṇi*
e. *cipa-yi icayi yaṇi ṭuku-yu yaun-tu*
f. *yaṇi icayi cipa-yi yaun-tu ṭuku-yu*

In the literature published since the original formulation of non-configurationality, there has been a lot of debate about how the notion should be defined, and which of the characteristics (including discontinuous NPs) are really a necessary condition to call a language non-configurational. I will not go into this question any further in this context, but the reader is referred to Jelinek (1984), Austin & Bresnan (1996), Nordlinger (1998b), Baker (2001), Baker (2002), Evans (2002) and Pensalfini (2004) for alternatives to the original position, and to Croft (2007: 25–30) and Nordlinger (2014: 227–232, 237–241) for overviews. In spite of a growing consensus that non-configurationality really concerns the absence of a VP constituent rather than the absence of an NP constituent (e.g. Nordlinger 2014: 230), the idea that there are languages without NPs remains, especially for the languages of Australia.

This idea has also found its way into the general typological literature, like Rijkhoff's typological survey of the noun phrase, where several languages are classified as having 'non-integral' NPs (2002: 19–22). These are "languages in which noun modifiers (if we can still call them that) are not fully integrated constituents of the noun phrase," but rather in apposition to each other (Rijkhoff 2002: 19). In Rijkhoff's analysis, absence of NP constituency can be a general feature of a language (Rijkhoff only mentions some Australian languages to illustrate this possibility) or it can be restricted to certain types of nominal expression. For example, when a language has restrictions on the number of prenominal modifiers, it only allows extra modifiers to occur in apposition, usually following the head noun (Rijkhoff 2002: 11). In Yimas, for instance, an NP can maximally consist of two elements. A structure like (111a) is not allowed: any extra modifiers are separately marked and occur in apposition, as in (111b or c) (Foley 1991: 4, 184, 188; referred to in Rijkhoff 2002: 20).

(111) Yimas (Indo-Pacific; Foley 1991: 184–185)
    a. *yua kpa impram
       good big basket
    b. *[yua-m   [kpa impram]]*
       good-VII.SG big   basket.VII.SG
    c. *[[yua impram]   kpa-m]*
       good basket.VII.SG big-VII.SG
       'a good big basket'

In her typological survey of the noun phrase in South American languages, Krasnoukhova (2012: 177–181) adds to this point by showing that some languages have 'non-integral' NPs for certain types of modifiers. For instance, Hixkaryana only allows nominal possessors to be integrated in the NP, while other modifiers like demonstratives form separate NPs (Krasnoukhova 2012: 178–179), as reflected in their flexible order (compare (112a) with (112b)) and separate case marking (as illustrated in (112c), where the noun and the demonstrative each have a separate comitative marker).

(112) Hixkaryana (Cariban; Derbyshire 1985: 53, 1979: 68, 40; cited in Krasnoukhova 2012: 178–179; glossing by Sergio Meira)
a. **ow-oti**   **mosoni**   ø-ar-ko   ha
2-meat.food   DEM:PROX:AN   3-take-IMP   INTENS
'Take this meat for you.'
b. *Kaywana y-omsï-r*   *y-oknï*   **mokro**   **kaykusu**
Kaywana LK-daughter-POSSD   LK-pet:POSSD   DEM:MED:AN   dog
'That dog is Kaywana's daughter's pet.'
c. *k-omok-no*   **moson**   **y-akoro**   ro-he-tx   y-akoro
1SA-come-IMMPST   DEM:PROX:AN   LK-COM   1-wife-POSSD   LK-COM
'I have come with this one, with my wife.'

One feature of 'non-integral' NPs that is particularly salient in the literature is that the noun and its semantic modifiers need not be adjacent and can occur discontinuously. Australian languages are (again) the prototypical example in the literature, but discontinuity has also been used as evidence for non-integral status of NPs in other languages, e.g. Krasnoukhova (2012: 176) on Mosetén.

For several languages in which discontinuity has been observed, the phenomenon has been associated with specific functions, like contrastive contexts or the marking of focus (see the references in Rijkhoff [2002: 258–259] and in Schultze-Berndt & Simard [2012: 1038]). A classic example is Polish, for which Siewierska (1984) argues that discontinuous NPs are only found in contexts where the elements of an NP have different information structural functions, viz. where one element of the NP is in focus, while the other is topic (most commonly a contrastive or a new topic). This is illustrated in (113), which shows a double contrast: *beautiful* is paired with *garden*, *house* with *crummy*. The first discontinuous NP in (113b) has *house* in pre-verbal position (associated with topic – we are still talking about the house, though in contrast with *garden* in the following clause), and *crummy* in post-verbal position (associated with focus). The second discontinuous NP in (113b) then has *beautiful* in topic position (continuing the topic in (113a), and contrasting with *crummy* from the previous NP) and *garden* in focus position (as it is new information) (Siewierska 1984). In other words, this study suggests that discontinuity is not free but has a function.⁷¹

(113) Polish (Indo-European; Siewierska 1984: 60)
  a. *Podobno   mają piękny   dom.*
     apparently have beautiful house
     'Apparently they have a beautiful house.'
  b. *Nieprawda!* **Dom** *mają* **kiepski**, *ale* **piękny** *mają* **ogród**
     untrue   house have crummy but beautiful have garden
     'Rubbish! Their house is crummy, but they have a beautiful garden.'

As is clear from the discussion above, Australian languages feature prominently in both the theoretical and typological literature as languages lacking NP units, with characteristics like flexible word order in NPs and discontinuity (e.g. Blake 1983; Hale 1981, 1983; Heath 1986; Nash 1986; Blake 1987: 77; Harvey 1992; Himmelmann 1997; Rijkhoff 2002: 19–22, 255–257). One problem with much of the general literature is that it has a limited empirical basis, with claims that are usually based on the same handful of languages, like Warlpiri, Kalkatungu and Nunggubuyu.⁷² If we look at individual grammars of Australian languages, the picture is very mixed. Many grammars explicitly discuss the question of constituency – reflecting its prominence in the theoretical literature – but not all come to the same conclusion. Some descriptions clearly confirm that a 'classic' NP constituent is absent (e.g. Evans [2003a: 227–234] on Bininj Kunwok; Campbell [2006: 57] on Giimbiyu; Harvey [2001: 112] on Limilngan). For instance, Bininj Kunwok is argued to lack strict NP structures, in which elements that semantically belong together "are related paratactically and the relations between them are worked out from pragmatics rather than syntax" (Evans 2003a: 227). The reasons for this analysis include the fact that elements that semantically belong together need not occur contiguously, and that there are no strict ordering tendencies within the nominal expression (Evans 2003a: 227–234). Other grammars, by contrast, provide evidence in favour of NP constituency (e.g. Bowe [1990] on Pitjantjatjara; Gaby [2017: 195–197] on Kuuk Thaayorre; Nordlinger

---

[71] Rijkhoff argues that this type of discontinuity is different than from what is found in some Australian languages, because in those languages the elements do not form integral NPs anyway (2002: 255–257).
[72] At least one exception is Pensalfini's (1992) work on word order in a sample of 16 Pama-Nyungan languages, arguing for an implicational relation between 'free' discontinuity and flexible word order in the NP.

[1998a: 131] on Wambaya). For instance, Kuuk Thaayorre is argued to have NP constituents because case markers are attached to the final eligible element of the NP (i.e. they serve as boundary markers), because there is a relatively strict internal word order, and because the NP has a single intonation contour (Gaby 2017: 195–197). Finally, there are languages for which different analyses are available. Even for Kalkatungu, for instance, which is considered the prototypical example of a language lacking integral NPs, there is an analysis that argues for determiners as (optional) head of the NP and head-dependency relations as part of its internal structure (Blake 2001).

The diversity of arguments in individual grammars, together with the narrow empirical basis of general claims made in the literature, suggests that there is a genuine need to study this question in a systematic way, using a broad range of languages. This is the subject of chapter 6, where I use my sample of 100 Australian languages to show that the evidence against NP constituency in Australian languages is not as strong as it has often made out to be. There are, in fact, a number of interesting leads for this in the Australianist literature (McGregor 1989, 1990, 1997a; Schultze-Berndt & Simard 2012; Croft 2007), where several authors have proposed alternative analyses for some of the phenomena that are often taken as strong evidence against NP constituency, like flexible ordering and discontinuity. For instance, McGregor (1990) uses data from Gooniyandi to show that apparent flexibility of word order can be resolved by looking at functional categories instead, and thus need not be an argument against constituency. For example, an attributive nominal can precede or follow the head nominal. This is not a matter of free variation in order, however. McGregor shows show this difference can be related to a difference in function: in pre-head position the attributive nominal acts as Classifier, in post-head position as Qualifier. Thus, in (114a), the attributive nominal *thiwa* 'red' helps to identify a subtype of women (according to race or cultural group), while in (114b) it describes a property of the referent (the colour of the flower). (See further in chapter 6; see Harvey [1992] for a critique of this analysis.) This is a good illustration of how the tension between word class and functional structure is manifested in the languages of the sample, and how focusing on either of the two produces different results in the analysis.

(114) Gooniyandi (McGregor 1990: 272)
    a. Classifier – Entity
       thiwa goornboo
       red   woman
       'a white woman'

b. Entity – Qualifier
jiga   thiwa
flower red
'a red flower'

Second, on discontinuity, McGregor (1997a) and Schultze-Berndt & Simard (2012) use data from Gooniyandi and Jaminjung to argue that discontinuity of nominal expressions is actually restricted to certain formal and functional contexts and is a "meaningful option" (McGregor 1992: 316) rather than a free variant of contiguous expressions (much as argued by Siewierska for Polish; see above). For instance, one of the functions of discontinuous NPs in Jaminjung is contrastive argument focus. The example in (115) is an extract from a mythical narrative that accounts for the differences between the brolga and the emu. In this example, the number of their offspring is contrasted (two vs. many children). In the first intonation unit, the NP *jirrama jarlig* 'two children' is split, with the quantifier *jirrama* 'two' occurring in initial position (the position associated with focus), as it contributes to the contrastive interpretation (Schultze-Berndt & Simard 2012: 1034–1035).

(115) Jaminjung (Schultze-Berndt & Simard 2012: 1035)
   ^***jirrama*** *ganuny-ma-ya*   ***jarlig****, gumurrinyji orait,*
   two   3SG>3DU-have-PRS child   emu   all.right
   ^*bardawurru gana-ma-ya* \ .. *jarlig* \
   many   3SG>3SG-have-PRS child
   'She (the brolga) has two children. The emu, all right, she has many, children that is.'

In chapter 6, I show that such clear functional differentiation for discontinuous structures suggests that discontinuity need not be regarded as evidence against NP constituency, but rather indicates that these structures are distinct constructions which need to be analysed separately from contiguous structures. I argue that this is actually a good way to deal with the Australian data overall: analysing a language in terms of different construals (i.e. structural possibilities) can offer a much more fruitful perspective than analysing it in terms of the presence or absence of 'classic' NPs.

Part II: **NP constituency and determination**

The second part of this study takes up the two questions that were introduced in the final chapter of Part I, viz. the status of determining elements and the issue of NP constituency. While all of the questions addressed in the previous chapters require more work, determination and NP constituency constitute the most obvious gaps in the literature – one because it is only rarely discussed in grammars or more general studies, and the other because it is frequently discussed, but has never really been tested on a larger scale. The next two chapters investigate these two questions in detail, and propose an in-depth analysis for each of them.

The question of NP constituency is taken up in chapter 6, where I use a set of concrete parameters to determine whether there is evidence for syntactic unithood of nominal expressions in the languages of the sample. I show that there is clear evidence against the widespread idea that Australian languages generally lack phrasal structure for nominal expressions. As an alternative, it may be more interesting to typologise languages in terms of where and how they construe sequences of nominals as NPs than in terms of a simple yes-no distinction, and I also apply this idea to discontinuous structures. Chapter 7 examines the status of determining elements. I show that a determiner slot can be identified in about half of the languages of the sample. I also investigate which elements can occur in determiner slots, with a special focus on elements that can be used both inside and beyond these slots, demonstrating once again how category and functional structure do not necessarily align.

Unlike in the survey chapters, the analysis in these chapters is intended to be as exhaustive as possible for the sample, at least as far as the sources allow this. Accordingly, the data are treated differently here. The text of the chapters discusses the basic arguments and categories, with relevant examples, and the maps provided summarise the relevant information for all sample languages. Details of the analysis for each individual language are also included as an Appendix at the end of the book, in the form of tables that categorise all languages in the sample, with reference to the specific part of the source materials on which the analysis is based. This allows the reader to trace back decisions for each language in the sample.

6 Noun phrase constituency

1 Introduction

As[73] discussed in chapter 5 (section 2), it has often been argued that Australian languages show unusual syntactic flexibility in the nominal domain, and may even lack clear noun phrase structures altogether (see also McGregor 1997a: 84; Cutfield 2011: 46–50; Nordlinger 2014: 237–241, for overviews and more general discussion of claims to this effect). This idea is based mainly on features like flexibility of word order and the availability of discontinuous nominal expressions, as illustrated in the examples in (116)-(118) below.

(116) Bininj Kunwok (Evans 2003a: 707, 207)
    a. *"wanjh,* **an-dehne gukku** *nga-bo-bawo-n*   *bedberre*
        well   VE-that   water   1-liquid-leave-NPST   for.them
        munguih-munguih"
        for.ever
        'Yeah, I'll leave that water for them forever...'
    b. **gun-barlkbu**   **an-ege** *bi-rrerlme-ng*
        IV-digging.stick   VE-that   3/3H.PST-throw-PST.PFV
        'She threw that digging stick at him.'

(117) Warlpiri (Hale 1983: 6)
    wawirri   *kapi-rna*   *panti-rni*   **yalumpu**
    kangaroo   FUT-1SG.SA   spear-NPST   that
    'I will spear that kangaroo.'

---

[73] This chapter is written in first person singular, for reasons of consistency, but it is an extended version of an article co-authored with Jean-Christophe Verstraete (shared first authorship), published as: Louagie, Dana & Jean-Christophe Verstraete. 2016. Noun phrase constituency in Australian languages: A typological study. *Linguistic Typology* 20: 25–80. The chapter is different from the published paper in some respects: a few languages changed categories after further investigation (see footnotes 85 and 91 for more information), I included maps and some notes on the distribution of features across the continent, the chapter now includes extra examples and a note on adpositions, the discussion of diagnostic slots has been extended, and references to the literature or to alternative analyses have been added in different places

https://doi.org/10.1515/9781501512933-008

(118) Kalkatungu (Blake 1983: 145)
   a. ***cipa-yi ṯuku-yu yaun-tu*** *yaŋi*   *icayi*
      this-ERG dog-ERG big-ERG white.man bite
      'This big dog bit/bites the white man.'
   b. ***cipa-yi ṯuku-yu*** *yaŋi icayi* ***yaun-tu***
   c. ***ṯuku-yu cipa-yi*** *icayi yaŋi* ***yaun-tu***
   d. ***yaun-tu cipa-yi ṯuku-yu*** *icayi yaŋi*
   e. ***cipa-yi*** *icayi yaŋi* ***ṯuku-yu yaun-tu***
   f. *yaŋi icayi* ***cipa-yi yaun-tu ṯuku-yu***

The two Bininj Kunwok structures in (116) show that nominal word order is flexible, in that, for instance, the demonstrative can both precede and follow its nominal head. The Warlpiri structure in (117) shows how a modifier, again a demonstrative, can be detached from its apparent nominal head in a discontinuous construction. These two properties are taken to their extremes in the oft-cited Kalkatungu example in (118) (repeated from (110)), which allows at least six different structures for a demonstrative, adjective and nominal head, in different orders and with different modifiers separated from their apparent heads. The features of word order flexibility and discontinuity illustrated in (116)-(118) have been regarded as indications that languages like Bininj Kunwok or Kalkatungu lack phrasal structures in the nominal domain, without obvious internal structure or cohesion to suggest that a noun and its semantic dependents form a constituent in the 'classic' sense (e.g. Evans 2003a: 227–234; Blake 1983: 145).

As already mentioned, the existing literature about NP constituency in Australian languages is strongly embedded in theoretical debates about non-configurationality (e.g. Hale 1981, 1983; Blake 1983; Heath 1986; Austin & Bresnan 1996; Nordlinger 1998), and often also has a limited empirical basis, with claims that are based on only a handful of languages (typically including the well-known cases of Warlpiri, Nunggubuyu or Kalkatungu). The aim of this chapter is to check how valid general ideas about NP constituency in Australian languages really are, i.e. whether nominal elements that belong together semantically show any evidence for syntactic unithood. I try to answer this question by addressing the two main problems in the existing literature. On the one hand, the issue is disentangled from the wider theoretical debate on non-configurationality by focusing on the question of NP constituency in its own right (following Nordlinger [2014]), breaking it down into a set of concrete parameters that can be checked in a consistent way over a range of languages. On the other hand, the empirical basis is broadened by the use of my sample of 100 Australian languages. The results of my analysis show that there is no evidence for any widespread absence of NP constituency across Australia, rather on the contrary. In this sense, this survey confirms earlier analyses that provide alternative perspectives on NP structure in Australian languages (e.g. McGregor [1990] on Gooniyandi), or that give clear evidence in favour of 'classic' NP constituency (e.g. Bowe [1990] on Pitjantjatjara). More generally, the results also imply that specific grammatical descriptions may have to be revisited on this point, and that theoretical or typological work (for instance on non-configurationality) should not take simple generalisations about NP structure in Australian languages for granted. In addition, an alternative perspective to this question is proposed: the results show that NP constituency is not an all-or-nothing phenomenon, and they suggest that it is more interesting to look at the different structural possibilities languages have available rather than just presence or absence of 'classic' NPs.

The rest of this chapter is structured as follows. Section 2 presents the set of parameters used for determining constituency status, discussing the rationale behind each parameter. Section 3 analyses the results, showing that especially the parameters of word order and locus of case marking provide clear evidence against the idea that Australian languages generally lack noun phrase structures. Section 4 zooms in on discontinuous structures, examining the motivations for discontinuity where they are available, and arguing that the existence of discontinuous constructions is not invariably an argument against NP constituency. Section 5 wraps up with some conclusions, including the argument that it makes more sense to typologise languages on the basis of where and when elements that belong together semantically are construed as NPs, rather than on a yes-no answer to questions of constituency or (dis)continuity.

2 Parameters

In order to study whether elements that semantically belong together can be construed as one syntactic unit, i.e. an NP, I break down the concept into a number of concrete parameters that define constituency, which can be checked across the sample in a consistent way. Obviously, the sources do not allow me to check these criteria exhaustively for all languages, but there are a number of criteria for which there is good information across the entire sample. I distinguish between external and internal criteria for constituency. External criteria, discussed in section 2.1, identify a constituent in terms of its interaction with the structure of the clause, while internal criteria, discussed in section 2.2, identify a constituent in terms of its internal structure.

Just as a reminder, this chapter uses the term NP only for nominal expressions that show evidence for syntactic constituency (unlike in the other chapters in this book). When generally referring to a group of elements in the nominal domain that belong together semantically, regardless of whether or not they form a syntactic unit, I use the term 'nominal expression' (NE).[74] Another convention concerns the NP/NE templates provided throughout the text, as explained in chapter 1: (G) indicates that the template was provided in the grammar, (W) indicates that the grammar provides word orders, which I put in template format, and (E) indicates that the template is based on examples throughout the grammar. Within the templates I refer to word classes, but as already mentioned, I use them in a broad functional sense (see chapters 1 and 3).

2.1 External parameters

External criteria for constituency focus on the interaction of a constituent with the structure of the clause: where case markers are located (section 2.1.1), where nominal expressions can occur relative to diagnostic slots for constituency (section 2.1.2), and how prosody suggests unithood (section 2.1.3). In addition to showing if nominal expressions are treated as one unit in the clause, in some cases these criteria also provide a clear delimitation of (one of) the edges of the nominal expression.

2.1.1 Locus of case marking

The marking of (relational) case in a nominal expression is a first criterion that may tell us something about its status as a syntactic unit. In the sample, there are three basic options (see also Blake 1987: 78–91 and Dench & Evans 1988): marking of one element in the nominal expression, marking of all elements, or no marking at all.[75]

---

[74] I will not go into the question whether nominal expressions are better analysed as DPs (determiner phrases) or NPs. The focus is on syntactic unithood; a study of headedness would go beyond the scope of this book. See footnotes 67 (chapter 5) and 112 (chapter 7) for more context.

[75] In addition to bound case markers, several languages have one or a small set of adpositions, although for many of these the exact syntactic status of these elements is unclear (e.g. some are described as preposition-like adverbials, locational words or particles). Evans (2003a: 256) argues that prepositions are an areal feature of Arnhem Land, but I found examples across Australia. The majority of them express location in general or more specific locational relations, and some express comparison ('like') or temporal relations ('before', 'until'). Pre- and postpositions occur roughly equally across the languages; in some languages, like Bardi (Bowern 2012: 346–347), Emmi (Ford 1998: 103–104) and Mangarrayi (Merlan 1989: 25–26), the same element can be used as preposition and as postposition (and has not grammaticalised yet into a fixed position). Adpositions are not further investigated in this study.

The first option is for case to be marked on only one element of the nominal expression, i.e. phrasal marking (see also Blake 1987: 78–86). The selection of one element for case marking implies that the nominal expression is in fact one syntactic unit, which is marked for its role in the clause through one of its constituent parts.[76] In addition, if case is marked at either the left or the right edge of the nominal expression, then this also serves to mark one of the boundaries of the NP. An example is Yandruwandha, where the ergative case suffix is attached at the right edge of the nominal expression, as in (119), thus showing that the noun and its modifier can be analysed as a single NP, with the modifier forming its right edge.

(119) Yandruwandha (Breen 2004a: 77)
 ngala **wathi malkirri-li** nganha ngarndangarndamaritji
 then tree many-ERG 1SG.ACC block:RDP:CAUS:UNSP:EMPH
 'A lot of trees blocked me from getting through.'

Another option is for case to be marked on each element of the nominal expression, i.e. word marking (see also Blake 1987: 86–91). In itself, this does not say anything about constituency, because there can be more than one reason for word marking. One reason may be that the elements are separate nominal expressions in apposition, which have the same case marker because they have the same function in the clause. This is how Blake (1983; see also 1987: 89–90) analyses the structure in (118) above from Kalkatungu (not in the sample, but see footnote 93), repeated below as (120): the demonstrative, the adjective and the noun are analysed as three elements in apposition, each of which is a dependent of the verb, and therefore receives its case marker directly from that verb.

(120) Kalkatungu (Blake 1983: 145)
 cipa-yi ṭuku-yu yaun-tu yaɲi icayi
 this-ERG dog-ERG big-ERG white.man bite
 'This big dog bit/bites the white man.'

---

[76] This is the main reason why McGregor (1990: 276) analyses case markers as postpositions in Gooniyandi. They are bound forms and do not always occur at the end of the NP (see further section 3.2), so in my view, they are different from what is referred to in the preceding footnote (viz. independent forms following the nominal expression). See also Schultze-Berndt (2000: 52) for a short discussion on analysing case markers as suffixes or postpositions in Jaminjung. Other grammars where bound case markers are referred to as postpositions include McGregor (2011: 160) on Nyulnyul, Hamilton (1996: 12) on Oykangand, Sommer (1998) on Umbuygamu and Alpher (1973: 13) on Yir Yoront.

Another possible motivation for word marking may be that the elements of a nominal expression have the same case marker due to a process of agreement within a single NP. In such cases, there is usually other evidence for constituency, as in Yingkarta, illustrated in (121) below. In this language, word order is quite fixed, with modifiers preceding the nominal head, which constitutes independent evidence for constituency (see also section 3.1 below). Moreover, case may also be marked on only one element of the NP in this language, as in (121b), which further confirms that word marking in the structure in (121a) really is agreement rather than apposition of separate NPs.

(121) Yingkarta (Dench 1998: 19, 49)
    a. *kutharra-lu mayu-ngku pinyarri-nyi*
       two-ERG   child-ERG   fight-PRS
       'Two children are fighting.'
    b. *Kurrika milyura-lu wintirri-lpurru wurrayi wura.*
       one   snake-ERG   bite-PST   many   dog
       'One snake bit several dogs.'

Next to phrasal marking and word marking, the third option is that case is not marked in nominal expressions at all. This is often the case in head-marking languages (most of the non-Pama-Nyungan languages in the sample), where the core argument relations are marked on the verb, and corresponding nominal expressions remain unmarked (especially for core arguments, but possibly also non-core arguments or adjuncts). An example of such a language is Ndjébbana, where case is generally not marked in the nominal expression, as in (122), although case affixes are available for certain roles (e.g. ablative, purposive or object of hunt; McKay [2000: 155, 191]).[77]

(122) Ndjébbana (McKay 2000: 191)
    karrddjúnja *njana-bá-la-yángaya*
    stingray   1MIN.OBJ<MIN.A-bite-REM-3MIN.F.A
    'A stingray bit me.'

These options are not mutually exclusive and could all at the same time apply in a given language. It is particularly common to find languages that allow both phrasal marking and word marking, as already mentioned for Yingkarta

---

[77] Whether these show phrasal marking or word marking is unclear: no relevant examples can be found in the grammar.

above. Relative frequencies and functions of the two alternatives are discussed in more detail in section 3.2. More generally, the locus of case marking is also one of the criteria for which good information is available across the entire sample, and thus will serve as one of the central criteria in the analysis in section 3.

2.1.2 Diagnostic slots

This criterion concerns the existence of so-called diagnostic slots in clausal morphosyntax, which are defined in terms of constituency. The best-known example is when a language has an element that obligatorily comes in the second position of the clause, following the first constituent. Evidently, this criterion is more limited in the sample than the previous one, as only some languages have such slots, but there are some famous cases like Warlpiri, where the verbal auxiliary has a fixed position as the second element in the clause, following the first constituent (e.g. Hale et al. 1995: 1431). This implies that all elements occurring in the first position before the auxiliary have to be analysed as one constituent. Accordingly, in example (123), the nominal *wawirri* and the demonstrative *yalumpu*, both preceding the second position auxiliary, must be analysed as forming a syntactic unit.

(123) Warlpiri (Hale 1983: 6)
wawirri yalumpu kapirna panti-rni
kangaroo that AUX spear-NPST
'I will spear that kangaroo.'

Obviously, this criterion can only determine the constituency status of nominal expressions occurring in this slot, but not in other positions, so it is slightly less conclusive than the previous criterion. Even so, the existence of slots defined in terms of constituency in a particular language does suggest quite strongly that construal as an NP is at least available in this language.[78]

2.1.3 Prosody

A final 'external' criterion concerns prosody, more specifically the expectation that constituents will tend to form one prosodic unit, and will allow less easily for prosodic breaks. This criterion should be used with caution, however. For instance, Himmelmann (2013) argues that using prosodic evidence for determining

---

[78] This type of slot can often also take other elements than nominal expressions, which may eliminate the degree of circularity in the argument (thanks to Hendrik De Smet and Freek Van de Velde for pointing out this potential problem).

phrase structure is problematic, because prosody really is a tool for packaging information structure, and there is no necessary one-to-one mapping to (morpho)syntax. This is also the external criterion that is least widely applicable in my sample: most of the grammars provide little or no information concerning prosody. Still, as prosody can be crucial in distinguishing several types of constructions (cf. e.g. Schultze-Berndt & Simard 2012, see also in section 4), I will refer to prosodic information whenever it is available.

2.1.4 Other

There are some other external parameters that have traditionally been used to diagnose constituency, like substitution ('constituents can be replaced by one lexical element') or coordination ('constituents of the same type can be conjoined') (see also chapter 5, section 2). While such criteria are often part of the basic toolkit of initial fieldwork, they rarely find their way into grammars, which means they are difficult to apply to the sample.[79] More generally, some of the traditional tests may also be problematic for typological reasons, like a lack of NP-level coordinators in Australian languages (Sadler & Nordlinger 2010), or interference with the very topic to be studied (e.g. movability tests and discontinuity, compare Bowern 2012: 328). For these reasons, these traditional criteria have not been used in this study.

2.2 Internal parameters

In addition to the external criteria, there are also two criteria that probe the internal structure of nominal expressions to diagnose constituency: contiguity, discussed in section 2.2.1, and word order, discussed in section 2.2.2.

2.2.1 Contiguity

The relevant criterion here is whether the elements of a nominal expression are contiguous, i.e. adjacent, or not. This criterion goes back to Behaghel's first law, which says that what belongs together semantically tends to occur together (Behaghel 1932: 4). When the elements are contiguous, they are most likely one unit (though this is not necessarily the case, as they could also be analysed as several single-item NPs in apposition, see also example (120) above, and

---

[79] Two sources in my sample that do at least discuss the criteria, and identify a number of difficulties with them, are Bowern (2012: 328–329) on Bardi and Spronck (2015: 37) on Ungarinyin.

sections 3.2 and 4 below). When they are not contiguous, however, as in the Garrwa structure in (124) below, this has often been interpreted as evidence against NP constituency. Thus, for instance, Mushin (2012: 260) argues on the basis of structures like (124) that "the capacity for discontinuity suggests that nominal groups do not constitute a clearly defined syntactic unit."[80]

(124) Garrwa (Mushin 2012: 259)
  nayinda langi-na   **wirringarra** badajba=yi
  this   north-ABL cyclone   come=PST
  'This cyclone came from the north.'

The question is, however, whether this always follows when a language has discontinuous structures. I believe that the presence of discontinuous constructions in a language does not necessarily imply that contiguous constructions in the same language cannot be analysed as genuine NPs (see further in section 4 on this argument). Therefore, I investigate discontinuity separately in section 4 below.

2.2.2 Word order

Word order is the most important internal criterion for constituency in this chapter, because there is at least some information for almost all languages of the sample.

If nominal expressions have a fixed internal order in a language, this is evidence for constituency, in the sense that the existence of a clear internal structure for a nominal expression points towards unithood. This is the case, for example, in Umpithamu, as illustrated in the NP template in (125a) and the structure in (125b).

(125) Umpithamu (Verstraete 2010: 11, 7)
  a. Template (G):
     [N N A Num]-case Pron
  b. **wantya**   **waarruthu** **uutherri** wuna-n=ula   / weerra
     old.woman   no.good   two   lie-PST=2DU.NOM / sleep
     'Two old ladies were sleeping (there).'

---

[80] However, Mushin does attribute some "phrase-like" qualities to nominal groups: "The observed patterns of ordering and contiguity of nominal groups in the corpus suggests a preference for co-referential members of a nominal group to stick together and for the least prominent common nominal to occur last in the group. Consistent case marking of this group's elements also suggest that speakers treat these as items contributing to the elaboration of a semantic role (whether a core argument or an oblique role)." (Mushin 2012: 260)

Flexible word order, by contrast, has often been regarded as one of the main arguments against NP constituency in Australian languages. When looked at in more detail, however, word order flexibility is not as straightforward a phenomenon as it might seem to be: it covers a range of different types of flexibility, and conclusions concerning constituency status for the nominal expression differ accordingly. As I show in section 3.1 below, much of the flexibility in nominal expressions in Australian languages is actually constrained, and some of these restrictions even provide evidence for, rather than against, syntactic unithood. An example is Umpila, as illustrated in (126) below, where the order of the head noun and the modifier is fixed, while the determiners (personal pronoun, demonstrative, quantifier or possessive pronoun) can occur at either edge of the nominal expression. The choice between pre-head and post-head position for determiners is both syntactically and interactionally determined (Hill 2018: 149–154; see also chapter 7, section 2.3).

(126) Umpila/Kuuku Ya'u (Hill 2018: 123)
 Template (G):
 (Det) (Entity) $\begin{Bmatrix} (Mod) \\ (Det) \end{Bmatrix}$

 Det: [(Pron) (Dem) (Quant)], or [Poss.Pron]

This can be called flexibility, but it does not point towards the absence of internal structure, and therefore also the absence of constituency. On the contrary, it preserves the edges of the nominal expression, and therefore shows that the nominal expression is one unit. There are, of course, also languages that show genuine word order flexibility for nominal expressions, i.e. where there are no clear restrictions whatsoever, but at best some tendencies. An example is Warrongo, where demonstrative, head noun and adjective can occur in different orders, as illustrated in (127) below, and for which Tsunoda (2011: 347) argues that "the relative order of NP constituents is not fixed, and it is difficult to generalize about it." This is really the only type of language where flexibility could provide evidence against constituency, in which case the co-referential elements would only be loosely related to each other (i.e. only in terms of semantics and not in terms of syntax).[81]

---

[81] One reviewer notes that if a language with flexible order does not allow discontinuity, this in itself may be sufficient evidence that the elements form a syntactic unit (i.e. because elements are always contiguous). As mentioned in section 1, however, I think it is necessary to study discontinuity as a separate issue (see section 4 for more detailed argumentation). I do believe that it is possible for a language to have syntactic NP units with flexible order,

(127) Warrongo (Tsunoda 2011: 688, 596, 348)
    a. *gaya-na-ø   ngaygo / mayga-lgo* **yarro-wo yamba-wo**
        father-KIN-ACC 1SG.GEN tell-PURP   this-DAT   camp-DAT
        jarribara-wo *yani-yal.*
        good-DAT   come-PURP
        'I will tell my father to come to this good camp.'
    b. *ngaya* **bori-ø   ngona-ø gagal-ø** *wajo-n   ngaya*
        1SG.ERG fire-ACC that-ACC big-ACC burn-NFUT 1SG.ERG
        yori-ø   goyba-lgo bori-wo
        kangaroo-ACC throw-PURP fire-DAT
        'I made a big fire so that I could throw a kangaroo to the fire.'
    c. ***jarribara-ø yarro-ø banggo-ø***
        good-NOM   this-NOM hollow-NOM
        'This nice hollow.'

2.2.3 Other

Two other criteria that are sometimes mentioned in the literature are noun class and number agreement (see chapter 2, section 4; chapter 4, section 1.1.2; and chapter 5, section 2). However, it is not clear what they can tell us about NP constituency, as they mark dependency relations rather than constituency, and are not even limited to the nominal domain. The only instance where this type of agreement could be interesting is when it is tied to case marking and changes location along with it – in which case it really is an instance of the criterion of locus of marking mentioned in section 2.1.1 above. This is found, for instance, in Arabana/Wangkangurru (Hercus 1994: 63) and in Warlpiri (Nash 1986: 174), where number (if marked at all) is marked on the same element(s) as case. Example (128) from Arabana/Wangkangurru shows this clearly, with number and case both marked at the right edge of the NE in (128a) or on each element of the NE in (128b).[82]

---

although it is likely that in such cases word order is not completely free. See section 3.5 for two potential examples (Bardi and Ngan'gityemerri/Ngan'gikurunggurr).

[82] An alternative analysis for example (128b) could be that there are in fact two separate units, which are each marked for number and case. (Thanks to an anonymous reviewer for pointing this out.) See section 3.2 for more discussion on this issue with respect to case marking.

(128) Arabana/Wangkangurru (Hercus 1994: 63)
 a. *Mathapurda kumpira-kumpira-**kari-ri** ngunta-ka.*
    old.man   dead-dead-PL-ERG   show-PST
    'The old men, long dead, told me this.'
 b. *Mathapurda-**kari-ri** kumpira-kumpira-**kari-ri** ngunta-ka.*
    old.man-PL-ERG   dead-dead-PL-ERG   tell-PST
    'It was the old men who told me this, the old men long dead.'

A third potential criterion concerns internal complexity of the NE, for instance, whether it can include embedded NEs or adjective phrases. On the one hand, the availability of embedded NEs shows that there is structure at a higher level, and can provide a good argument against so-called 'flat' structure of NPs (e.g. Gaby 2017: 197 on Kuuk Thaayorre). On the other hand, it is not always clear if the availability of structures such as adjective phrases implies the presence of structure at a higher level, since it need not per definition entail that these structures are part of a larger NP unit. There is often too little evidence either way in the sample, and other types of evidence need to be taken into account. Accordingly, this question is not investigated in any more detail in this book, which is limited to a study of simple NEs in any case (see chapter 1, but see chapter 3, section 2.2, for some comments on adjective phrases).

2.3 Overview

Table 6 provides an overview of the parameters uses in this study. As already mentioned, a distinction has to be made between those criteria for which there is good information across a large part of the sample (locus of case marking, word order, and contiguity), and those criteria for which there is only information in some languages (prosody and diagnostic slots).

Table 6: Parameters for constituency.

	External parameters	Internal parameters
Used for all languages	Locus of case marking	Word order
		Contiguity
Used where applicable or where information is available	Prosody	/
	Diagnostic slots	

3 Results

This section discusses the results of the analysis for four of the five criteria discussed in the previous section. I show that there is little (or at best only moderate) evidence against NP constituency across the sample, and that many languages have NP constituents available, even though this is often not the only option. Sections 3.1 and 3.2 discuss word order and case marking, the two criteria for which I have most information. This is followed by a discussion of occurrence in diagnostic slots and prosody in sections 3.3 and 3.4. In section 3.5, I investigate how the results cluster on a language-by-language basis, and what this can tell us about NP constituency. The final criterion, which relates to discontinuity, is discussed separately in section 4.

3.1 Word order

Before the results for this criterion can be discussed, two methodological notes are in order. One of these concerns the units whose order is analysed. In the large majority of the grammars in the sample, word order for nominal expressions is described in terms of word classes, like demonstrative, noun, adjective, etc. This is not the ideal basis for a description of word order, however, as ordering patterns typically concern slots that can be filled by words of different classes (see also chapter 3, section 2.1, example (61), and chapter 4, section 2.1, example (92c)). This has been demonstrated convincingly by McGregor (1990), who shows that noun phrases in Gooniyandi can be described in terms of a functional template, listed below in (129a) (see also chapter 2, section 2.1.2, and chapter 5, section 2). One functional role can be realised by elements from different word classes, and elements from one word class can have different functional roles, like the nominal *nyamani* 'big', which functions as a Quantifier in pre-head position, as illustrated in (129b) (repeated from (99)), or a Qualifier in post-head position, as illustrated in (129c).

(129) Gooniyandi (McGregor 1990: 253, 260, 265)
    a. Template (G):
       (Deictic) (Quantifier) (Classifier) Entity (Qualifier)

b. *nyamani   gamba*
      big   water
      'a lot of water'
   c. *yoowooloo nyamani*
      man   big
      'a big man'

From the perspective of word order, this also implies that in a language like Gooniyandi, apparent flexibility in terms of word classes can actually be resolved in terms of functional roles, i.e. there is a fixed role order (see also chapter 5, section 2). Ideally, therefore, checking the criterion of word order across the sample would involve functional classes and not word classes. However, there is very little functional information available overall in the sample: only 14 grammatical descriptions use functional role order; the rest describe word class order. Whenever there is an analysis in terms of functional classes for a language, I use it, but for the rest I have to rely on analyses that are exclusively based on word classes.[83] It is, of course, not unlikely that in such cases apparent flexibility could be resolved in terms of functional classes, as for Gooniyandi, but I take the more cautious perspective here, and do not go beyond any generalisations allowed by the grammars I use. In chapter 7, I investigate one of these functional roles, viz. determination, for all the languages of the sample.

The second methodological note concerns the quality of the data (see also chapter 1, section 2.2). While all grammars provide basic information about word order in the nominal domain, the information is sometimes quite limited. For instance, some grammars only discuss word order for one modifier at a time (rather than longer nominal expressions), and only focus on adjectives and demonstratives (omitting modifiers such as possessive pronouns, personal pronouns or numerals). This implies that for such grammars the explicit description of word order found in the text is not sufficient; in those cases, I rely on an analysis of examples throughout the grammar to supplement the basic description. Whenever I have had to do this, this is marked explicitly in table 10 (Appendix).

Overall, languages in the sample can be categorised in terms of three basic types of word order, discussed in sections 3.1.1 to 3.1.3 below: fixed order, restricted flexible order, and flexible order. At least for the first two types, which together cover 65 languages, patterns of word order provide

---

83 Note that I use the traditional term 'word order' as a convenient short-hand term for both word class order and functional role order.

evidence for NP constituency.[84] Map 9 shows the spread of the word order types across the sample; see the following subsections for further discussion. An overview of my analysis for each individual language can be found in table 10 (to be found in the Appendix at the end of the book), including references and more details.[85]

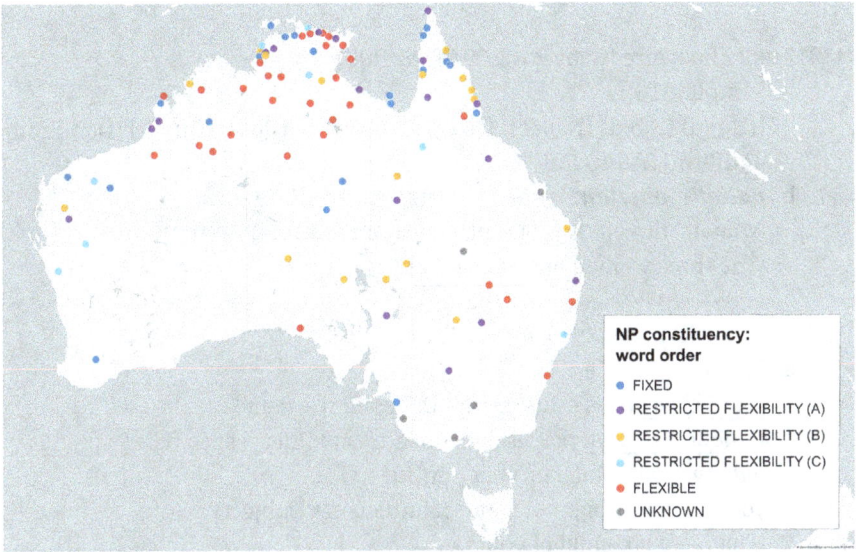

Map 9: Word order in the NE. For an online, dynamic version of this map, see: http://bit.ly/wordorder-NP. For additional notes and references, see table 10.

---

[84] Incidentally, most languages of the sample seem to follow general word order tendencies for nominal expressions as discussed in Dryer (2007b: 111–113) and Rijkhoff (2002: 327–332). For instance, when a demonstrative and an adjective both precede the nominal head, the demonstrative comes first, and where they both follow the nominal head, the demonstrative usually – but not always – comes last (cf. Greenberg's universal 20 [1966: 87] and Dryer's discussion [2007b: 111–113]). Unfortunately, for many languages there is only limited information about word order in NEs with more than one modifier, or about the position of numerals in the NE. Where information is available, it seems that almost all languages follow the tendencies described above.

[85] Two languages have changed categories compared to the published paper, viz. Muruwari and Bundjalung. Bundjalung remains in the category of restricted flexible order, but is now analysed as belonging to a different subtype, based on the analysis of a larger number of examples. Muruwari was first analysed as having restricted flexible order, but has been moved to the flexible category; this decision is based on the analysis of extra examples, which show a more flexible order of determiners than first assumed (though many are ambiguous).

3.1.1 Fixed word order

In the sample, there are 21 languages that have fixed word order, which shows that at least in terms of their internal structure, nominal expressions form a syntactic unit (i.e. an NP). One example is Kuuk Thaayorre, which has fixed word order for NEs, illustrated in the template in (130a) and the example in (130b). A second example is Nyungar, which also shows fixed order in NEs, as illustrated in (131).

(130) Kuuk Thaayorre (Gaby 2017: 297–298, 300)
    a. Template (G):
        ((Ngen) (Ngen) (Nspec)) ((Deg) Adj (Deg))* (Poss) (Quant) (DemPron/ IgnPron) (AdnDem)[86]
    b. **paanth pinalam** ith   ngamal.katp-rr-ø peln
       woman three(NOM) DEM:DIST hug-RECP-NPST 3PL(NOM)
       'The three women hug each other.'

(131) Nyungar (Douglas 1976: 44–45)
    a. Template (G+W):
       Word class: poss – N(s) – [A – intensifier] – dem
       Functional class: possession – head – modifier – specifier
    b. njunaŋ nop kumpaṛ meṭ al(-itj)
       your child big very that(distant)(-subject)
       'That very big child of yours...'

Some of these languages allow a change in word order for emphasis or focus, as in Tiwi, where the head noun normally occurs in penultimate position, as shown in (132a), but can be fronted for focus or for stylistic effect, as in (132b) (Lee 1987: 222, 243 note 5). Since such changes have a clear functional motivation and are not the default, I do not regard this as counter-evidence for NP constituency.

(132) Tiwi (Lee 1987: 222, 224)
    a. Template (G):
       (Limiter) (Definitive) (Dem) (Quantifier) (Descriptive) (Head) (Exposition)

---

[86] See chapter 7, section 2.4 on one potential exception to the fixed template: personal pronouns often occur as independent units (as in (130b)), but in some cases they also seem to occur as part of a higher-level NP.

b. *pilayiki yirrara*
   flag(M) two(M)
   'two flags'

The map above shows that fixed order (in dark blue) is not restricted to a particular area but spread out across the continent. Several, but not all, of the Paman languages (Cape York) have fixed order, as do the Tangkic languages on the nearby Gulf of Carpentaria and the two Arandic languages in the sample. In the west and north of Australia, languages with fixed word order stand out amongst the many languages with restricted flexible or completely flexible orders. Interestingly, these are mostly languages that have been described in terms of functional roles in the grammars (e.g. Nyulnyul, Gooniyandi, Martuthunira, Gaagudju), which suggests that the results for some of the genetically related languages could look quite different if they too were to be analysed in terms of functional roles.

3.1.2 Restricted flexibility

There are 44 languages with some degree of flexibility in word order for nominal expressions, but where the flexibility is such that it cannot be regarded as evidence against NP constituency – rather on the contrary. In this section, three subtypes are distinguished, showing for each how flexible word order is compatible with, or even evidence for, NP constituency.

A first subtype ((A) on the map above) is flexibility that is clearly limited in frequency, i.e. where the language has one dominant general NP template, but where other orderings are also possible to a limited extent. This is the case for 19 languages in the sample. An example is Yingkarta, for which Dench (1998: 50–51) argues that 90% of the NPs follows the pattern in (133a), while there is also a minor pattern illustrated in (133b). Another example is Biri, where demonstratives "always" precede the noun and adjectives "usually" or "typically" do so as well, as illustrated in (134) (Terrill 1998: 29, 45, 47).

(133) Yingkarta (Dench 1998: 50)
   a. Template (G):
      (Determiner) (Modifier) Head
   b. *Wanthawu yurlu-ja nyintangu?*
      where   camp-DEF 2SG.GEN
      'Where is your camp?'

(134) Biri (Terrill 1998: 47, 29, 74)
  a. Template (W):
     dem – N
     A – N (usually), or N – A
  b. **yinhami manhdha** yuga-lba-ŋ-aya   guya ...
     this.ABS   food.ABS   eat-CONT-PRS-2SG.S/A bad
     'this food I'm eating is bad'
  c. ŋaya   naga-lba-ya   **binbi waynmari-gu**
     1SG.S/A   see-CONT-1SG.S/A good girl-DAT
     'I see a nice girl.'

Given the difference in frequency, it is quite likely that minority patterns correlate with changes in meaning or function, in which case they could be like (132) in the previous category, or could even allow for an analysis in terms of functional classes. The necessary functional information to support this hypothesis for the languages in this category is wanting, but there are hints of meaning changes correlating with minor word order patterns for some. In Yingkarta, for instance, Dench suggests that the minor pattern of a possessive pronoun following a head noun in (133b) has a marked interpretation, glossed as 'that X of yours' (Dench 1998: 51).

The other two subtypes both show word order flexibility that is edge-preserving. In the languages in these categories, word order is flexible for some elements, but in such a way that one (or both) of the edges of the nominal expression are preserved and thus clearly delineated, which suggests that the nominal expression is treated as one unit.

One subtype ((B) on the map above) shows flexibility of determining elements (such as demonstratives)[87] at the edges of the nominal expression, while other modifiers have a fixed position closer to the head. There are 17 languages showing this type of flexibility, illustrated for Worrorra in (135a), where the deictic element can either come at the left edge (135b) or the right edge (135c) of the nominal expression. The same applies to Umpila, as illustrated in in (126) above.

(135) Worrorra (Clendon 2014: examples, 144, 428; own glossing for b)
  a. Template (E):
     dem / poss – N – A – dem / poss

---

[87] The possessive pronoun usually behaves in a similar way, but not always: there are a couple of languages in this category where the possessive pronoun has a fixed position, while the demonstrative and the personal pronoun have flexible positions at the edges. See more on determiner and alternative functions of determining elements in chapter 7.

b. *inja   eeja   i=raarreya*
   3SG.M.DEF man 3SG.M=big
   'the big man'
c. ***kanbanerri birdeen-ya aaya*** rlerlewa ka-ø=murrka-rla-eerri
   crab   small-3SG.M 3SG.M.REF crawl 3SG.M-3=go.to-PST-PROG
   'A little crab went crawling up to him.'

The other subtype ((C) on the map above) has flexibility of adjectival modifiers with respect to the head, while determining elements[88] have a fixed position at one of the edges. There are 8 languages that show this type of flexibility. An example is Mawng, where modifiers such as adjectives and quantifying nominals occur at either side of the head, while determiners (demonstrative and third person pronoun) have a fixed position at the left edge (Forrester 2015: 45), as shown in the template in (136a). The flexible position of the adjective is illustrated in (136b). Another example is Mayi, where demonstratives and other determining elements are fixed at the left edge, while qualifying nominals can occur at either side of the head nominal (Breen 1981b: 63; see the template in (137a)), as illustrated in (137b-c).

(136) Mawng (Forrester 2015: 45, 46)
   a. Template (G):
      (art) (determiner) (art) (determiner) (art) (modifier) (art) head (art) (modifier)
   b. ***Taka-pa   wurt wumawurr anyak*** ang-ngurri–ngung
      DEM:DIST.LL-EMPH tiny creek   little.bit 3LL-flow-PST.CONT
      'The small creek was flowing.'

(137) Mayi (Breen 1981b: 63, 61; own glossing for b)
   a. Template (W):
      dem / pron / interr – num – N*
      with N*: N.qual – N.head or N.head – N.qual
   b. *waṭi panʸa tʸalu-ŋku*
      that woman small-ERG
      'that small woman'

---

[88] Again, the possessive pronoun usually behaves in the same way as demonstratives, but in some languages, it has a flexible position (like the adjectival modifier). See chapter 7 (section 3.5).

c. *waṭi miṭan yalmir /kuŋkun-kali ṉanti-ṉanti-ŋu*
   that tall man spear-?   hold-hold-PRS
   'that tall man is holding a spear'

Taken together, this implies that there are 44 languages for which apparent flexibility actually supports NP constituency. The map (with purple, orange and light blue representing the different subtypes) shows that they are even more spread out across the continent than the previous category, and that it is hard to discern any clear areal or genetic patterns.

3.1.3 Flexibility

30 languages show flexibility that is less restricted or not restricted at all, which can provide evidence against NP constituency (although not necessarily so, depending on evidence from other parameters, see also footnote 81, or on whether an analysis in terms of functional roles results in clear ordering patterns). There is, however, quite a bit of variation here, in that very few of these languages allow the full flexibility that is often posited in general statements about non-configurationality in Australian languages (see, for instance, the structures in (127) above for Warrongo). Most languages in this category show flexibility of more than one type of modifier, not necessarily of the edge-preserving kind (e.g. both adjectival modifiers and determining elements can occur on either side of the nominal head). Even here, there appear to be some restrictions, going from general tendencies to very strict rules for some of the modifiers. Some of these languages could perhaps even be re-categorised under the previous type, but I adopt the more cautious approach here and put a language in this category whenever in doubt. The types of restrictions on flexibility in this category are diverse, so rather than giving a list, I illustrate this with some examples from the sample, going from languages that are closest to the previous category to those that are furthest from it.

A first example is Bardi (Bowern 2012: 331–336). At first sight, word order is quite free: all types of modifiers (personal pronoun, demonstrative, adjective, nominal modifier, quantifier, possessive pronoun) can precede or follow the head, and elements preceding the head can come in almost any order (e.g. both dem-A-N and A-dem-N are possible). However, there are four important qualifications. First, when a modifier follows the nominal head, it has a non-restrictive or contrastive meaning (Bowern 2012: 335), which provides a functional motivation for at least some of the flexibility. Second, the possessive pronoun always occurs in the outer layer of the NP (Bowern 2012: 332–333), which delineates the boundaries of the NP. Third, the personal pronoun and the demonstrative do not co-occur, i.e. they seem to be in complementary distribution; the same goes for the demonstrative and the possessive pronoun (Bowern p.c.). And finally, there is a restriction on the number of modifiers in the NP (Bowern 2012: 329). These features even lead the author to questioning a 'flat structure' analysis for nominal expressions in Bardi (Bowern 2012: 329), although I still decided to put Bardi in the 'flexible' category because it does not meet my own criteria for restricted flexibility.

A second example is Garrwa (Mushin 2012: 256–257, examples throughout grammar), where word order again seems to be quite free, with all types of modifiers preceding or following the head. However, in this language the demonstrative and the possessive pronoun clearly show a preference for the position preceding the head (Mushin 2012: 256–257). In addition, if a demonstrative and an attributive modifier both occur on the left side of the head, the demonstrative occurs at the edge and the attributive modifier closer to the head (Mushin 2012: examples throughout grammar). This shows again that flexibility is not absolute, but unlike with Bardi there is no indication to suggest that the restrictions in Garrwa provide any evidence for NP constituency.

A final example is Bilinarra (Meakins & Nordlinger 2014: 103–104). As can be seen in (138), the NE template is very general and allows for a high degree of flexibility. However, even in this case, there are certain restrictions, for instance, on the number of modifiers that can precede and follow the head, and the position of the demonstrative and the possessive pronoun, which tend to precede the head rather than follow it.

(138) Bilinarra (Meakins & Nordlinger 2014: 103–104)
    Template (G):
    (modifier) (modifier) head (modifier) (modifier)

The map above shows that flexible order (in red) is mainly found in the north of Australia, but there is no clear-cut correlation between flexible order and the non-Pama-Nyungan families, as many non-Pama-Nyungan languages belong to the other categories described above, while several Pama-Nyungan languages also belong to this category.

3.2 Locus of case marking

This section discusses the locus of case marking in contiguous nominal expressions (see section 4 on discontinuous structures). As already mentioned, the basic options here are phrasal marking (case marked once in the NE), word marking (case marked for all elements in the NE)[89] or no case marking at all (at least for core arguments). Languages in the last category sometimes do have some peripheral (e.g. local) case markers. Whenever this is the case, table 11 mentions whether they use phrasal or word marking, but I do not regard this as sufficient evidence to put them in, say, the 'phrasal marking' category on a par with languages that use phrasal marking throughout, for both core and peripheral case markers. Table 11 (Appendix) provides details and references for my analysis of each individual language.

An overview is given in map 10 below. It is hard to detect strong areal or genetic tendencies for location of case: phrasal marking (blue and purple, together 57 languages) is available across the continent, as is word marking (purple and red). Languages without core case marking (dark grey) are only found in the north of Australia, especially in the Top End.

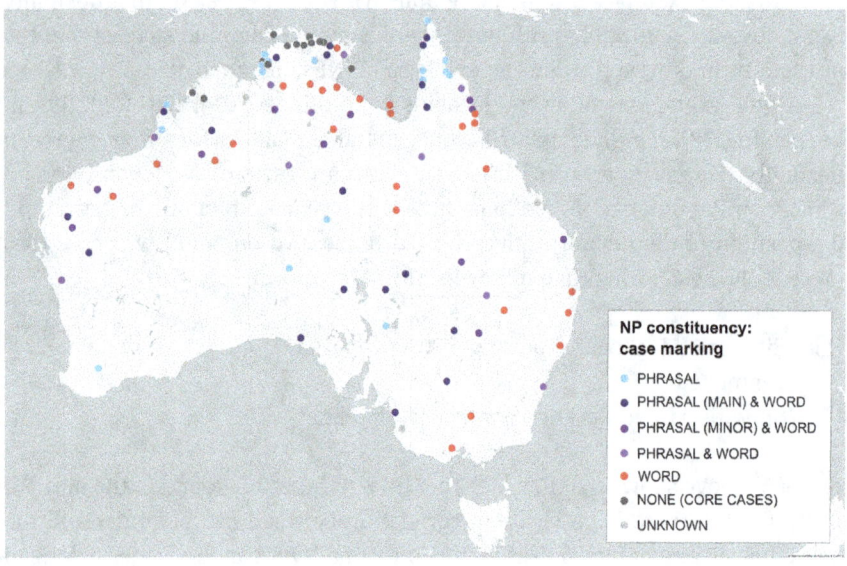

Map 10: Locus of case marking. For an online, dynamic version of this map, see: http://bit.ly/case-NP. For additional comments and references, see table 11.

---

89 As discussed in section 2.1.1, word marking can be interpreted in largely two ways: as agreement within one syntactic unit or as separate single-word elements each marked for their role in the clause. It is often not possible to determine which of these is the case in a given language (or a given example).

In the sample, there are 57 languages for which phrasal marking is an option: 17 that have only phrasal marking, as illustrated for Yawuru in (139), and 40 that have a choice between phrasal marking and word marking, as illustrated for Wirangu in (140).

(139) Yawuru (Hosokawa 1991: 81)
    a. *manydya-yi wamba*
        many-DAT   man
    b. **manydya-yi wamba-yi*
        many-DAT   man-DAT
        'to/for many people'

(140) Wirangu (Hercus 1999: 48)
    a. **garba marnaardu-gu** *wina-rn*
        house big-ALL   go-PRS
    b. **garba-gu marnaardu-gu** *wina-rn*
        house-ALL big-ALL   go-PRS
        'We are going to the big house, the community hall.'

Phrasal case marking is at least one of the options in 57 languages or more than half of the sample, which is clear evidence for NP constituency. Of these 57 languages, 43 have case marked at the (left or right) edge,[90] marking one of the boundaries of the NP and thus providing additional evidence for constituency. For the other languages, which have only word marking or no marking at all, the location of case marking is a neutral feature with respect to constituency (see section 2.1.1).

Within these results, it is remarkable that two thirds of the languages allow both phrasal marking and word marking for case. There is at least one language in the sample for which there is a detailed analysis of this alternation, viz. Gooniyandi. McGregor (1989) shows that phrasal marking is the default option in Gooniyandi, while 'phrase fracturing' has a special functional motivation, viz. to give equal prominence to each constituent of the phrase (e.g. contrastive focus), usually in a phrase consisting of two elements. An example of phrase fracturing for contrastive focus can be found in (141). Interestingly, McGregor (1989, p.c.) takes a stronger position than I do here. He argues that adding a case marker to

---

[90] Some of these languages show variation in the location of the case marker, either between the left and the right edge, or between one of the edges and another element (e.g. the head).

each element of the expression in effect breaks it into two (contiguous) units, i.e. it gives each element the status of a phrase, although they "share a second constituency analysis as complex units" (McGregor 1989: 220). In other words, these case markers do not simply realise agreement in one NP (i.e. word marking), but constitute a complex phrase consisting of two phrases. In this analysis, 'word marking' is not an actual possibility; rather, there is only phrasal marking, and the difference is between one multi-word unit and several co-referential single-word units. A similar syntactic analysis is proposed by Bowe (1990: 53) for Pitjantjatjara, a close variety of Yankunytjatjara. Bowe argues that a noun and adjective each marked for case are separate, apposed NPs, because they can occur in either order relative to each other (as in 142a-b), whereas a noun-adjective sequence with a single, right-edge case marker is fixed (142c). The apposed NPs in (142a-b) do form a constituent at a higher level, since they cannot be separated by a second position pronominal clitic (as in 142d), but have to occur as a single constituent in first position. (Note that for some languages there is evidence the other way; see below on register variation in Djabugay.)

(141) Gooniyandi (McGregor 1989: 213)
thaarri   nganyi-ngga   gardlooni /
mistakenly.believed I-ERG   I:hit:him
ngoorroo-ngga   yaanya-ngga   gardbini /
that-ERG   other-ERG   he:hit:him
'It was mistakenly believed that I had hit him, but it was really that other person who hit him.'

(142) Pitjantjatjara (Bowe 1990: 53)
   a. *Minyma-ngku waṟa-ngku-ṉi nya-ngu.*
      woman-ERG   tall-ERG-1SG.ACC see-PST
      'The woman, the tall one, saw me.'
   b. *Waṟa-ngku minyma-ngku-ṉi   nya-ngu.*
      tall-ERG   woman-ERG-1SG.ACC see-PST
      'The tall one, the woman, saw me.'
   c. *Minyma waṟa-ngku-ṉi   nya-ngu.*
      woman tall-ERG-1SG.ACC see-PST
      'The tall woman saw me.'
   d. **Minyma-ngku-ṉi   waṟa-ngku nya-ngu.*
      woman-ERG-1SG.ACC tall-ERG see-PST
      (intended) 'The woman, the tall one, saw me.'

Unfortunately, there is only limited information on this alternation for most other languages of the sample. There are some tendencies, however. For instance, the options do not seem to have an equal status in most languages: phrasal marking is the basic option in 18 languages, while 11 have word marking as the basic option (for the other 10 that have both options, it is unclear which is the basic one). The less frequent option usually seems to occur in specific environments. In Oykangand, for instance, case is normally marked on the right edge of the NE, as in (143a), but when the NE of a demonstrative and a noun, it can also be marked on the initial element or on both elements, as in (143b, c) (Hamilton 1996: 19–20). Another example is Duungidjawu, where case is marked on each element of the NE, as in (144a), except for the comitative, which only occurs at the right edge, as in (144b) (Kite & Wurm 2004: 37, examples).

(143) Oykangand (Hamilton 1996: 20; own glossing)
    a. *aber   unggul-gh   uw*
       woman DEM:DIST-PURP give
       'Give it to that woman there.'
    b. *aber-agh   unggul   uw*
       woman-PURP DEM:DIST give
    c. *aber-agh   unggul-gh   uw*
       woman-PURP DEM:DIST-PURP give

(144) Duungidjawu (Kite & Wurm 2004: 34, 37)
    a. *guyur ŋa-dju binda-yi **guyum-gu yo:-rinj-gu** meŋ*
       food 1SG-ERG send-PST camp-ALL 3SG-GEN-ALL today
       'I sent food to his camp today.'
    b. *woŋan man bun-du barandje-nge guyum-u*
       woman DEM knee-INS stand-IPFV camp-LOC
       gandan   ŋa-rinj-baɲu
       younger.sister 1SG-GEN-COM
       'That woman is kneeling at the fire with my younger sister.'

The grammatical descriptions that give more detailed information on the function of the alternation tend to mention emphasis or contrast as a motivation for word marking in a language that normally marks case once per phrase (e.g. [Hercus 1994: 283] for possessive modifiers in Arabana/Wangkangurru; [Oates 1988: 68] for dative case markers in Muruwari; [Hercus 1999: 48] for Wirangu). An example is given for Diyari in (145) below.

(145) Diyari (Austin 2011: 144, 97)
    a. ***kanku kundrukundru-nthu-yali*** *nganha yakalka-yi*
       boy   cough-PROP-ERG   1SG.ACC ask-PRS
       'The boy with a cough is asking me.'
    b. ***kinthala-li nhungkarni-yali*** *nganha matha-rna wara-yi*
       dog-ERG   3SG.NF.DAT-ERG   1SG.ACC bite-PTCP   AUX-PRS
       'HIS DOG bit me'

On the other hand, the use of phrasal marking in a language that normally marks case on each element is sometimes associated with casual speech (e.g. Patz 1991: 290 for Djabugay); as mentioned above, register variation like this can provide evidence that word marking really is agreement rather than apposition of single-word units in this language (compare the discussion on Gooniyandi above).

3.3 Diagnostic slots

At least 19 languages[91] in the sample have a diagnostic slot that can be used for testing NP constituency, in the form of a second position auxiliary or second position clitics that occur after the first constituent, as in Warlpiri (see example (123) above) and in Kuuk Thaayorre (146) (Gaby 2017: 154). Usually, the diagnostic elements are pronominal markers, but other types also occur, e.g. discourse clitics in Lardil (Klokeid 1976: 261), as illustrated in (147) below for the clitic *thada* 'meanwhile'. An overview can be found in table 12 (Appendix) and in map 11 below. The map shows that diagnostic slots occur in different families and areas across the continent (e.g. Ngumpin-Yapa, Kartu, Western Desert, Garrwan, and some south-eastern languages).

(146) Kuuk Thaayorre (Gaby 2017: 458)
    pam   ***ith=ul***   *yarra yan*
    man(NOM) DEM:DIST=3SG(NOM) away go.NPST
    patp-nhan=okun=ul
    camp-GO&:NPST=DUB=3SG(NOM)
    'maybe that chap will hive off and pitch camp'

---

91 This number is slightly higher than the number mentioned in the published paper; Bunganditj, Kuuk Thaayorre, Wajarri, Wathawurrung and Yankunytjatjara have been added.

(147) Lardil (Klokeid 1976: 261)
yalange   wurtuu   <u>thada</u>   niya   waa
other.LOC corner.LOC meanwhile 3SG.NOM go
'Meanwhile, he went over to another corner.'

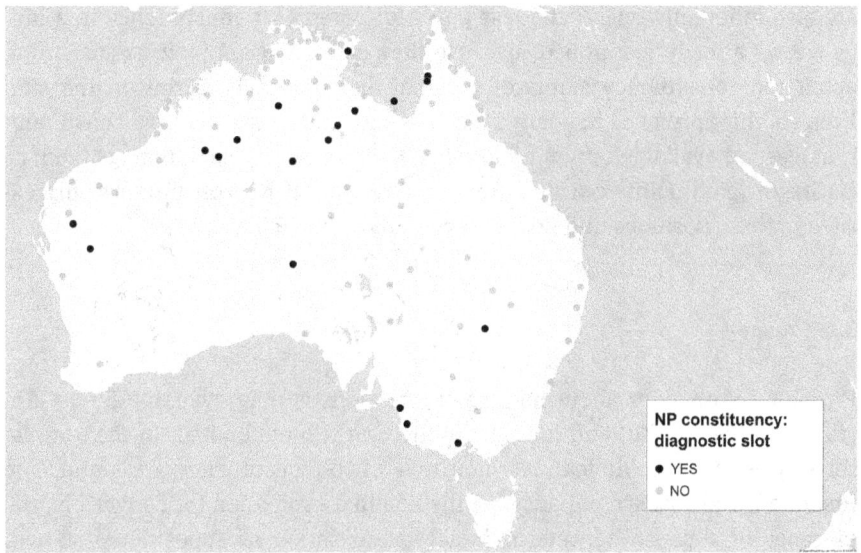

Map 11: Diagnostic slots. For an online, dynamic version of this map, see: http://bit.ly/diagnostic-slot. For additional information and references, see table 12.

There are a few languages (e.g. Wangkajunga, Walmajarri, Wajarri) where the diagnostic element can also follow the first word of a multi-word NE. Logically, two analyses are possible: one where the diagnostic element shows variation in position, either following the first constituent or the first word (whether or not this is part of a larger constituent), and another where the diagnostic element, fixed in 2nd position, 'splits up' the NE (see section 4 for an example of Warlpiri that is analysed this way).[92] There are also a few languages, like

---

[92] I have found no further claims to this effect in my sample, but there may be more languages in the sample that show this variation. Incidentally, there is one other language in the sample – Lardil – that has two sets of clitics, one following the first constituent and another following the first word (Klokeid 1976: 261–262). Evidently I only focus on the first set here (see example (147)).

Wangkajunga and Warlpiri, where the diagnostic element can occur in third position instead of second, but this seems to occur only in specific contexts (see table 12 for more details). Obviously, this implies that the criterion is somewhat weaker here than in the other languages, as it does not invariably identify the first constituent.

In fact, although diagnostic slots are much discussed in the literature, they are also inherently one of the less powerful criteria for constituency in a language, as already mentioned, because they can really only tell us something about the constituency status of nominal expressions occurring in the slot. Even so, their presence in a language does show that construal as a constituent is at least an available option for nominal expressions in that language (and, as McGregor [p.c.] points out, it would be surprising if NP constituents only existed in these positions and not elsewhere in the language).

3.4 Prosody

Prosodic information about nominal expressions is only available for 19 languages in the sample, and for most of these, it is quite limited. In the sample, three types of prosodic features indicative of NP constituency are found. The first one is the absence of pauses in the nominal expression (or conversely, the presence of a pause between nominals as a marker of appositional status), which is mentioned for 11 languages. For instance, in their analysis of Bilinarra, Meakins & Nordlinger (2014: 102–103) use the presence or absence of a pause between nominals as a defining criterion for constituency:

> Coreferential nominals which are separated by a pause are not considered to belong to a single NP but are treated as nominals in apposition. (...) They do not occur in the same intonational phrase and are therefore considered separate NPs in apposition. If they were not separated by a pause (...) the nominals would be considered a single NP.

A second feature, mentioned for 11 languages, is that the nominal expression occurs under a single intonation contour. In Umpila/Kuuku Ya'u, for example, "the NP is typically produced under a single intonation contour" (Hill 2018: 126), which is taken as criterion for the identification of NPs (Hill 2018: 126). The third feature is that the nominal expression has a single stress peak, which is mentioned for one language, Kuuk Thaayorre, together with the two other features described above: "Prosodically, the noun phrase is characterized by: (a) a lack of planned pauses; (b) a single intonation contour; (c) a primary stress peak" (Gaby 2017: 196). An overview can be found in table 13 (Appendix).

3.5 Conclusion

In themselves, the results discussed in the preceding sections are telling: internally, about two thirds of the languages show fixed or restricted flexible word order, and externally, more than half of the languages have at least an option for phrasal case marking. On top of this, several languages in the sample show prosodic evidence for NP constituency or allow the use of nominal expressions in diagnostic slots. These findings show quite clearly that it is not the case that Australian languages generally lack NP structures, and that there is evidence for the availability of classic NP construal in a majority of languages in the sample.

What I have not yet examined, however, is how the different criteria interact on a language-by-language basis, and what this says about the precise role of NP construal in each language. Is it a default option or rather a marginal phenomenon in the language? Table 7 provides an overview of the four criteria discussed in the previous sections, organised mainly around word order and locus of case marking, with underlining for presence of diagnostic slots and italics for prosodic evidence. (Analyses in terms of functional classes are marked with * following the language name.)

What this table suggests is that we can distinguish roughly between three major types of languages in the sample (leaving aside the 'unknown' categories at the edges); see map 12 below for an overview. First, there is a set of 15 languages for which all internal and external evidence points to NP constituency in the classic sense: these are the languages that have fixed or restricted flexible word order, and only phrasal case marking. An example is Arrernte, which shows fixed word order and right-edge phrasal marking of case (Wilkins 1989: 102–103). The map (type A, in blue) shows that these languages are mainly situated in Cape York, and only a few in central and north Australia.

Secondly, there is a set of 49 languages for which all internal evidence points to NP constituency, with fixed or restricted flexible word order, but externally there is a choice between word and phrase marking, or only word marking (or no marking at all). Given that there is internal evidence for NP constituency, these are languages for which word marking probably cannot be analysed in terms of apposition, and may have a functional motivation if there is an alternation with phrase marking (see section 4.2 above). An example is Diyari, which has restricted flexible order (with determining elements at either edge of the NP) and right-edge phrasal case marking; in contexts of emphasis or contrast, each element of the NP can be marked for case (Austin 2011 97–100, examples). The map (type B, orange) shows that these languages occur across the continent.

Table 7: Results for NP constituency.

	phrasal marking	phrasal + word marking			word marking	no marking	unknown
		main phrasal	minor phrasal	unclear			
fixed word order	Arrernte *Dalabon* * *Kuuk Thaayorre* Marrithiyel Nyungar * Umbuygamu Umpithamu *	Alyawarra Anguthimri *Gooniyandi* * Ngarrindjeri *Nyulnyul* * Uradhi			Dyirbal Kayardild * Lardil *Martuthunira* * Panyjima *	*Gaagudju* * *Limilngan* * Tiwi *	
restricted flexible word order	*Atynyamathanha* Kala Lagaw Ya Kugu Nganhcara Malakmalak *Umpila/Kuuku Ya'u** Wadjiginy Yankunytjatjara Yawuru	Arabana/ Wangkangurru Diyari Mathi-Mathi /Letyi- Letyi/ Wati-Wati Oykangand *Paakantyi* Tharrgari *Wajarri* *Warray* Yandruwandha Yir Yoront	Djabugay Duungidjawu Kuku Yalanji Ngiyambaa Yindjibarndi Yingkarta *	Guugu Yimidhirr Karajarri Mayi Nhanda	Alawa Biri Bundjalung *Dhuwal* Gathang Mangarrayi Pitta-Pitta Yalarnnga Yanyuwa Yidiny	Emmi Matngele Mawng * Ndjébbana Worrorra	Rimanggudinhma

flexible word order	Bardi	*Djinang*	*Bilinarra*	Dharrawal/	Gumbaynggir	Burarra	Miriwung
	Ngan'gityemerri/	Rembarrnga	<u>*Garrwa*</u>	Dharumba/	<u>Jaru</u>	Bininj	
	Ngan'gikurunggurr	Wirangu	Walmajarri	Dhurga/	*Marra*	Kunwok	
			<u>Warumungu</u>	Djirringanj	Nyangumarta	Anindilyakwa	
				Jaminjung	Wambaya	Giimbiyu	
				Jingulu	<u>*Wangkajunga*</u>	Ungarinyin	
				Muruwari	*Wardaman*		
				(equal)	Warrongo		
				<u>Ritharngu</u>	Yuwaalaraay		
				Warlpiri			
word order unknown			Margany/		<u>Wathawurrung</u>		<u>Bunganditj</u>
			Gunya		Yorta Yorta		Dharumbal

Italics: prosodic evidence; underlining: presence of diagnostic slots; *: analysis in terms of functional classes.

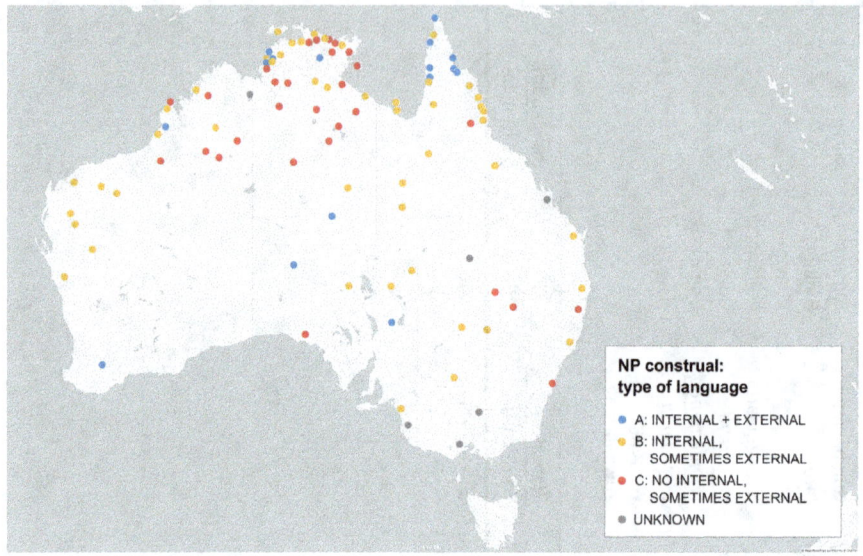

Map 12: NP construal: types of languages. For an online, dynamic version of this map, see: http://bit.ly/NPconstrual.

Finally, there is a set of 29 languages with flexible word order, for which the internal structure does not point towards NP constituency.[93] The map (type C, red) shows that a majority of these is situated in one single zone in the north and north-west of Australia (see section 3.1.3 on the spread across language families). Not surprisingly, there are not many languages in this category which only have phrasal marking (i.e. that show unambiguous external evidence for constituency): the only two that do, viz. Bardi and Ngan'gityemerri/Ngan'gikurunggurr, actually also have some indications of edge-preserving word order flexibility (i.e. internal evidence), though in a different way than the criteria I used in section 3.1.2.[94]

---

[93] The introduction to this chapter mentioned three languages which played a prominent role in the non-configurationality debate: Warlpiri, Nunggubuyu and Kalkatungu. Only Warlpiri is part of my sample, but readers may be interested to know that the other two languages would fit into this last group as well. Nunggubuyu and Kalkatungu both show flexible word order, but unlike Warlpiri, they have only word marking and no evidence from diagnostic slots (see Heath [1986: 377–381], and Blake [1979a: 108–109, examples; 1983: 144–145]).

[94] In Ngan'gityemerri/Ngan'gikurunggurr, the head has a fixed initial position, while the modifiers seem to be flexible with respect to each other (Reid 1997: 267). In Bardi, the possessive pronoun always occurs at the outer edge of the nominal expression (Bowern 2012: 333). In addition, there are several other restrictions on word order flexibility in Bardi nominal expressions (see further in section 3.1.3 above). Because of these restrictions on word order flexibility,

The rest has only word marking, or an alternation between word and phrasal marking; moreover, this is also the category that has the most diagnostic slots in the sample. An example is Bilinarra, which shows flexible word order (see also section 3.1.3) and word marking, but sometimes also head marking for case; additionally, constituents can be identified in a diagnostic slot (preceding bound 2nd position pronouns) and by prosodic means (Meakins & Nordlinger 2014: 102–106). On the one hand, this suggests that for these languages, word marking could – at least in principle – be analysed as evidence for apposition, unlike the languages in the second category. On the other hand, the availability of phrasal marking and quite a few diagnostic slots also shows that constituency is not completely absent from these languages. Unlike in the first two categories, it may not be the dominant way to organise nominal expressions, but NP construal is available at least as an option (albeit sometimes only a peripheral one): through phrasal case marking, via construal in a diagnostic slot, or both.[95] In this sense, NP constituency is not an all-or-nothing phenomenon: some languages have it as the dominant way to organise the nominal domain (which, incidentally, also seems to be the case in 'traditional NP languages' like English or Dutch), while others have it as an option available in only a few circumstances.[96] This suggests that the question which was the starting point of this study, viz. whether Australian languages have clear NP constituents or not, is not the most interesting question to ask. It is difficult to give a straightforward answer for many languages, and it glosses over differences between languages in terms of how

---

in addition to phrasal marking throughout, these languages could alternatively be analysed as type B languages (also because NP construal is not a marginal possibility as in other type C languages, but rather a dominant pattern). However, since I want to apply my criteria on flexibility of word order strictly (see also section 3.1.3) I have decided to choose the cautious approach and keep these two languages in type C.

95 There are 9 languages in the sample that do not have any options for NP construal at all, according to my criteria, and could therefore be regarded as lacking NPs altogether (i.e. across the whole language system). In the table, these would be the languages with flexible word order, and without phrasal marking, diagnostic slots or prosodic evidence (Gumbaynggir, Nyangumarta, Warrongo, Yuwaalaraay, Burarra, Bininj Kunwok, Anindilyakwa, Giimbiyu and Ungarinyin). Even here, however, it is not unlikely that there are other, perhaps more marginal, options for NP construal in the language. This is the case, for instance, in Bininj Kunwok, where against the "anarchic background" (Evans 2003a: 244) of flexible word order, the indefinite marker stands out in that it has a fixed position at the start of the nominal expression (Evans 2003a: 244). See also chapter 7, section 4.

96 Additionally, as a reviewer points out, it may be the case that one sequence is interpretable both phrasally and non-phrasally. This is not further addressed in this book, because it is hard to tell based on grammars (but see section 3.2 for some comments on different interpretations of word marking).

dominant or peripheral NP construal is. In this sense, a far more interesting perspective to take is to look at the range of nominal structures a language has available and how 'classic' NP construal fits in. In the next section, I show that this is also a useful perspective to deal with discontinuity, which can also be analysed as a distinct construction type that is available in a range of options to organise nominal expressions.

4 Discontinuous structures

In the previous section, I focused on contiguous constructions, and came to the conclusion that only a minority of Australian languages may lack NP structures overall, which means that the idea from the literature that Australian languages generally lack NP structures is an overstatement. I deliberately left out the issue of discontinuous structures, which are often regarded as a typical feature of the nominal domain in Australian languages, and a strong argument against NP constituency. I believe that discontinuous structures should be treated separately, for two reasons. One is theoretical: the existence of discontinuous structures in a particular language does not necessarily imply that contiguous constructions in the same language cannot be analysed as genuine NPs; at best, it shows that a language allows nominal expressions to be construed as NPs or not (see also Croft [2007: 27–30] for a similar argument; see also LFG accounts like Simpson [1991: 257–294] on Warlpiri). The second is empirical: where they are available, discontinuous structures are generally less frequent than contiguous structures, and they have specific functions, often in the domain of information structure, as shown convincingly in McGregor's (1997a) and Schultze-Berndt & Simard's (2012) detailed discourse-based studies of discontinuity in Gooniyandi and Jaminjung. This suggests that discontinuous structures are not simply variants of contiguous structures, but distinct construction types, with a distinct form encoding a distinct meaning. From this perspective, it makes sense to discuss discontinuous structures in their own right, rather than as variants of the structures discussed in the previous section.

Before I move on to the analysis, a methodological note is in order about the identification of discontinuous constructions. As argued convincingly by Schultze-Berndt & Simard (2012), it is important to distinguish 'genuine' discontinuous structures from structures that are really two (or more) separate, though co-referential, NPs. Co-referential NPs can be used, for instance, in dislocation and afterthought constructions, as in the Bilinarra example in (148), where a co-referential NP is added after the clause to further clarify the referent, viz. whose house the speaker is talking about (Meakins & Nordlinger 2014: 352). Co-referential NPs can also be used to describe multiple characteristics of a referent, especially where there is a restriction on multiple qualifiers in one NP, as has been noted for a range of languages (e.g. Paakantyi [Hercus 1982: 99], Rembarrnga [McKay 1975: 70], Umpila/Kuuku Ya'u [Hill 2018: 140–144] and Yuwaalaraay [Williams 1980: 96]; see also chapter 3, section 2.2). This is illustrated in the Umpila example in (149) (repeated from (65)), where it is difficult to have the two qualifiers 'old' and 'big' in the same NP (as in 149b), and they have to be split over two NPs, as in (149a). While such structures may look like discontinuous constructions at first sight, they fall outside the scope of the argument about constituency, since they can simply be analysed as consisting of more than one NP.

(148) Bilinarra (Meakins & Nordlinger 2014: 352)
 ngurra-nggurra=rna=rla ga-nggu, **ngayiny-jirri,** warrba=ma
 house-ALL=1MIN.S=3OBL take-POT 1MIN.DAT-ALL clothes=TOP
 'I'm going to take them to the house, to my (house), the clothes I mean.'

(149) Umpila/Kuuku Ya'u (Hill 2018: 142; p.c.)
 a. kampinu-lu tha'i-na pu'ala yilamu /mukana
  man-ERG hit-NFUT drum old big
  'the man hit the big old drum'
 b. ?kampinu-lu tha'i-na pu'ala yilamu mukana
  man-ERG hit-NFUT drum old big
  'the man hit the big old drum'

Leaving aside such structures, discontinuity is distributed as follows in the sample. It is mentioned and/or attested for 49 languages, while it is explicitly said to be impossible for 19 languages. For the other 32 languages, no mention is made in the grammatical descriptions, nor have I found any unambiguous examples. Of course, these are only rough numbers, as much depends on the analytical choices of the fieldworkers, and the detail of the information that is available (for instance, some people analyse constructions as discontinuous even if they look very much like dislocation or afterthought constructions). Even so, the evidence suggests that about half of the languages in the sample allow some kind of discontinuity in the nominal domain, and the other half do not. While not all grammars provide detailed information, a number of generalisations can be made about the nature of discontinuity as found in the sample. As will be shown, all of these suggest that discontinuous structures are separate construction types rather than variants of contiguous structures, which implies that they cannot be used as evidence against the constituency status of the latter.

A first generalisation is that discontinuous patterns are usually far less frequent than contiguous patterns in the languages where they occur, indicating that they are not merely free variants that can be used anytime. In Jaminjung, for example, discontinuous NPs are only approximately 1% of all NPs in discourse (Schultze-Berndt & Simard 2012: 1032), in Mawng they represent 1.41% of all NPs (Forrester 2015: 58), in both Wardaman and Gooniyandi they make up 3% of all NPs, and 11% and 17% of multi-word NPs respectively (Croft 2007: 6; McGregor 1997a: 92). Other descriptions do not mention percentages, but often simply state that discontinuous structures are "much less common" than contiguous structures (Gaagudju; Harvey [2002: 316]), or that co-referential elements occur contiguously "[i]n perhaps the majority of the examples," though "they may occur separately" (Warrongo; Tsunoda [2011: 348]).

Secondly, discontinuity is not unconstrained, but appears to show some formal restrictions. For instance, McGregor (1997a) shows that discontinuity in Gooniyandi is generally restricted to one structure per clause, and that discontinuous structures rarely have more than two words. The sample can add some other types of restrictions. For one thing, discontinuity seems to be far more frequent for nominal expressions in core argument roles than for adjuncts, as stated explicitly for Dhuwal (Djambarrpuyngu) by Wilkinson (1991: 125): "Discontinuity is particularly a feature of nominal expressions coding core roles. Those coding peripheral roles have a greater tendency to be juxtaposed." In addition, discontinuity appears to be more typical for some word classes than for others. Thus, for instance, quantifiers, like numerals or elements meaning 'many' or 'some', appear to be particularly prone to occur discontinuously (as observed by Bowern [2012: 336–338] for Bardi, Evans [2003a: 242] for Bininj Kunwok, and Evans [1995a: 250] for Kayardild). This seems to be the case especially in contexts where the number of the referent(s) is emphasised, as in the Wambaya example in (150). Other elements that are often split off in instances of discontinuity in the sample are different types of determining elements, e.g. demonstratives, as in (151), possessive pronouns, as in (152), and personal pronouns, as in (153).

(150) Wambaya (Nordlinger 1998a: 133)
    garngunya   gin-aji   yabu **garirda-rdarra**   garndawugini-ni
    many.II(ACC) 3SG.M.A-HAB.PST have wife.II-GROUP(ACC) one.I-LOC
    'One (man) used to have many wives.'

(151) Tharrgari (Klokeid 1969: 38)
  yiṉa ṯaRi-da-nma   ŋadi **pawa**, makadbu ŋadi paja-lariŋu.
  that cold-VBLZR-IMP 1DU water so   1DU drink-INTENTV
  'Cool this water, so we can have a drink.'

(152) Atynyamathanha (Schebeck 1974: 74, 109)
  yata   naku-ankat-aṯu **vanʸtʸuṟu**
  ground see-PST-1SG.A   his
  'I have seen his ground'

(153) Yingkarta (Dench 1998: 52)
  pinya-tha   yanma-nu-nyi   **muntungu**
  3SG.NOM-DEF go.IMMPST-AFF-*nyi* European
  'Them fellas have all gone.' ('That (group of) Europeans has gone.')

In combination with low frequency, the existence of formal restrictions on discontinuous structures suggests quite strongly that they also have a specific function. This is, in fact, what is shown in the two detailed discourse-based studies available in the sample, viz. McGregor (1997a) on Gooniyandi and Schultze-Berndt & Simard (2012) on Jaminjung, both of which identify specific information-structural functions. For instance, Schultze-Berndt & Simard show convincingly that discontinuity is not semantically neutral, but serves to mark focus. This can be contrastive argument focus, as in (154a) below, where the discontinuous element *gujugujugu* 'big' is highlighted in contrast with the much smaller size of the tents that were used earlier. Alternatively, it can mark sentence focus, which typically involves out-of-the-blue statements that "alert the hearer to the presence or appearance of an entity with a particular property, or in a particular quantity" (Schultze-Berndt & Simard 2012: 1041), as in (154b).

(154) Jaminjung (Schultze-Berndt & Simard 2012: 1038, 1041)
  a. **bulayi**   yirra-ma-na   ^***guju~gujugu*** na \
     fly/tent 1PL.EXCL-have-IPFV PL~big   now
     'We had *big* tents then.'
  b. ***jarndu*** ga-ram   **luba** mangurn=mij!
     boat   3SG-come.PRS big white.person=COM
     'There comes a big boat with white people!'

Obviously, such detailed analyses are unavailable for many languages in the sample, but if authors mention anything about discontinuity, they often suggest information-structural functions. Thus, for instance, Evans (1995a: 249–250) links the use of discontinuous structures for qualifiers in Kayardild to functions of contrastive focus and emphasis. Similarly, according to Merlan (1994: 242), discontinuity in Wardaman is associated with a focus-presupposition structure, the first element usually being presupposed and the last one as "more in-focus for one reason or another e.g., because it is contrastive, or otherwise the less presupposable element of the theme as a whole." Bowern (2012: 328–329) also associates the use of discontinuous structures with focus in Bardi: in (155), for instance, the contiguous structure in (155b) is pragmatically neutral, while the discontinuous structures in (155a) and (155c) focus on 'two' and on 'fish', respectively. Finally, discontinuity in Warlpiri can be also linked to information-structural features, as argued by Simpson (2007). In Warlpiri, prominent information precedes the 2nd position auxiliary, but what is prominent need not coincide with a whole nominal expression. This is illustrated in the question-answer pair in (156), where only the modifying elements *nyajangu* 'how many' (A) and *panu* 'many' (B) are presented as prominent. Non-prominent material which is at the same time new information will precede the main predicate (but follow the auxiliary), as *karli* 'boomerang' in the question in (A), while non-prominent material which is given information will follow the main predicate, as *karli* in the reply in (B).

(155) Bardi (Bowern 2012: 329)
    a. *gooyarra i-na-m-boo-na aarli*
       two   3-TR-PST-spear-REMPST fish
       'He speared two fish.'
    b. *gooyarra aarli i-na-m-boo-na*
       two   fish 3-TR-PST-spear-REMPST
    c. *aarli i-na-m-boo-na gooyarra*
       fish 3-TR-PST-spear-REMPST two

(156) Warlpiri (Simpson 2007: 510)
    A. **Nyajangu**=ngku **karli**   yu-ngu nyuntu-ku;
       how.many=2O   boomerang give-PST you-DAT
       kirdana-rlu nyuntukupalangu-rlu?
       fater-ERG   your-ERG
       'How many boomerangs did he give you, your father?'
    B. **Panu**=ju yu-ngu **karli**;   **panu** nganta=ju yu-ngu
       many=1O give-PST boomerang; many seems=1O give-PST
       kirdana-rlu ngajukupalangu-rlu **karli**   *ngaju-ku.*
       father-ERG my-ERG   boomerang me-DAT
       'He gave me many boomerangs; my father gave me many.'

Additionally, examples from grammatical descriptions that do not discuss discontinuity in detail, often seem to fit the analyses of contrastive argument focus and of sentence focus made by Schultze-Berndt & Simard (2012) and McGregor (1997a), though of course these intuitions would need to be confirmed by detailed discourse studies for individual languages.

Overall, therefore, whenever there is relevant information in my sample, it suggests that discontinuous structures are not simply formal variants of contiguous structures, but distinct constructions with a distinct meaning (in addition to other structures the language may have available, like NP construal, fracturing, etc.). They are typically formally constrained and less frequent, which reflects a specific discourse function. Their status as a separate construction type also suggests that they cannot be used as arguments against the constituency status of contiguous nominal expressions. Such an argument could only work if contiguous and discontinuous structures are genuinely free variants, with no formal constraints or meaning differences.[97]

---

[97] There is only a small set of languages in the sample where I cannot detect any constraints on discontinuity. In such languages, nominal expressions may be 'split' into more than two parts, as in the Jaru structure in (ii), or there may be multiple discontinuous structures in a single clause, as in the Dyirbal example in (iii). Given the nature of the examples, one wonders in how far such structures are attested beyond elicitation.

(ii) Jaru (Tsunoda 1981: 94)

  jalu-ŋgu lani-i **mawun-du** ḍaḍi **jambi-gu**
  that-ERG spear-PST man-ERG kangaroo big-ERG
  'That big man speared a kangaroo.'

(iii) Dyirbal (Dixon 1972: 107)

  a. **bayi**   **waɲal**   **baɲul**   **yaṟaɲu**   **bulganu**
     there.NOM.I   boomerang.NOM   there.GEN.I   man.GEN   big.GEN.I
     baŋgun   ḍugumbiṟu   buṟan
     there.ERG.II   woman.ERG   see.PRS/PST
     'woman saw big man's boomerang'
  b. **bayi**   **yaṟaɲu**   **ḍugumbiṟu**   buṟan   **waɲal**
     there.NOM.I   man.GEN   woman.ERG   see.PRS/PST boomerang.NOM
     baŋgun   baɲul   bulganu
     there.ERG.II   there.GEN.I   big.GEN.I
     'woman saw big man's boomerang'

5 Conclusion

To round off this chapter, I would like to highlight a few points. The main conclusion is, obviously, that the case for the absence of clear NP structures in Australian languages is over-stated, and probably results from over-generalisation based on a handful of languages. If concrete criteria for NP constituency like word order, locus of case marking, diagnostic slots or prosody are applied to a broad sample of Australian languages, there is no strong evidence against NP constituency at all, quite on the contrary. As shown in the summary in section 3.5, about two thirds of the languages in the sample show good evidence for NP constituency. In this sense, theoretical or typological work (for instance on non-configurationality) cannot take simple generalisations about NP structure in Australian languages for granted.

Apart from this obvious conclusion, there are some other points that emerge from this study. Perhaps the most important one is that questions about the presence or absence of NP constituency are not really sensible questions to ask about a whole language system (see also Himmelmann 1997: 136). Even in those languages in the sample that seem to conform to received ideas about 'flexible' nominal expressions (about one third of the sample), NP constituency is not completely absent, although these languages obviously have a different profile than languages with a more dominant pattern of NP construal. As shown in section 3.5, most of these allow nominal expressions to be construed as NPs in some form, either in diagnostic slots or with phrasal case marking. What this suggests is that it may be more interesting to typologise languages on the basis of where and how they allow NP construal. Almost all of the languages in the sample seem to have NP construal in some form, but in some languages, it is the dominant way to deal with nominal expressions, while in others it may be more marginal, manifested in specific contexts. This conclusion is compatible with the one reached by Himmelmann (1997), who proposes to couch such differences in terms of differential grammaticalisation of syntactic structure.[98] The same argument can be made a fortiori for discontinuity, traditionally regarded as one of the strongest arguments against NP constituency. Again, the presence of discontinuity in a particular language cannot serve as evidence against constituency for the language as a whole. Since discontinuous structures are usually

---

98 In other words, the more dominant NP construal is in a language, the more strongly we could regard its NE as grammaticised. In this perspective, NP constituency is a gradient concept. However, I do not think such gradient approaches capture all the relevant differences: I think it is just as useful to focus on where and when NP construal is allowed, as on how dominant it is in the overall language system.

quite distinct formally and functionally, it makes more sense to regard them as a separate type of construal in the nominal domain, in addition to NP construal and other types of construals that may be available (i.e. it is just one of the structural possibilities). In this sense, languages should really be typologised in terms of the range of nominal construals they have available, and the division of labour between them, rather than on the basis of a simple yes-or-no answer to the question of constituency or (dis)continuity. I believe this applies not just to languages for which NP constituency has been questioned, like Australian languages or some South American languages (Krasnoukhova 2012: 177–181; see also chapter 5, section 2), but also to many languages for which NP constituency has been assumed as the default (compare, for instance, work on discontinuity in German, e.g. De Kuthy [2002]).

In order to develop such a typology, however, the analysis has also shown quite clearly that much more careful discourse-based work on nominal expressions is needed, in the line of studies like McGregor (1989, 1997a), Simpson (2007) or Schultze-Berndt & Simard (2012). It is only when one looks at what types of nominal construal there are, and what their functions are in discourse, that it becomes clear how they divide up the nominal domain, and where a particular language fits in the typology of nominal construal. This type of work is not only needed for Australian languages, of course, but also for better-described languages, where corpus-based work on narrative and interactional data could reveal more variation in nominal construal than has traditionally been assumed. This may also lead to a further re-assessment of where Australian languages stand in the typology of nominal construal, and if and how they are really different from other types of languages.

7 The status of determining elements

1 Introduction

As pointed out in chapter 5, Australian languages generally lack many of the features that define a prototypical determiner system, like specialised word classes or obligatoriness of use. This chapter[99] investigates whether Australian languages can be said to have any kind of determiner system, and if so, what it looks like in structural terms. This links in with the idea that in some languages, NPs can be analysed in terms of functional-structural slots, as discussed in chapter 6 (section 3.1). In this chapter, I focus on one of these slots, viz. the determiner slot, and I investigate its presence in the languages of the sample. If a language has a determiner slot, this implies that it is part of a larger syntactic unit, at least for those nominal expressions which have such determiners (but not necessarily for other nominal expressions, as will be shown for Bininj Kunwok in section 4.1). As this chapter remains agnostic about whether there are structural slots for other functions, I do not further discuss the implications for NP constituency here.[100] The results of this chapter and the previous one are brought together in chapter 8.

Unlike prototypical determiner languages, Australian languages do not usually have word classes that are specialised in determiner functions (see also e.g. Lyons 1999: 49; Dixon 2002: 66–67; Stirling & Baker 2007; Baker 2008). Some elements, like demonstratives, do typically have determining functions (e.g. they can specify identifiability based on distance relations or anaphoricity), but they can also have other functions, typically in other positions. This is illustrated in (157) from Gaagudju, where demonstratives can be used both as determiners, in initial position (157b), and with other modifying functions, following the head noun (157c) (see the general NP template in (157a)).

---

[99] This chapter is a significantly extended version of a journal article, published as: Louagie, Dana. 2017. The status of determining elements in Australian languages. *Australian Journal of Linguistics*. 37(2). 182–218. The chapter is different from the published paper in a number of respects. Most importantly, it includes a discussion of languages without determiner slots. In addition, the criterion of edge position is discussed more critically and I have added a summarising discussion on elements which fill determiner slots. The chapter now also includes more examples, and I have added a map and accompanying discussion on the distribution of the different types of determiner slots across Australia. Finally, the discussion of one language (Kuuk Thaayorre) is somewhat different (see section 2.4), following the more recent analysis in Gaby (2017)
[100] Consequently, the remainder of this chapter again uses the term 'noun phrase' or NP in a general sense, and not in a strictly syntactic sense (unlike in the previous chapter).

(157) Gaagudju (Harvey 2002: 316–317)
  a. Template (G):
     (Deictic(s)) Entity (Qualifier)
  b. ***magaadja njinggooduwa*** *ø-iinj-ma ø-baalgi njoogi*
     that:II   woman   3I<3F-got I-lots   white.ochre
     'That woman got lots of white ochre (too).'
  c. *gooyu* ***djaarli naarri*** *biirda ibárdbi i-rree-nj-dja*
     mother meat   I:here   tough   NEG   3I<1-FUT-eat
     'Mother, this meat here is tough. I cannot eat it.'

Furthermore, modifiers with a determining function are rarely obligatory in Australian languages (see, for instance, Stirling & Baker [2007]), and they tend to co-occur rather than compete. A frequent combination, for example, is that of an adnominal demonstrative and a personal pronoun (cf. also Blake 2001: 424; Stirling & Baker 2007; Stirling 2008 for examples), as illustrated in the Kala Lagaw Ya structure in (158) below. In the same language, there is no element that is obligatory to distinguish definite from indefinite NPs: a bare noun can be interpreted as either (Stirling & Baker 2007: 2–3).

(158) Kala Lagaw Ya (Stirling & Baker 2007: 3)
  ***Thana   sethabi   moegithap** uruy-n*   *poyzen mabayg-aw*
  3PL.NOM 3PL.DEM:REM tiny   creature-ERG poison person-GEN
  kulka-nu   wan-an.
  blood-LOC put-NFUT
  'These tiny creatures put poison into a person's blood.'

In this chapter, I investigate whether Australian languages can be said to have determiner systems at all, and if so, what these look like in structural terms. I show that a determiner slot can be identified in half of the sample, which can be filled by a range of different elements. On the other hand, there is also a group of 25 languages which show (some) evidence against the presence of a determiner slot. In practical terms, I first compare the position of what are cross-linguistically prototypical determiners (like demonstratives or personal pronouns) and what are cross-linguistically prototypical modifiers (like adjectives), in contiguous NPs. If a clear pattern emerges, with different positions for the two categories, there is structural evidence for a determiner slot. For the languages in which such a slot can be distinguished, I then look at what types of elements can occur in this slot, regardless of their cross-linguistic prototypicality as determiners. Obviously, this procedure is somewhat circular, but this is inevitable for languages without specialised determiners. Moreover, it also has an advantage in that it casts a wide net, and brings to the surface many instances of atypical determiners from various word classes. As I will show in section 3, this offers an interesting window into the semantics of determination, as it allows us to contrast determiner uses with non-determiner ones, and tease out features that are crucial in either use.

The rest of this chapter is structured as follows. In section 2, I look at evidence for identifying determiner slots in the languages of the sample, and I investigate a notable feature found in the sample, viz. optionality of determiners. Section 3 investigates which elements can occur in determiner slots, showing that most of them are not specialised in this slot but can also be used in non-determiner positions. I focus on the semantics of these elements, investigating what makes them eligible for use as a determiner, or alternatively, as a non-determining modifier. In section 4, I look in some more detail at the languages for which I was not able to identify a determiner slot.

2 Structural determiner slots in the sample

In this section, I investigate the presence of a structural slot for determiners in the languages of the sample. There are 14 languages in the sample for which the grammatical description has already identified a determiner slot; these are marked with a * following the language name in the corresponding tables (see section 3.1 in chapter 6 for more information on analyses in terms of functional roles). In Gooniyandi, for instance, McGregor (1990) identifies a fixed NP template in terms of functional roles (shown in (159a), repeated from (129a)). Each functional slot can be filled with elements from different word classes, and one word class can occur in several slots. For example, the number word *yoowarni* 'one' can occur in the Deictic[101] slot (159b) (repeated from (92c)), functioning as an indefinite determiner (McGregor 1990: 258), or in the Quantifier slot (159c), indicating a specific quantity (McGregor 1990: 259–260, 270–271).

(159) Gooniyandi (McGregor 1990: 253, 374, 260)
    a. Template (G):
        (Deictic) (Quantifier) (Classifier) Entity (Qualifier)

---

101 Some analyses use the term Deictic, which seems to be equivalent to what I call determiner. For instance, the Deictic slot in Gooniyandi serves to "contextualise the phrase, relating it to the linguistic or extralinguistic context, thus facilitating the identification of its referent" (McGregor 1990: 257), or similarly in Gaagudju to "contextualis[e] the noun phrase" (Harvey 2002: 317).

b. *Yoowarni-ngga* / ***yoowarni-ngga gardiya*** /
   one-ERG   one-ERG   white.person
   cherrabun bore / *warangji* / *gamba bambimnga-wirrangi*
   <place name>   he:sat   water he:pumped:it-for:them
   boorloomani-yoo /
   bullocks-DAT
   'There was a white man at Cherrabun Bore pumping water for the cattle.'
c. *yoowarni gamba*
   one   water
   'one (glass of) water'

For the other languages in the sample, I identify a structural slot by both syntagmatic and paradigmatic means. A syntagmatic perspective focuses on the position of elements in the NP as evidence for the presence of a structural slot. I distinguish two syntagmatic criteria, one relative and one absolute. The first criterion looks at whether the elements under scrutiny are in a position that is clearly delimited from the nominal head and other modifiers, which would suggest a separate slot in the NP. In Dyirbal (Dixon 1972: 60–61, examples), for instance, the nominal head of the NP divides the 'demonstrative noun marker'[102] on its left side from the adjective(s) on its right side, as shown in the NP template in (160a) and the example in (160b). However, the demonstrative noun marker is not the only element that can occur to the left of the head: possessive pronouns can occur in the same position, as shown in (160c). What the elements on the left side of the head have in common is that they encode the identifiability status of the referent, i.e. they both have a determining function, and occur in the same position. This suggests the presence of a determiner slot at the left edge.

(160) Dyirbal (Dixon 1972: 60, 61, 105; own glossing)
   a. Template (W):
      demonstrative noun marker – noun – adjective(s)
   b. ***bayi*** *yaṟa bulgan baniɲu*
      there.NOM.I man.NOM big.NOM is.coming
      'big man is coming'

---

[102] This name suggests that they are mainly markers of noun class membership, but they also indicate deictic contrast (although the distal form is also used "when no specification of visibility/ proximity is intended" [Dixon 1972: 46]). They also seem to have a link with personal pronouns, and are called "pseudo-pronouns" by Dixon at one point (1972: 244).

c. ɲinda **ŋaygu** **bayi** **galbin** balgan
   2SG.A 1SG.GEN there.NOM.I child hit.PRS/PST
   'you hit my son'

The second syntagmatic criterion looks at whether (potential) determiners occur at the edge of the NP, as would be expected according to Rijkhoff's (2002: 313) Principle of Scope (see chapter 5, section 1). This can be illustrated with Panyjima (Dench 1991: 186), where the demonstrative occurs at the left edge, and the attributive nominal may precede or follow the head, as in the template in (161a). When these two modifiers both occur on the left side of the head, the demonstrative occurs furthest from the head, as in (161b). This is indicative of a determiner slot (although edge position in itself is probably insufficient and needs to be combined with evidence from other criteria; see section 4.1 for some comments on languages that only have evidence from this criterion).

(161) Panyjima (Dench 1991: 186, 219)
    a. Template (W):
        dem – quant/log – attr.N/poss – head.N – attr.N/poss
    b. *mirlima-larta kangkuru-ku miyinma-larta nhupalu*
        spear-FUT kangaroo-ACC provide-FUT 2DU
        nyiya-jirri-ku kamungu-ku juju-ngarli-ku panti-jangu
        this-PL-ACC hungry-ACC old.man-PL-ACC sit-REL
        nhangu-yu pili-ngka-ku.
        here-ACC cave-LOC-ACC
        'You two spear kangaroos to provide for these hungry old people here in the cave.'

If both these syntagmatic criteria are met, we can identify a structural determiner slot. By contrast, if neither of them is met, there is no determiner slot. This is the case, for instance, in Ngan'gityemerri/Ngan'gikurunggurr, in which the NP shows a "loose ordering of modifiers" following a fixed-initial head (see the NP template in (162a)) (Reid 1997: 167). For instance, an adjective and a demonstrative can occur in either order following the head, including a non-edge position for the demonstrative (162b-c).

(162) Ngan'gityemerri/Ngan'gikurunggurr (Reid 1990: 291; 1997: 167, 168, 201)
    a. Template (W):
        generic – specific – modifier(s)

b. *mi-menem   yerr=syari yerr=kinyi*[103]
   VE-billygoat.plum TREE=dry   TREE=this
   'this dry billygoat plum tree'
c. *mi-menem   yerr=kinyi yerr=syari yubu-ket-ø*
   VE-billygoat.plum TREE=this   TREE=dry   2SG.S:AUX-cut-IMP
   'Chop down this withered billygoat plum tree!'

If only one of these criteria is met, the analysis is more problematic and depends on the weight one wishes to give to each criterion. The edge criterion is potentially the weaker one: one may wonder whether this is not merely a crosslinguistic tendency, an epiphenomenon of their semantic scope, rather than a necessary condition.[104] This is further discussed in section 4, where I look at several languages that have only evidence from one of the criteria and no or conflicting evidence from the other one.

A paradigmatic criterion for slots is whether the elements compete for the same position or co-occur in it. As discussed in chapter 5, section 1, complementary distribution is often seen as the only scenario that provides evidence for a determiner slot, and co-occurrence as evidence for different slots. However, I believe that co-occurrence does not necessarily provide evidence against a determiner slot: some languages in my sample have determiner 'zones', where 'determiner complexes' form functional units and as a whole say something about the identifiability status of the referent (see also chapter 5, section 1). Co-occurrence of determiners is a common feature of many languages in the sample, which will be discussed in section 3.8.

The rest of this section looks at what evidence there is for a structural determiner slot in the languages of my sample. There are 28 languages in the sample that show convincing evidence for a determiner slot, and an additional 22 languages with some evidence for a determiner slot, which is either more limited or slightly different from that of the 'prototypical' case. There are four ways in which the determiner slot is attested in these 50 languages, which I now discuss in turn. An overview can be found in table 8, and in map 13 in section 2.5.

---

103 See chapter 2, section 5, example (43) on the variable gender agreement between head and modifiers in this example.
104 Thanks to Birgit Hellwig and Hendrik De Smet for pointing this out.

Table 8: Determiner slots.

type	generalised template	number of languages
1	**determiner(s)** – HEAD – modifier(s)	5 (+2)
2	**determiner(s)** – modifier(s) – HEAD – modifier(s)	7 (+8)
3	**determiner(s)** – HEAD – modifier(s) – **determiner(s)**	11 (+7)
4	**determiner(s)** ... modifier(s) – HEAD (or HEAD – modifier(s) ... **determiner(s)**)	5 (+5)

2.1 Type 1: determiner(s) – HEAD – modifier(s)

The first type of language has a determiner slot on the left side of the head and other modifiers on the right side of the head. The determiner slot occurs at the edge, is clearly delineated from other modifiers, and can involve competition or co-occurrence. There are five languages that are definitely of this type, and two that are most likely of this type, but with slightly weaker evidence. An overview can be found in table 14 (Appendix), where the second column shows the elements that can occur in the determiner slot or zone, also indicating patterns of competition or co-occurrence (see also section 3).

An example of this type is Uradhi, for which the author proposes an NP template as in (163a) below. The template is defined in terms of word classes, but I argue that all the modifiers found on the left side of the head form a determiner zone, in which the demonstrative and 3rd person pronoun are in competition for the initial slot, followed by a genitive NP or a possessive pronoun (Crowley 1983: 371, 377, examples).[105] This analysis is supported by (i) left edge position, (ii) clear delimitation from other modifiers with the head as barrier,[106] and (iii) the common feature of 'identifiability' in demonstratives, personal pronouns and possessives (see further in section 3). Additionally, the grammar

---

[105] This analysis is slightly different from Crowley's (1983: 371), who characterises only the initial slot (filled by a demonstrative or personal pronoun) as a determiner slot, presumably because the possessive is not in complementary distribution with either of these. This is at least what the description and template suggest (Crowley 1983: 371), but unfortunately there are no examples of either a demonstrative or a personal pronoun co-occurring with a possessive in the grammar. Note that the available data is overall limited for Uradhi.

[106] Note that the possessive can sometimes follow the head noun (Crowley 1983: 377). A logical explanation would be that in this position it does not have a determiner function (see section 3.4), or that exceptional order is related to discourse-functional factors (see chapter 6, section 3.1, esp. the example of Tiwi).

also has an example with *uɲa* 'other' in this position (see (163b)), which implies that this element can also be used as determiner.

(163) Uradhi (Crowley 1983: 371, 377, 393)
 a. Template (G+W):

$$\begin{bmatrix} \text{dem} & \text{(gen NP)}^{107} & \text{(N) (Adj)} \\ \text{3pron} & & \\ & & \text{(N) (gen NP)} \end{bmatrix}$$

 b. *uɲa-ŋku mata-ŋku*
  other-INS hand-INS
  '[He used] the other hand.' (after having burnt his one hand)

Another good example of this type of language is Gaagudju, for which the author also identifies a determiner slot in the grammar (Harvey 2002: 316–320) (see the template in (164a)). Elements which can occur in this slot are the demonstrative, the pronoun (as in (164b)), the numeral 'one' (meaning 'a certain (amount)/same' in this slot), interrogative-indefinites and the element *noondji* 'other'. It is possible to have more than one determiner at the same time. More specifically, the combination of a 'definite Deictic' followed by an 'indefinite Deictic' is allowed, most commonly 'that other', as in (164c) (Harvey 2002: 318). Most, if not all, of these elements can also occur outside this slot, i.e. following the head noun, but then they have a Qualifier function, as described in more detail in Harvey (2002: 317–320). The relationship between parts of speech and functional slots is further explored in section 3.

(164) Gaagudju (Harvey 2002: 316, 317, 318)
 a. Template (G):
  (Deictic(s)) Entity (Qualifier)
 b. **ngaayi aardi** m-balbarraaga
  1MIN clothes IV-torn
  'My clothes are torn.'
 c. njinggooduwa=ngaayu ø-an-galeemarr-wa=nu **magaarra**
  woman=3FDAT IV-3M-jealous-AUX:PST.PFV=3MIO that:I
  ngoondji djirriingi
  other man
  'He is jealous of that other man over the woman.'

---

107 Double possessives are also possible, e.g. *atumu-:namu pana-:namu miṇa* [1SG.GEN-GEN friend-GEN meat] 'my friends meat' (Crowley 1983: 377).

In addition to the clear cases, there are two further languages that look like the others in this category, but with limited (frequency-related) flexibility. In Djapu, for instance, the elements occurring on the left side of the head (see the NP template in (165a)) all mark the identifiability status of the referent in some way (see also section 3),[108] which, in combination with their edge position, argues for a determiner zone. In this zone, the personal pronoun can co-occur with a demonstrative, in this order (Morphy 1983: 84), as in (165b). This structure is very similar to what we have seen before, with one difference: unlike in Uradhi, the NP template in Djapu is only "usually" adhered to, with only the personal pronoun and the dual/plural marker having a fixed position, and quantifiers, numerals and locational modifiers being entirely "free" (Morphy 1983: 82–87, examples).

(165) Djapu (Morphy 1983: 82–87, examples, 84)
    a. Template (W+E):
       3pron – dem, indef/hypothetical det, N-PROP, genitive/inalienable PR – N(s) – du/pl modifier – modifying nominal
    b. *bala [ŋayi   ŋunhi-ny-dhi   yolŋu-ny]s   marrtji*
       then 3SG.NOM that.ABS-PRO-ANAPH person.ABS-PRO come.UNM
       'Then that person comes along'

2.2 Type 2: determiner(s) – modifier(s) – HEAD – modifier(s)

In a second group of languages, determiners are found on the left side of the head, and other modifiers can occur on either side of the head. When both categories co-occur, determiners are furthest from the head. In other words, there is a determiner slot (or zone) at the left edge, which is delineated from other modifiers (in that it has a fixed position with respect to the head whereas other modifiers are flexible), and which allows competition or co-occurrence. Seven languages are

---

108 One possible exception is the noun marked with a proprietive suffix, as shown in (iv), which may be a compound-like or classifying construction.

(iv)   Djapu (Morphy 1983: 85)
      nhä-ma   ŋali   [gundirr-mirr   wäŋa]$_{OBJ}$
      see-UNM 1DU.INCL.NOM antbed-PROP.ABS place.ABS
      'We saw a place with a lot of antbed'

definitely of this type, while an additional eight show some evidence, which is either more limited or mixed. An overview can be found in table 15 (Appendix).

A language which clearly belongs to this type is Mayi (166a).[109] The grammar suggests (Breen 1981b: 63, examples) that the demonstrative, personal pronoun and interrogative compete for the initial slot, as for instance in (166b-c). As these elements also share a feature of identifiability, this can be analysed as a determiner slot. It is unclear whether the numeral on the left side of the head could be part of a larger determiner zone (i.e. having a kind of determining function), or whether it has a purely quantifying function. (It should be noted that the position of the numeral is "not definitely established" [Breen 1981b: 63].) One reason why I have chosen not to include numerals as determiners in this case is that for the purposes of this study I do not want to go beyond anything I can infer from the grammar.

(166) Mayi (Breen 1981b: 63, 66, 55)
    a. Template (W):
        dem/pron/interr – num – N.qual – N.head – N.qual
    b. **kula kaṯi** wamuran^y-pir
        this meat crow-ALL
        'This meat is for the crows.'
    c. **pala yampi** paṯa-mp-iŋu
        3DU dog bite-RECP-PRS
        'The dogs bit [sic] one another.'

Another example of this type is Martuthunira (167), which has also been analysed as such in Dench (1994: 189–198), with a left-edge determiner slot, and several other pre- and post-head modifiers. Elements which can function as determiner in Martuthunira are demonstratives, possessive pronouns, *yarta* 'other one' and *yartapalyu* 'others, other group' (Dench 1994: 190). It is unclear whether these elements are in competition or can co-occur in this slot.

(167) Martuthunira (Dench 1994: 189, 190)
    a. Template (G):
        (Determiner) (Quantifier) (Classifier) Entity (Qualifier(s))

---

109 A caveat should be added that the grammar of Mayi is a salvage grammar, so the data on which the analysis is based is relatively limited.

b. ***Nganaju yaan*** *yungku-lha murla-a **yartapalyu-u***
   1SG.GEN wife give-PST meat-ACC others-ACC
   kanyara-ngara-a.
   man-PL-ACC
   'My wife gave meat to the other men.'

There are two further sets of languages which may belong to this type, but less clearly so. First, there is a set of three languages with mixed evidence, in that they seem to mainly follow the type as described above, but with some exceptions. For instance, the template of the Bundjalung NP is described by Sharpe (2005: 98) as in (168a). This is very similar to the template of Mayi as in (166a) above, with probably at least the demonstrative and the possessive pronoun in a determiner zone at the left edge, as in (168b). However, a few examples with N-dem or N-poss order have been found in the grammar, as in (168c). It is unclear whether this implies that there is a second determiner slot following the head noun (as in type 3, section 2.3) or whether the demonstrative could have a qualifying function in this position (as is the case in Martuthunira). See also footnote 133 on this analytical issue.

(168) Bundjalung (Sharpe 2005: 98, 99, 37)
   a. Template (W):
      dem – poss – num – A – N – A
   b. *munah-mba ngañah bulahbu bargan*
      those.NVIS-LOC 1SG.POSS two boomerang
      'those two boomerangs (that I had)'
   c. *Mahñ dabahy yung-ba-le-hla* ***gibam-bu mali-yu***.
      those dog bark-say-ANTIP-PROG moon-INS that-INS
      'The dogs are barking because of the moon.'

Second, there is also a set of five languages for which there is only information on NPs of two elements, and not on relative order in the case of multiple modifiers, which implies there is no evidence concerning possible edge position. However, the information there is points to a distinction between determiners and other modifiers, in that the former have a fixed position with respect to the head and the latter a flexible position. An example is Mangarrayi (see the template in (169a)), where the demonstrative, interrogative-indefinite pronoun and possessive pronoun (all typical encoders of identifiability, see section 3) seem to have a fixed initial position (as in (169b)), while the adjective is flexible (as shown in (169c-d)).

(169) Mangarrayi (Merlan 1989: 29–30, 51, examples, 41, 107, 142)
    a. Template (W+E):
       dem – N; interr-indef – N; poss – N
       A – N or N – A; Num – N or N – Num
    b. **Ṉaḻi-nara-bayi ṉaḻa-bugbug**   mir?   wuran-ṉa-ni-wa.
       F.NOM-DIST-FOC   F.NOM-old.person   know   3SG/3DU-AUX-PST.CONT-NARR
       'That old woman knew those two.'
    c. *yar̠?*   *ja-ø-war̠*   **ṉa-gaya-ṉayawu ṉa-balayi.**
       cover   3-3SG/3SG-AUX   N.ERG-hair-hers   N.ERG-big
       'She is covering it up with her big (mop of) hair.'
    d. **ø-balayi ø-ṉanan**   ŋanba-wu.
       N.ABS-big   N.ABS-money   2PL/1SG-give.IMP
       'Give me a lot of money.'

2.3 Type 3: determiner(s) – HEAD – modifier(s) – determiner(s)

The third type of language is almost a mirror image of the previous type, viz. determiners are flexible with respect to the head and other modifiers have a fixed position (for most languages this is on the right side of the head). When co-occurring, determiners are further from the head than other modifiers. In other words, these languages have two determiner slots, at the edges of the NP and clearly delineated from other modifiers in that they are the only modifiers to occur in pre-head position. Again, both competition and co-occurrence are possible. There are 11 languages that are clearly of this type and another seven that are likely candidates, though with somewhat weaker evidence. An overview can be found in table 16 (to be found in the Appendix at the end of the book).

A good example of this type is Guugu Yimidhirr (the NP template can be found in (170a)). Haviland (1979: 104) describes the NP as having a 'core' consisting of one or more of the following elements: generic, specific, inalienable part and adjective (incl. numeral), in this order. At either side of this 'core' are the possessive pronoun, demonstrative, or logical or quantifying nominal (i.e. elements such as *wulbu* 'all' or *yindu* 'a different one'), as in (170b-e). These elements appear to have a common function of identifiability (see also section 3), and they have a similar distribution at the edges of the NP, which seems to be good evidence for identifying two determiner slots. In addition, a personal pronoun can occur at the left edge,[110] as in (170d), which is also a determining element in terms of its function (see section 3.3).

(170) Guugu Yimidhirr (Haviland 1979: 104, examples, 102, 122, 157, 116)
    a. Template (W+E):
    pron – poss/dem/log/quant – [gen – spec – inal.part – adj/num] – poss/dem/log/quant
    N – pron
    b. **Nhanu-umu-n gudaa-ngun warrga-al** nganhi dyinda-y.
       2SG.GEN-*mu*-ERG dog-ERG big-ERG 1SG.ACC bite-PST
       'Your big dog bit me.'
    c. *Wanhdhu* **gudaa nhanu** *gunda-y?*
       who.ERG dog.ABS 2SG.GEN.ABS hit-PST
       'Who hit your dog?'
    d. **Nyulu nhayun waarigan** gada-y waarnggu=wunaarna-y
       3SG.NOM that.ABS moon.ABS come-PST sleep=lie.RDP-PST
       '[Then] the Moon came and lay down to sleep.'
    e. **Gamba-gamba nhayun** yinil dyaarba-angu.
       old.woman.ABS that.ABS afraid.ABS snake-PURP
       'That old lady is afraid of snakes.'

Another language of this type is Umpila/Kuuku Ya'u, which is also analysed as such by Hill (2018). The template can be found in (171a) (repeated from (126)), showing that determiners can occur at either edge; these determiner slots are mutually exclusive (see also footnote 133 for more discussion). These slots can be filled by one of two sets of elements which are in competition: the first includes personal pronouns, demonstratives and quantifiers, as illustrated in (171b-c), and the second consists of possessive pronouns, as illustrated in (171d-e). Interestingly, Hill (2018: 149–154) gives an account of the syntactic and interactional motivations for the choice between initial and final position for determiners. Basic determiners (i.e. pronoun, demonstrative and quantifier) are normally placed initially, but occur in final position in three specific contexts, viz. (i) when the NP is the subject of a non-verbal predicate (as in (171c)), (ii) in coordination structures (i.e. complex NPs), and (iii) when the NP adds extra specifications about a previously established referent (e.g. in afterthoughts). For

---

[110] The personal pronoun seems to have a less flexible position than the other determiners and mainly occurs in initial position, but some examples of a noun-pronoun sequence have been found as well.

possessive pronouns, there is a very strong correlation between the position and the person-number features of the pronoun: first singular possessives are almost always in initial position (as in (171d)), whereas other possessives are almost always in final position (as in (171e)).

(171) Umpila/Kuuku Ya'u (Hill 2018: 123, 124, 149, 137)
    a. Template (G):
        (Det)   (Entity) $\left\{ \begin{array}{l} \text{(Mod)} \\ \text{(Det)} \end{array} \right\}$

        Det: [(Pron) (Dem) (Quant)], or [Poss.Pron]
    b. ***ngulu***   ***nga'al***   ***pulthunu mukan*** nhiina-na
        3SG.NOM DEM:DIST1-DM boy   big   sit-NFUT
        'That big boy sat.'
    c. ***thul'i***   ***nga'a-l***   waangka mukamukana
        stomach DEM.DIST1-DM clay/mud RDP.big
        'that stomach is really muddy' (talking about body paint)
    d. Rattler ***ngathangku kul'a***   paalnta-nya
        Rattler 1SG.GEN   money/stone steal-NFUT
        "Rattler stole my money"
    e. *nga'a-lu*   ***ngaachi pulangku*** kalma-na chinchanaku
        DEM:DIST1-DM place   3PL.GEN   come-NFUT night.island
        'that one came from their country, Night Island'

There are seven other languages that seem to fit in this category, but with mixed and/or limited evidence. Evidence is mixed when not all potential determiners have the same distribution. Only some of them may be flexible at the edges, while others are fixed at one edge, as in Duungidjawu (172). Alternatively, none of the elements may be flexible at the edges, but they are fixed at one edge each, as in Nyungar (173). In other words, unlike in the other languages of this type, not all determiners can occur in each of the two slots, which provides somewhat weaker evidence for these slots, although I think both can still be characterised as determiner slots generally.

(172) Duungidjawu (Kite & Wurm 2004: 96, examples, 95, 96, 50)
    a. Template (W + E): N – A – degree modifier
                          pron – N
                          interr – N
                          dem – N or N – dem
                          poss – N or N – poss

b. *djaŋar [mowanin wunba]*
   limb [big   very]
   'very big limb'
c. *goro:man mana*
   kangaroo DEM
   'that/the kangaroo'
d. *gari-ŋi   ŋa:m ŋin-du   badji-ø   **mana guyur***
   DEM-LOC   1DU   2SG-ERG   find-GENRL   DEM   thing
   'We (incl.) found that thing there.'

(173) Nyungar (Douglas 1976: 44–45)
   Template (G+W):
   poss – N(s) – [A – intensifier] – dem

Evidence is limited when there only is information about two-word NPs, as can be seen for Duungidjawu (172) above. Even though edge position is uncertain, determiners are delimited from other modifiers (i.e. adjectives), in that they can all occur at least before the head, while modifiers are not attested in that position.

2.4 Type 4: determiner(s) ... modifier(s) – HEAD (or reverse)

Finally, there is a group of languages that have fixed word order in the NP with the head at one edge, and the other modifiers going from the adjectival modifier closest to the head to the demonstrative or personal pronoun at the other edge. For these languages, the exact delimitation of a possible determiner slot is more difficult than for the languages described above, as it is unclear where the 'cut-off' point is in the string of modifiers. Still, there is usually some other evidence to argue for a determiner slot. There are five languages that definitely belong to this type, and five languages that probably do, though with less certain evidence. An overview can be found in table 17 (Appendix).

A good example is Marrithiyel (174). As Green (1997: 246) puts it: "NP modifiers fall into two broad groups. The first consists of (general) adjectives and quantifiers. The second consists of demonstrative adjectives, numerals and possessive adjectives. Members of the first group tend to occur immediately following the NP head, while members of the second cluster in NP-final position." In addition, the numeral has an interchangeable position with the demonstrative and the possessive pronoun, and the demonstrative and possessive pronoun never co-occur (Green 1989: 48). Taken together, these properties show that there is a final determiner slot with at least the demonstrative or possessive pronoun as fillers, and possibly also the numeral.[111]

(174) Marrithiyel (Green 1997: 246)
Template (W): generic – specific – A/quant - ⎡num – dem/poss.pron
⎣dem/poss.pron – num

Another language of this type is Umpithamu (Verstraete 2010), where the final position in the NP is analysed as a slot for "identification". Personal and possessive pronouns are in competition for this slot, as shown in the NP template in (175a) and in the examples in (175b-c). This slot falls outside the case marking of the NP.[112]

(175) Umpithamu (Verstraete 2010: 11, 4, 10)
   a. Template (G+W):
      [N   N A   Num]-case Pron/poss
      (classification) X modification number   identification
   b. *Yintyingka*   *aakurru* *athuna,* **omoro-mun** **athuna**
      Yintyingka   home   1SG.GEN father-ABL   1SG.GEN
      angkutha-mun   *athuna*
      father's.father-ABL 1SG.GEN
      'Port Stewart is my home, from my father and my father's father.'
   c. **minya**   **ina**   *iya-n=ina*
      game.animal 3PL.NOM go-PST=3PL.NOM
      'All the animals left.'

---

111 When the numeral is the final element, the case marker moves to the penultimate element instead of the final one, indicating that perhaps the numeral is not part of the NP in this case.

112 As pointed out by a reviewer, this could be evidence for an analysis in terms of a determiner phrase (DP), where the inner constituent (which is the domain of case marking) is an NP, and the NP and determiners together form a DP. As mentioned in footnotes 67 and 74, this book does not further investigate NP versus DP analysis, because there is overall insufficient information in the sample to draw any conclusions on this matter.

There are five languages that show mixed evidence for this type. Three of these, Kugu Nganhcara, Kuuk Thaayorre and Oykangand, have a fixed template, with the exception of the personal pronoun, which can occur at either side of the head (at the edges of the NP in Kuuk Thaayorre; in the other two languages, the position with respect to other modifiers is unknown). One possibility is that the personal pronoun is actually not part of the NP, but co-referential to it. If this is the case, the NP has a fixed template with the head at one edge, which makes these languages clear members of this type. Another possibility is that there is a second determiner slot, which can only be filled by the pronoun. This would imply that these languages belong to type 3, discussed in section 2.3. In fact, the personal pronoun in Kuuk Thaayorre can be used both as part of the NP and as a separate, co-referential NP, which leads Gaby (2017: 216) to argue that it is "midway between heading an independent, apposed phrase and being integrated into a higher-level phrase."

The other two languages, Yingkarta and Kala Lagaw Ya, have an NP template that is very similar to the ones described above, but which allows for limited flexibility of the modifiers with respect to the head. In Yingkarta, for instance, 90% of the NPs follow the template as described in (176) (repeated from (133)), and there are indications that the opposite pattern has a more marked interpretation (Dench 1998: 51).

(176) Yingkarta (Dench 1998: 50–51, examples)
    Template (G+E):   (Determiner) (Modifier) Head
                        with Determiner: dem, poss, pron

2.5 Discussion

Overall, there is structural evidence for the presence of a determiner slot for half of the languages in the sample (i.e. 50 languages, 28 of which show good evidence and 22 weaker evidence; note that some analyses are based on salvage grammars). I distinguished four ways in which the determiner slot is manifested, in each of them at the edge of the NP. An overview can be found in table 8 above and map 13. The map also shows the languages that have no determiner slot, the languages which show mixed evidence, and the languages for which there is not enough information to decide either way (see section 4 for more on these languages).

2 Structural determiner slots in the sample — 181

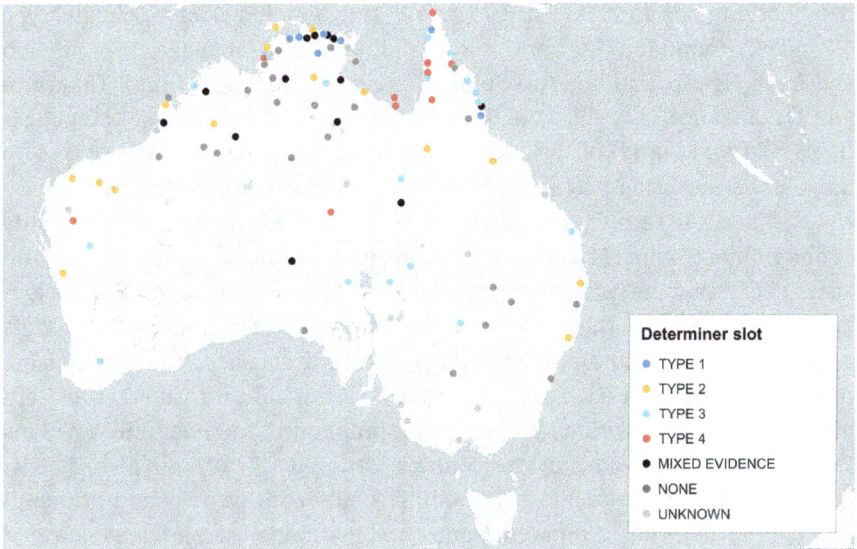

Map 13: Determiner slots. For an online, dynamic version of this map, see: http://bit.ly/determiner-overview. For more detailed information and references, see the tables in the Appendix.

The map shows some patterns in the spread of the four types. Type 1 is found in several languages, but only in the north of the continent, both in Cape York and in the Top End. Type 2 is more widespread, found in the Ngayarta languages (Panyjima, Yindjibarndi and Martuthunira) and Nhanda in the west of Australia, as well as in several unrelated languages in the northwest of the country, and in some languages of different Pama-Nyungan subgroups in the east and on the south-east coast. Type 3 is clearly represented in Cape York and central Australia, as well as some languages scattered across the continent. In Cape York, a type 3 determiner slot is found in three languages of the Yimidhirr-Yalanji-Yidinic subgroup (Guugu Yimidhirr, Kuku Yalanji, Djabugay),[113] and in Yir Yoront, Umpila and Anguthimri (belonging to different subgroups). In central Australia, type 3 is found in three Karnic languages (Arabana/Wangkangurru, Diyari, Yandruwandha),[114] as well as in the

---

[113] The fourth language of this group in the sample, Yidiny, can possibly also be analysed as having a type 3 determiner slot, but with mixed evidence (see table 18).
[114] Again, the fourth Karnic language in the sample, Pitta-Pitta, also shows some evidence for a type 3 analysis, but it is mixed (see table 18).

neighbouring but unrelated languages Yalarnnga and Paakantyi. Finally, type 4 is mainly found in Cape York: in two Middle Paman languages (Umpithamu and Kugu Nganhcara) and two Southwest Paman languages (Kuuk Thaayorre and Oykangand), as well as in Kala Lagaw Ya. The two Tangkic languages (Kayardild and Lardil) of the sample also have type 4 determiner slots, as do three other, unrelated languages (Marrithiyel, Arrernte and Yingkarta).

Within these results, one feature that stands out is the overall optionality of determiners, which is interesting because it is not normally associated with 'classic' determiners (see chapter 5, section 1). In fact, there are only three languages in the sample that have an obligatory determiner, in the sense that its absence also marks the absence of the feature it encodes. The "definitising pronoun" at the right edge of the Arrernte NP is an obligatory marker for definiteness, i.e. an NP without a definitising pronoun is "non-definite" (Wilkins 1989: 165), as illustrated in the contrast between (177a) and (177b) below. Similarly, in Kuku Yalanji, a bare noun "usually conveys new and/or indefinite reference," while a pronoun-noun combination is used for "anaphoric or definite reference" (Patz 2002: 202). In Marra, the use of the article marks discourse topicality, while its absence indicates focus or contrast (see further in section 3.1).

(177) Arrernte (Wilkins 1989: 129, 194)
    a. **Artwe itne** no ahel-irre-ke   **artwe mperlkere ikwere**.
        man   3PL.S no angry-INCH-PST.COMPL man   white   3SG.DAT
        'The men didn't become aggressive towards the white man.'
    b. *The* **ayeye ampe-kweke-kerte** *ile-me*   ampe mape-ke.
        1SG.A story child-little-PROP(OBJ) tell-NPST.PROG child PL(GROUP)-DAT
        'I'm going to tell a story about a baby to the kids.'

Beyond the category of determiners, there are some other examples of obligatoriness of identifiability markers in the sample. In Ngiyambaa, for instance, the 3ABS personal pronoun is obligatory for definite absolutive NPs (i.e. its use makes the following NP definite), as illustrated in the contrastive examples in (178a-b) (Donaldson 1980: 128). However, while this pronoun is syntactically and functionally a proclitic to the NP, it is morphologically enclitic to the previous element in the clause (i.e. it is a ditropic clitic; see Cysouw [2005] and Himmelmann [2014: 945–949] for other examples and discussion of the origin of such structures). As it is not fully part of the NP, it is not a determiner in the sense in which I use the term here.

(178) Ngiyambaa (Donaldson 1980: 128)
   a. *miri-gu=**na**   **bura:y**   gadhiyi*
      dog-ERG=3.ABS child.ABS bite.PST
      'The dog/ a dog/ (some) dogs bit the child.' (*a child)
   b. *miri-gu   **bura:y**   gadhiyi*
      dog-ERG child.ABS bite.PST
      'The dog/ a dog / (some) dogs bit a child/(some) children.' (*the child)

For all other languages, determiners are not obligatory. In other words, a bare noun can have both definite and indefinite interpretations. This is a feature that has been highlighted in the existing literature on determiners on Australian languages. For instance, it is one of the key features of Stirling & Baker's (2007) category of 'topic determiners', which are "much more at the speaker's discretion" (Stirling & Baker 2007: 5) (see chapter 5, section 1, for more details).

3 Elements which fill determiner slots

Now that I have identified a determiner slot or zone in half of the languages of the sample, I can turn to the second main question: which elements can occur in these determiner slots? As already mentioned, Australian languages are generally quite different from typical 'determiner languages', in that they have very few elements which are specialised in the determiner slot (such as articles). There is, however, a whole range of elements that can occur both in the determiner slot and elsewhere, which allows us to contrast these two uses and gives us an interesting window into determiner semantics.

    Elements that are attested in a determiner slot in the languages of this sample are articles, demonstratives and other 'locational' elements, 3rd person pronouns, possessive pronouns, interrogatives, 'ignoratives' and indefinites, quantifiers and numerals, and comparative qualifiers.[115] As they can all occur in the same slot, I assume they must share a particular function, and thus have a particular semantic feature in common which allows them to take up this function, whether it is a prominent part of their semantics or not. I argue that this is 'identifiability' (see also chapter 5, section 1). I use this concept not just in the classical sense, viz. encoding whether the referent(s) of the NP is/are identifiable or non-identifiable, but also

---

[115] The main focus of this book is 'simple' NPs (as discussed in chapter 1), i.e. I will not discuss embedded or complex modifiers such as possessor NPs.

include other types of identifiability, such as identifiability of the reference mass (i.e. the intended referent is not identifiable in itself, but it is directly related to a reference mass which is identifiable), following Langacker (1991) and Davidse (2004).

In the rest of this section, I discuss each of the different categories that can occur in determiner slots, analysing how their semantics fits in with determiner uses as well as other uses. The order in which I discuss the categories relates to how typical they are as determiners: I start out with categories that occur most typically (or even exclusively) as determiners, and gradually move on to categories that are less typical as determiners, and more often used in other functions. Information about which elements can occur in the determiner slot in each language can be found in tables 14 to 17 at the end of this chapter, as well as in the online version of map 13, by clicking on individual data-points.

3.1 Articles

Articles, as a specialised category of markers, have often been regarded as the prototype for determiners, even though they are far from universal (see e.g. Lyons 1999: 48–51). A definite article is formally defined by Himmelmann (2001: 832–833) as (i) a grammatical element which occurs only in nominal expressions, (ii) with a fixed position, and (iii) which is obligatory in grammatically definable contexts.

For only two languages in the sample does the grammatical description posit a separate part of speech with the label 'article'. The article in Marra (Heath 1981: 64, 68–70, 270; Baker 2008) is a marker of discourse topicality (as opposed to a zero for focus or contrast), and is also used in certain polarity contexts (Baker 2008: 139, 142–147). It is specialised in the determiner slot and never occurs elsewhere (see (179) for an example; the article is glossed TOP for topic).[116]

(179) Marra (Baker 2008: 153)
ŋapa **nana** ø-juntuɲuka wa-ø-ciɲca-jiɲca ø-wiici,
also M.TOP M-turtle NPST-3SG.S-DISTR-eat.PRS M-grass,
ø-maca
M-sea.grass

---

[116] Marra does not belong to one of the four types discussed in section 2. However, there is some evidence for positing a determiner slot at least for the article, which has a fixed initial position (whereas all other modifiers are flexible with respect to the head). See section 4.1.

ṉana	ø-waḻca,	wa-ø-ciṉca-jiṉca		ṉana	ø-wiici
M.TOP	M-dugong	NPST-3SG.S-DISTR-eat.PRS		M.TOP	M-grass

'The turtle/turtles eat grass, sea grass [that is]. And dugongs, they eat grass [too].'

In the other language, Mawng, the article is "on the path of grammaticisation between a generic article and a noun marker" (Forrester 2015: 92), occurring not only NP-initially but also between other elements, and thus as not (or no longer) being a determiner.[117]

In addition, there are a handful of languages where either a third person pronoun or a demonstrative has been characterised as 'general definite determiner' or 'similar to the English article *the*' in the grammatical descriptions, because they show some signs of grammaticalisation (such as semantic bleaching). This suggests they may be changing word class. The proximal demonstrative =*n* in Worrorra, for instance, is mainly used as a definite article according to Clendon (2014: 160): "the main and most frequent function of =*n* in Worrorra appears to be to grammaticise identifiability (cf. Lyons 1999: 278); in Lyons' terms, =*n* occupies a structural position activating definiteness in the NP in which it occurs."

Another example is Nyulnyul, where the third person minimal pronoun *kinyingk* in adnominal use is in fact analysed by McGregor as a separate, homophonous "non-demonstrative determiner" marking definiteness (2011: 124–125, 158–159). One reason for McGregor's analysis of adnominal *kinyingk* as a determiner rather than a pronoun is that it can be used for non-minimal referents as well as for inanimate referents, as in (180), which is impossible for the free pronoun. In addition, the pronoun has a suppletive oblique, whereas the determiner does not.[118]

---

[117] A different analysis was proposed by Singer (2006: 49–54), who makes a distinction between the initial article, which has a function relating to information structure, and linking articles which occur between elements of the NP. In this scenario, the initial article can be analysed as a filler of the initial determiner zone, since it occurs in fixed initial position (similar to the demonstrative and personal pronoun, and contrary to other modifiers which can precede or follow the head, see also section 2.2). The main reason why Forrester (2015: 67–92) discards this distinction between initial article and linking article is that a new analysis of data has shown that all articles are optional (instead of just the initial article, as Singer argued) and thus have the same status.

[118] Section 3.3 discusses another pathway of grammaticalisation for the adnominal pronoun (apart from the one leading to a general determiner): in Djapu, the adnominal pronoun shows signs of having grammaticalised into a number marker. See also footnote 123 on Gooniyandi, and see Louagie & Verstraete (2015: 179–183) on incipient grammaticalisation affecting personal pronouns, which includes discussion of Djapu, Nyulnyul and Gooniyandi.

(180) Nyulnyul (McGregor 2011: 158)
 kinyingk bilabil bardangk-ukun riib arri layib
 DEF   leaf   stick-ABL   bad not good
 'The leaves of that tree are poisonous.'

Whatever the status of these elements in terms of word class (a detailed study is beyond the scope of this chapter), they are elements which seem to be specialised fillers of the determiner slot(s) posited for these languages.

3.2 'Ignoratives', interrogatives and indefinites

Another set of elements that are found in the determiner slot are interrogatives and indefinites. Most interrogatives can also occur on their own (i.e. as head of a NP), but there are no examples of interrogatives or indefinites occurring in a non-determiner modifier slot, i.e. when used adnominally they are specialised in the determiner slot.[119] This is not surprising considering their rather specialised semantics of (non-)identifiability (though in addition some forms can also mark different 'knowledge categories', cf. Mushin [1995: 7–20]). Interrogatives encode that the speaker is not able to identify the referent but that the hearer possibly can (and thus invite the hearer to provide this information). Indefinite markers encode, simply stated, that the speaker assumes the referent is not identifiable by the hearer.[120]

Australian languages often (though not always) take the interrogative and indefinite sense together in one element; these are the so-called 'ignoratives' or 'epistememes' (see e.g. Mushin 1995). Unfortunately, there is limited information on the adnominal use of these elements in my sample, especially in their indefinite sense (if it is at all possible to distinguish between the two senses). An example of an adnominal interrogative occurring in the determiner slot, can be found in (181) from Nyulnyul (McGregor 2011: 405). Two possible examples

---

119 In languages that have two determiner slots, the interrogative/indefinite form is usually (but not always) restricted to the initial slot. Note that for many languages, it is unknown whether interrogatives/ indefinites can be used as modifiers of nouns (e.g. it is not mentioned and there are no or few relevant examples in the grammars).
120 Davidse (2004: 522) argues that indefinites do encode identifiability, but of another type, viz. identifiability of type specifications: indefinites "instruct the hearer to conceptualize instances as corresponding to the categorization specified by the speaker" (cf. also Langacker 1991, Gundel et al. 1993).

of an ignorative used in the determiner slot in indefinite sense can be found in (182a) from Martuthunira and (182b) from Arabana/Wangkangurru.

(181) Nyulnyul (McGregor 2011: 136)
angka wamba juy
who man 2MIN.CRD
'Who are you?'

(182) a. Martuthunira (Dench 1994: 109)
Nhulaa kanyara thurlanyarrara ngaliwa-mulyarra kanarri-lha
near.you man poor.fellow 1PL.INCL-all come-PST
wawayi-l.yarra **nganangu juwayumarta-a.**
look.for-CTEMP someone.ACC doctor-ACC
'That poor man near you came to us looking for a doctor (assuming there might be one).'
b. Arabana/Wangkangurru (Hercus 1994: 299–300)
Nharla thangka-ka waru, kaRu mudlu-nga. Akuru
person sit-PST long.ago there sandhill-LOC over.there
ikara-nga Kuyani-na, **minha wangka nguRu**,
swamp-LOC Kuyani-EMPH what language other
Wardityi-karla-nganha, thadlu mathapurda, pinya.
Mulga-Creek-from only old.man vengeance.party
'Long ago some (Arabana Aboriginal) people stayed there on the sandhill. Further away over in the swamp there were Kuyani people, **speaking some language other (than ours)**; these were only grown-up men, they were a vengeance party.'

It is unclear whether the indefinites in the sample are used for specific, non-specific or even generic instances, or all of these.

3.3 Third person pronouns

A third person pronoun refers to non-speech act participants, and is further specified for number and possibly also gender. Lyons (1999: 26–32), following Postal (1970), attributes a feature of definiteness to personal pronouns (contrasting with indefinite pronouns such as *someone*), arguing for a close link between personal pronouns and definite articles. Himmelmann (1997:

218–219), by contrast, argues that the likeness between these two is only due to their common source,[121] and refers to the tracking use of personal pronouns as a possible starting point for their adnominal grammaticalisation.

Both definiteness and tracking are clearly related to identifiability, which explains why pronouns in adnominal use have their most natural position in the determiner slot, and indeed almost exclusively occur in this slot in the languages of the sample, as illustrated in (183)-(184).[122]

(183) Diyari (Austin 2011: 105)
nhani   mankarra nhintha pani
3SG.F.NOM girl.NOM   shame   none
'The girl is shameless.'

(184) Arrernte (Wilkins 1989: 499)
Elizabeth ne-ke   ingke utyene-kerte ante Elizabethe-ke
Elizabeth be-PST.COMPL   foot sore-PROP   and Elizabeth-DAT
newe-le   knge-ke   **crowbar ulthe-ntye**   **re-nhe**.
spouse-ERG take-PST.COMPL   crowbar press.down-NMLZ(heavy)   3SG-ACC
'Elizabeth had a sore foot and so her husband carried the heavy crowbar.'

This is confirmed in the functions identified for adnominal pronouns in the sample: they are markers of definiteness and/or specificity, or they have a function relating to discourse management. For example, structures like (183) from Diyari are analysed as follows by Austin (2011: 100): "Noun phrases in Diyari which contain a pronoun (...) are interpreted as definite, that is, the speaker assumes the hearer can uniquely identify the intended referent(s) of the NP (...). Third person pronouns without deictic or post-inflectional suffixes can be translated into English as 'the' when preceding other NP constituents."

---

121 Demonstratives are a typical source of personal pronouns, and therefore, it can sometimes be hard to distinguish between them. See Louagie & Verstraete (2015: 162–163) for some examples where third person pronoun forms appear to be demonstratives.
122 The adnominal use of third person pronouns is discussed in more detail in Louagie & Verstraete (2015). This paper identifies a determining function for these elements, based on distributional and functional properties, but remains undetermined about their precise syntactic status. This is resolved in the current chapter: their use in languages with a clear determiner slot is discussed in this section; additionally, third person pronouns can of course also be used adnominally in languages without a clear determiner slot (see section 4).

Functions relating to discourse management are, for instance, topic continuation in Guugu Yimidhirr (Haviland 1979: 156), and "reintroduction of major characters" in the narrative structure of Kala Lagaw Ya (Stirling 2008: 198). See Louagie & Verstraete (2015: 176–178) for more examples and a more detailed discussion.

There are only three languages in the sample where personal pronouns can also occur in another slot than a determiner one. In these non-determiner uses, it seems that other features of the pronoun's semantics are profiled, while the definiteness and tracking features are backgrounded. In Djapu (one of the Dhuwal varieties), it is the number value of the pronouns that is profiled, resulting in the use of dual and plural third pronouns as number markers. Number markers always immediately follow the head and take nominal (i.e. absolutive-ergative) case marking. This is illustrated in (185) in the form *walala-y*. In addition, adnominal pronouns in Djapu can also be used as determiners, in which case they occur in the initial slot and show the nominative-accusative alignment typical of pronouns. This is illustrated in (185) in the form *walal*. See Morphy (1983: 47–48) and Louagie & Verstraete (2015: 177–178) for a discussion. (See chapter 4, (71d) and (76) for other examples of the use of the pronoun as number marker.)

(185) Djapu (Morphy 1983: 48)
    nhina   *ŋanya*   *dhu_dakthu-n-a* *ŋunhi-yi*   *dhäruk*
    sit.UNM   3SG.ACC   learn-UNM-IMM that.ABS-ANA language.ABS
    walal   **mitjinarri-y**   **walala-y**
    3PL.NOM missionary-ERG PL-ERG
    'The missionaries are now learning this language.'

In the other two languages, Dalabon and Gooniyandi, the personal pronoun can be used as a qualifier. This use seems to relate partly to focus or emphasis, where the pronoun's inherent semantics of number or gender is potentially lost. This is also argued by Cutfield (2011: 54) for the Dalabon example in (186b), where the third person singular pronoun has "grammaticalized into a postnominal emphatic marker." In Gooniyandi, the adnominal personal pronoun *niyi*[123] regularly occurs in the post-head Qualifier slot, used when special focus is put on a previously mentioned referent (McGregor 1990: 270).

---

[123] McGregor (1990: 144–145, 170) analyses this form as a "distal endophoric determiner", i.e. as a part of speech separate from, but homophonous with, the personal pronoun. One reason is that they have different oblique forms. However, because there is a consistent pattern of personal pronouns functioning both as free forms and as determining modifiers in the NP across the sample, from the perspective of this study at least, this seems to be a systematic and motivated relation, rather than accidental homophony, possibly to be analysed in terms

(186) Dalabon (Cutfield 2011: 50–58, 113, 54)
    a. Template (G): (Deictic) Noun (Qualifier)
    b. bah **njel** *yibung* yala-h-bakah-ni-nj
        CONJ 1PL 3SG   1PL-R/A-many-sit-PST.IPFV
        'but there were a lot of us'

3.4 Demonstratives

If a language with a determiner slot has a separate category of demonstratives, they can always occur in this slot, but in some languages they can also occur as modifier outside this slot, although usually less frequently.[124] Both options reflect the inherent semantics of demonstratives. In broad terms, demonstratives specify that the speaker believes the hearer can identify the referent because (i) its location is specified (e.g. in terms of distance distinctions), (ii) it has been mentioned before, or (iii) it is shared knowledge (cf. Diessel 1999; Himmelmann 1997). In other words, the feature of identifiability is part of the semantics of demonstratives, and it is this aspect that is highlighted when the demonstrative is used in a determiner slot, its most natural position. However, the identifiability-component can also be backgrounded, and in such cases it is the location of the referent that is highlighted as an attribute of the referent, which explains its use in a non-determiner slot. This often happens in 'pointing' contexts, where the demonstrative literally points to a referent which is present in the context.

    The contrast between these two uses of the demonstrative can be illustrated with some examples from Gooniyandi. The NP template is given in (187a) (repeated from (159a)), an example of the regular determiner use of the demonstrative in (187b), and an example of qualifier use in (187c). This last example shows how the demonstrative is used in a 'pointing' context (and is even accompanied by lip-pointing); in this case, the demonstrative provides the location of the referent as an attribute. According to McGregor (1990: 267–268) this implies a predicative relationship: a paraphrase of (187c) might be 'the tobacco which is here'.[125] A similar

---

of grammaticalisation (see Louagie & Verstraete [2015: 183] for a more detailed argumentation, and see section 3.1 for a similar case in Nyulnyul).

124 In many, if not all, languages of the sample, demonstratives can also function as the 'head' of a NP (i.e. pronominal use). This, together with word order flexibility (both on NP level and on clause level) in some languages, sometimes makes it hard to distinguish adnominal and pronominal uses. I have followed the analysis of the author where available.

125 This is related to a general distinction between pre-head 'reference modification' and post-head 'referent modification' (Bolinger 1967; McGregor 1990: 267–268). Reference modification

functional analysis is given for Gaagudju (Harvey 2002: 316–320), Dalabon (Cutfield 2011: 122), and Limilngan (Harvey 2001: 112–113).

(187) Gooniyandi (McGregor 1990: 253, 254, 268)
    a. Template (G): (Deictic) (Quantifier) (Classifier) Entity (Qualifier)
    b. *ngoorroo garndiwirri yoowooloo gimangarna*
       that   two   man   bush:dweller
       'those two bushmen'
    c. **ngoonyjoo ngirndaji** *waranggila dina-yawoo*
       tobacco   this   I:hold:it   dinner-ALL
       'I keep this tobacco until dinner-time.' (accompanied by lip-pointing at the actual object)

3.5 Possessive pronouns

Together with demonstratives and personal pronouns, possessive pronouns are one of the most frequent fillers of the determiner slot in my sample, but they are also the least rigid of these three: they occur relatively frequently outside of this slot (both within and across languages), either in a qualifier slot (on a par with descriptive modifiers) or in a slot of their own. Thinking about an explanation for this flexibility, we can see that possessive pronouns encode identifiability, but they also contain a descriptive element, which is perhaps more salient here than, for instance, in demonstratives. A possessive pronoun marks the referent as identifiable because of its association with another, identifiable referent (see e.g. Rijkhoff 2002: 174–175; Willemse 2005; Langacker 1991), which is what motivates the use of possessive pronouns as determiners.[126] When used in

---

entails a selection of a subset of potential referents ("subclassification"), while referent modification involves a predicative relationship.

126 Himmelmann (2001: 839) notes that possessives can in some languages even grammaticalise further into articles. This happens, for instance, when the possessive is used in contexts beyond possession, like in (v), where the possessive affix has a larger situational use (referring to the river that is known to the whole speech community; the river is nobody's possession).

(v)   Indonesian (Himmelmann 2001: 839)
       *karena sungai-**nya** keruh*
       because river-3SG.POSS muddy
       '(We couldn't take a bath) because the river was muddy'

a qualifying slot, the fact that the referent is a particular person's possession is merely descriptive, in the same way that a descriptive adjective, for instance, attributes a particular quality to the referent.

The presence of these two components in the semantics of the possessive pronoun comes to the surface most clearly in languages that allow a choice between use of the possessive in either the determiner or the qualifier slot. An example is Martuthunira (cf. the NP template in (188a)). In the determiner slot, the possessive pronoun "narrows the reference of the phrase by contextual identification of the referent" (Dench 1994: 190), as in (188b) (repeated from (167b)), while in the Qualifier slot it "attribut[es] some characteristic to the referent of the noun phrase" (Dench 1994: 192), as in (188c).

(188) Martuthunira (Dench 1994: 189, 190, 192)
    a. Template (G):
       (Determiner) (Quantifier) (Classifier) Entity (Qualifier(s))
    b. **Nganaju yaan** *yungku-lha murla-a yartapalyu-u kanyara-ngara-a.*
       1SG.GEN wife give-PST meat-ACC others-ACC man-PL-ACC
       'My wife gave meat to the other men.'
    c. *Ngayu kanarri-lha nhuwana-a wangka-lu* **ngurra-ngka**
       1SG.NOM come-PST 2PL-ACC speak-PURP.SS camp-LOC
       nhuwana-wu-la *nyina-nyila-a.*
       2PL-GEN-LOC sit-PRS.REL-ACC
       'I came to talk to you sitting in camp, your camp'

3.6 Quantifiers and numerals

In most languages in the sample, quantifying elements have a distribution similar to attributive modifiers, or they have their own slot (see also chapter 4, section 2.1). However, there is also a handful of languages in the sample where they can occur in the determiner slot, and some more where they are flexible between the determiner slot and a non-determiner slot.

What is it in the semantics of quantifiers and numerals that allows them to be used not only as quantifiers or qualifiers, but also as determiners? At first sight, they simply encode the quantity of entities referred to, which explains their natural position in a separate quantifier slot. The quantity of entities can also be attributed to a referent, i.e. used as a descriptive feature, which explains its use as qualifier (similar to what we saw for qualifying demonstratives or possessive pronouns; see below for examples). The determiner use may seem hardest to explain, but if we look more closely, there is often some sense of identifiability in quantifiers as well, which can be profiled when used in a determiner slot. As argued by Davidse (2004), in an article that focuses on English but has much broader theoretical relevance, relative quantifiers select a subset of the set of potential referents (the 'reference set'). This selection may involve a part of the reference set (as with *most* or *some*), the whole set (as with *all*), or non-overlap (as with *none*) (Davidse [2004: 509, 521]; also referring to Langacker [1991] and Milsark [1977]). Since relative quantifiers compare the referent of the NP to a reference set, this implies that this reference set is identifiable (Davidse 2004: 521). Absolute quantifiers (like *many* or *two*), on the other hand, express cardinality or size (Davidse 2004: 509; cf. Langacker 1991, Milsark 1977), and are, according to Davidse (2004: 530), in complementary distribution with indefinite articles in English, in the sense that they can "ground" indefinite NPs. In other words, just like indefinite articles, absolute quantifiers "require the hearer to recognize instances as instances of T [i.e. type specifications, DL]," which implies that the general type or class of things referred to is identifiable (Davidse 2004: 530; cf. also section 3.2). Interestingly, absolute quantifiers can also act as non-determining modifiers in English, when combined with a definite determiner (such as a definite article), in which case they simply "count" the number of instances (Davidse 2004: 531).

Let us investigate this issue further, using two languages that can have quantifying elements both in a determiner slot and in a non-determiner slot as examples. The first is Umpila/Kuuku Ya'u (Hill 2018: 135–137), where quantifying elements are analysed as determiners, as can be seen in the template shown in (189a) (repeated from (126) and (171a)) and the example in (189b) – as the template suggests, anything to the left of the noun is a determiner. Interestingly, this example shows how the numeral is combined with a personal pronoun, which seems to be a definite determiner (i.e. marking or at least implying definiteness, based on the translation). Quantifiers can also, though much less frequently, occur in the modifier slot (Hill 2018: 141), where they "specify or emphasise the degree or number of the referent as an attribute, rather than employing the quantificational semantics as an identification tool" (Hill 2018: 141). For instance, in (189c), the numeral 'one' functions as description (as can be seen in the translation 'lone coconut'), not as determiner marking identifiability (Hill 2018: 141).

(189) Umpila/ Kuuku Ya'u (Hill 2018: 123, 135, 141)
    a. Template (G):

        (Det)   (Entity) $\begin{Bmatrix} \text{(Mod)} \\ \text{(Det)} \end{Bmatrix}$

    Det: [(Pron) (Dem) (Quant)], or [Poss.Pron]
    b. ***pula***   ***pa'amu***   ***ku'unchi***   *nhiina-na*
       3PL.NOM   two   old.woman   sit-NFUT
       'those two old women sat.'
    c. *nganan/*   ***kuunga nhi'ilama*** *paa'i-na*   *ngungku-lu*
       1PL.EXCL.NOM   coconut one   stand-NFUT DEM:DIST2-DM
       'Us lot (sat) by the lone coconut over there'

The second example is Gooniyandi (cf. the NP template in (190a), repeated from (159a) and (187a)), where number words can occur in the determiner slot, the quantifier slot or the qualifier slot. An example of each use can clarify the functional differences between them, which have been described in great detail by McGregor (1990) (further examples can be seen in (159) above). In (190b), the number word 'one' occurs in the determiner slot. Number words occur in this slot for instance when used "comparatively", either indicating – as in the example – "that reference is being made to precisely the same one, two, etc. entities already established" (i.e. similar to comparative modifiers, see section 3.7), or "to each member of the previously established set of entities" (i.e. like relative quantifiers *both* and *all* in English) (McGregor 1990: 258). The example also shows how in this use the number word is often suffixed with *-nyali* 'repetition' (McGregor 1990: 258). Example (190c) illustrates the more frequent use of number words in the quantifier slot, where it simply indicates the number of things referred to, in this way contributing to the selection of a set of referents (McGregor 1990: 270–271). Finally, in (190d), the number word occurs in the post-head qualifier slot, again indicating the number of things referred to, but here just as an attribute of the referent (McGregor 1990: 270–271). McGregor's work on Gooniyandi also shows that we need to be careful to distinguish between a determiner and a quantifying function, which can share the function of 'reference modification' (i.e. the selection of a referent). This distinction is not easy to make for many of the languages in the sample.

(190) Gooniyandi (McGregor 1990: 253, 258, 270, 272)
   a. Template (G):
      (Deictic) (Quantifier) (Classifier) Entity (Qualifier)
   b. *yoowarni-nyali mayaroo*
      one-REP   house
      'the same house'
   c. *milala   garndiwirri tharra ngaanggi*
      I:saw:it two   dog   yours
      'I saw two dogs of yours.' or 'I saw two of your dogs.'
   d. *ngarragi ngaloowinyi garndiwirri*
      my   son   two
      'the two of my sons, both of my sons'

Perhaps the most easily recognisable case of quantifying elements acting as determiners is the indefinite use of the numeral 'one'. This is only allowed in a few languages of the sample. An example is Bininj Kunwok (Evans 2003a: 244), which does not have a clear determiner slot, except in the case of the indefinite marker 'one, a certain', which has a clearly identifiable position (see further in section 4). It is used for "the explicit treatment of an entity as a new mention" (Evans 2003a: 247), and has a fixed initial position, while the numeral 'one' (same form) can occur either preceding or following the head. An example can be found in (191). Another example, from Gooniyandi, was given in (159b) in section 2.

(191) Bininj Kunwok (Evans 2003a: 681)
   "*Njamed,* **na-gudji nayin** *ga-yo!*"   *ba-mulewa-ni.*
   what   M-one   snake 3-lie.NPST 3PST-inform-PST.IPFV
   '"Hey, there's a snake here!" he'd say.'

3.7 Logical and comparative modifiers

This section concerns elements with meanings like 'same', 'another, other(s)', 'some, some other', 'other, a certain', etc. Some elements are purely comparative, while others have both a comparative and a non-comparative sense (hence the often-used label 'logical modifiers'). This non-comparative sense seems to involve indefiniteness (as with 'some') and/or specificity (as with 'a certain'), which can be linked back to the (semantic) discussions in section 3.2 and to some extent to section 3.6 above. As determiners relating to indefiniteness and specificity were discussed before, this section focuses on the comparative senses of these elements. Unfortunately, these modifiers are not often discussed explicitly in grammatical descriptions (especially in terms of their distribution in the NP). For 11 languages, there is a mention of these elements as having the same distribution as determiners or occurring in the determiner slot. It is unclear what the distribution of these elements is in other languages, although it is likely that they also often appear in non-determiner modifier slots.

The use of comparative modifiers in a determiner slot is not surprising if we look at their semantics, which again encode a feature of identifiability. The speaker believes the hearer can identify the referent because it is the same as one previously mentioned, or because it is another referent than the one mentioned before but, for instance, with similar characteristics. As argued by Breban & Davidse (2003) and Breban (2002, 2010) in studies on the determiner use of English and Dutch 'adjectives of comparison', this (post)determiner use is the result of a process of grammaticalisation (see also example (103) in chapter 5). It is unclear whether we can go this far for the languages of the sample; a discourse or corpus study of each individual language as well as diachronic information would be needed to answer this question. In a non-determiner modifier use, one can presume that the non-determining semantics is profiled, viz. the descriptive quality of difference or same-ness (cf. also the 'lexical' uses in English as described by Breban [2002]).

An example of a language where comparative modifiers are used in the determiner slot is Kayardild (Evans 1995a: 240). The NP template is given in (192a), and an example of *niid-a* 'same' filling the determiner slot in (192b). This element has a feature of identifiability as part of its semantics: "Here the speaker assumes that the hearer can identify the referent, because it is identical to something that has just been talked about" (Evans 1995a: 240).

(192) Kayardild (Evans 1995a: 235, 240; see also footnote 138)
    a. Template (G):
       (Determiner) (Number) (Qualifier) Entity (Modifier)
    b. (After talking about the responsibilities of the father-in-law):

rar-umban-ji	*dulk-i*	**niid-a**	**warngiid-a**	**mungkiji**
south-ORIG-LOC	country-LOC	same-NOM	one-NOM	own(NOM)
kardu	*kala-th*			
father-in-law.NOM	cut-ACT			

'In the south land (i.e. on Bentinck Island) the same one true father-in-law performed the circumcision.'

There are also examples of comparative modifiers occurring in the qualifier slot, e.g. (193b) from Uradhi (compare section 2.1 for an example of determiner use of 'other' in Uradhi). According to the template, 'other' is a qualifier in this position (viz. following the head), which would imply that it attributes a quality of being different to the referent, rather than having a determiner function. (Of course, in the absence of discourse information, this would need to be confirmed with a more detailed study.) There are also examples of these elements occurring as head in several languages (as in (193c)).

(193) Uradhi (Crowley 1983: 399)
(story of how the narrator signed up in the army and had to work as a cook)
a. *ayu*   *wa-ɣa:*   *wa-ɣa:*   *wa-ɣa:*   *ayi*
     1SG.NOM   cook-PST   cook-PST   cook-PST   food.ABS
     ula:mu   *umay-ku*
     3NSG.GEN.ABS   European-DAT
     'I cooked and cooked and cooked the food for the Europeans'
b. ***umaɲ***   ***uɲiṇa***   *ana-a:lu*   *ayi*   *ayu*   *u-ka:*
     European.ABS   other.ABS   go.PRS-HERE   food.ABS   1SG.NOM   give-PST
     'Other Europeans would come and I would give them food.'
     (. . .)
c. *ulaβa*   *ana-n*   ***uɲiṇa***   *ana-a:lu*
     3NSG.NOM   go-PST   other.ABS   come.PRS-HERE
     'They would go and others would come'

3.8 Conclusion

This section provided an overview of the categories of elements that can occur in determiner slots. Some elements more typically occur in determiner slots than others, which correlates with their semantics. For instance, articles and ignoratives/interrogatives/indefinites only encode the identifiability status of the referent and thus exclusively occur in the determiner slot when used adnominally (articles are even restricted to this adnominal use). Other elements, like third person pronouns and demonstratives, still have a prominent feature of identifiability in their semantics but also encode other things (like number or deictic contrast). Accordingly, they are most typically used as determiners, but they also allow non-determiner use in some languages. Finally, there are elements where the feature of identifiability is not very prominent, like quantifiers and numerals; accordingly, these are found only occasionally in a determiner slot.

Table 9 gives an overview of the typical behaviour of elements with respect to a determiner slot (for the languages that have a determiner slot or show mixed evidence of the first subtype, see 4.1 below). For each element, an indication is given of the number of languages in which it is specialised in a determiner slot, the number of languages in which it is flexible between determiner and a non-determiner slots in the nominal expression, and the number of languages in which it only occurs outside the determiner slot. Where a range is given, this indicates that it is uncertain whether the element is specialised in a determiner slot, or can also be used in a non-determiner position (i.e. is flexible). Obviously, the table does not include the following: (i) languages for which the analysis of a particular element as determiner is undecided or unknown, (ii) languages which do not have the relevant part of speech or do not allow it to be used adnominally, (iii) use as head of a nominal expression.

Table 9: Elements filling determiner slots: distribution in determiner versus other slots. See also map 13.

Element	Specialised in determiner slot	Flexible (determiner slot or elsewhere)	Only outside determiner slot	Total number of languages *
Article	1	/	/	1
Ignorative, interrogative, indefinite	28	/	/	28
Third person pronoun	29	3	/	32
Demonstrative	36–43	11–4	/	47
Possessive pronoun	23–26	9–6	7	39
Quantifier, numeral	3	4	18	25
Logical/ comparative modifier	4–6	8–6	7	19

*Total: languages which have the relevant part of speech and use it adnominally (and for which sufficient information is available).

This section has so far discussed each determiner type separately, but, as mentioned earlier, the co-occurrence of two, or even three, determiners is common in many Australian languages, and deserves some attention. Unfortunately, this phenomenon is rarely discussed in the grammatical descriptions, or only in broad terms, which means that my analysis is mostly based on examples found in grammars or texts rather than explicit analyses. I focus on distributional and general functional evidence, but this is a question that really needs more discourse-functional and especially diachronic work, which is beyond the scope of a typological study like this one. Nonetheless, there are some observations we can make about what determiner 'zones' in the sample look like.

First, there are different combinatorial possibilities. Commonly attested combinations are of a personal pronoun and a demonstrative, as in (194), and of a demonstrative and a possessive pronoun, as in (195). A demonstrative and a comparative modifier also often co-occur, as in (196).[127]

(194) Arrernte (Wilkins 1989: 121)
Nhenhe anteme kweke arntnerre-ntye ikwere-kerte
this now little crawl-NMLZR 3SG.DAT-PROP
***ayeye nhenhe re** ne-ke.*
story this 3SG.S be-PST.COMPL
'This then was about the crawling baby, that's what this story was.'

(195) Yalarnnga (Breen & Blake 2007: 30)
*Nhangu-ta nhawa nhina-ma **tjarru-nguta ngatha-langki-ya***
what-PURP 2SG remain-PRS this-LOC 1SG-LIG-LOC
mutu-ngka.
camp-LOC
'Why are you in my camp?'

(196) Umpila/Kuuku Ya'u (Hill 2018: 137)
***nga'a-lu** **wiiyama** pulthunu ngaachi-nguna-ma*
DEM:DIST1-DM another boy place-LOC-PRED
'That other boy was at the place.'

Second, determiner complexes display some clear ordering tendencies, which can also be seen in the examples above. Generally speaking, a personal pronoun occurs at the very edge, as in (194) above and (197a) below, although in a few languages, its position is interchangeable with that of the demonstrative, as in (197b). A demonstrative usually occurs further from the head than a possessive pronoun, as in (195) above and (198a) below, although some counter-examples have been found, as in (198b). Finally, comparative elements are always closer to the head than other determiners, as in (196) above and (199a) below, with Tiwi (199b) as the only exception (Lee 1987: 221–230). These ordering tendencies seem to reflect a cline from more general (furthest from the head) to more specific functions (closest to the head). This hypothesis is in line with Rijkhoff's Principle of

---

[127] It may not always be certain in a given example whether both elements are determiners or one element in fact has another function in the nominal expression (e.g. a qualifying one), especially in the case of less typical determiners like 'other'. In the example given here, however, it is certain: in Umpila, qualifying modifiers always follow the head noun (Hill 2018: 123).

Scope, which also includes a claim that 'discourse modifiers' (e.g. articles)[128] occur further from the head than 'localising modifiers' (e.g. possessives) (2002: 218–223, 229–231; see chapter 5, section 1).

(197) a. Anguthimri (Crowley 1981: 177)
 lu   dʳuʔa yeḍi   dʳe:ni-geni-ni
 he.s this   wind.s different-INCH-PST
 'The wind has changed (= is now different).'
 b. Mawng (Forrester 2015: 61)
 naka-pa   yanat–apa   wurakak awuni-arrikpa–n
 DEM:DIST.M-EMPH 3M.PRON–EMPH   crow   3M>3PL-ruin-NPST
 'That crow ruined them.'

(198) a. Bundjalung (Sharpe 2005: 98–99)
 munah-mba wangah bargan
 that.NVIS-LOC 2SG.POSS boomerang
 'that boomerang (that you had)'
 b. Duungidjawu (Kite & Wurm 2004: 45)
 guyum man ŋa-ri   miye-ni
 camp   DEM 1SG-GEN further.away-LOC
 'My camp is further away.'

(199) a. Gooniyandi (McGregor 1990: 259)
 niyi yaanya yoowooloo
 that other   man
 'that other man'
 b. Tiwi (Lee 1987: 225)
 yoni   awarra   murrukupuni
 other(M) that(M) country
 'that other country'

There are also some issues which cannot be resolved in a typological analysis, but that require deeper analysis of individual languages. One is structural: in some languages there is no clear boundary that separates the determiner zone from other modifiers. This is especially the case for some languages of type 2

---

[128] Rijkhoff also mentions comparative modifiers such as 'other' and 'same' as discourse modifiers (2002: 231). However, as just mentioned, these elements are found closer to the head than other determiners such as demonstratives in almost all of the languages of the sample (for which there is information on this combination of modifiers).

and type 4. An example is Kuuk Thaayorre, for which the NP template is given in (200) (in a simplified form, see also (130a)). All modifiers, except for the adjective, are potential determiners. Demonstratives and ignoratives are most likely part of a determiner zone, as these elements usually are in Australian languages, but it is unclear whether the quantifier and possessive pronoun are determiners here, as they are elements which are also often found in other functions across Australian languages.

(200) Kuuk Thaayorre (Gaby 2017: 195)
Template (G):
(N) ((Deg) Adj (Deg))* (Poss) (Quant) (DemPron/ IgnPron) (AdnDem)

Another interesting question concerns the functional motivation for using multiple determiners. A straightforward explanation is that each element contributes its own specific semantics (such as definiteness, possession or location), and in combination the elements 'determine' the NP, locating it in the context of the speech event or of the discourse. Interestingly, the use of multiple determiners also seems to correlate with certain functions in discourse. An example is the repetition of the same demonstrative in Ungarinyin, which serves to contrast two referents, as in example (201), where the name that JE mentions contrasts with the more specific names PN has in mind (Spronck 2015: 175–176).[129] In Bundjalung, the combination of a visible and a non-visible demonstrative serves to (re-)introduce a referent in (202) (Sharpe 2005: 51–52). It remains unclear for most languages, however, what the exact functions are of the use of multiple determiners (except perhaps in the case of demonstrative + comparative determiner), both in the NP and in the larger discourse context.

(201) Ungarinyin (Spronck 2015: 176)
(PN introduces the topic of stones (*rarrki di* 'rock') and states there are rocks with different names, prompting JE's suggestion in the first line.)
JE: *manjarn di*
stone N_W.ANAPH
'[You mean] *manjarn*, stone'

---

[129] Ungarinyin does not belong to one of the four types described in section 2, because almost all types of modifiers seem to have a flexible position with respect to the head (Spronck 2015: 37–38, 166, p.c.). However, more or less fixed 'determiner constructions' seem to occur, like NPs with the anaphoric pronoun or constructions with multiple determining elements (Spronck 2015: 167–168, 175–176, p.c.). See also section 4.1 and table 18.

PN: *aka* **kanda kanda w-alngun** *di* *wumankarr kanda*
   not.so N_W.DEM N_W.DEM N_W-name N_W.ANAPH black.rock N_W.DEM
   dinki munda kumbarru munda
   limestone N_M.DEM yellow.stone N_M.DEM
   'No, this name here: *wumankarr*, black rock, *dinki*, limestone and *kumbarru*, yellow stone'
JE: *ah yow*
   ah yeah
   'Oh, yeah'

(202) Bundjalung (Sharpe 2005: 51)
   Male munah baygal *yina-li-ja-hn.*
   that that.NVIS man lie.down-ANTIP-PST-IMPF
   'That man (previously referred to) was lying down.'

4 Languages without determiner slots

The previous sections identified a determiner slot or zone in half of the languages of the sample, and discussed the types of elements that can occur in it. In this section, I address the question of what happens in the other half of the sample. It is certainly not the case that all 50 languages show clear evidence against a determiner slot. For some of these languages there simply is not enough information available to decide either way (this is the case for 13 languages; see table 20 for an overview). Another group of 13 languages shows mixed evidence, and a set of 25 languages shows at least some evidence against a determiner slot (although in most languages, the available information is relatively limited, so additional evidence could perhaps modify these results). I now discuss these last two groups in more detail.

4.1 Languages with mixed evidence

There are 13 languages that show mixed evidence of different types. An overview can be found in table 18 (Appendix); see also map 13 above. These languages are mainly situated in the north-west of Australia, with a few other languages in the centre (Yankunytjatjara and Pitta-Pitta) and the northeast (Yidiny).

A subset of eight languages have a fixed edge position for one or two elements with a determining function (initial for seven languages), while all other modifiers (with determining or non-determining functions) have a flexible position relative to the head and usually also to each other.[130] These languages can be analysed as having an initial/final determiner slot with only one or two possible fillers. The difference with the languages discussed in section 2 is that not all elements with determining functions coalesce in one structural slot (which is why I take the more cautious approach and discuss them separately). In fact, what these languages illustrate is that the presence of a determiner slot may be restricted to certain NPs (which ties in with the idea of NP construal put forward in chapter 6); this is further discussed in chapter 8. This analysis was suggested for the indefinite 'one' in Bininj Kunwok in section 3.6.[131] Another example is Marra (Heath 1981: 64, 290; Baker 2008: 139), which was mentioned in section 3.1 as the only language of the sample that has an article. This article is the only element in the NP that has a fixed position, as shown in the NP template in (203). The Marra NP could be analysed as having an initial determiner slot, with the article and potentially even the demonstrative as fillers. Analysing the pre-head demonstrative as a determiner is supported by the fact that demonstratives more frequently precede the head, while attributive nominals and possessive pronouns usually follow. The post-head demonstrative would, under this analysis, function as qualifier (like the attributive nominal and possessive). This analysis cannot, however, be confirmed based on the available material, so I can only analyse the article as a determiner in this case, which is also why this language was not included in section 2.1.

(203) Marra (Heath 1981: 64, 290, examples)
　　　Template (W+E):　article – dem – head – attr N/poss
　　　　　　　　　　　(article) – attr N/poss – head[132]
　　　　　　　　　　　head – dem *(less frequent)*

The other five languages show a variety of features and different types of evidence, but it usually boils down to having positive evidence for one of the syntagmatic criteria and no information or conflicting evidence for the other one. Table 18 specifies the NP structure, a possible determiner analysis, and evidence for and against the identification of a determiner slot for each of these

---

130 Note that these are all type C languages in the analysis of NP constituency (see chapter 6).
131 Bininj Kunwok allows other determining elements to occur between the head and other modifiers, and thus also belongs to the category of languages with evidence against a determiner slot (see section 4.2; it is accordingly counted twice).
132 "The article (...) is omitted when the Genitive pronoun precedes the noun, and is often omitted when an adjective-like modifying noun precedes it (...)." (Heath 1981: 290)

five languages. I illustrate this situation with just one example, viz. Wardaman (Merlan 1994: 227–234, examples). The NP template is given in (204a), showing how all types of modifiers are flexible relative to the head, as illustrated in (204b-d). There is, however, a clear tendency for the demonstrative to occur in initial position, and a similar, but weaker tendency for the possessive pronoun (Merlan 1994: 229, 231). Additionally, if a demonstrative or possessive pronoun is combined with an adjective, the elements either occur on different sides of the head (as in (204b)) or on the same side with the demonstrative or possessive at the edge (as in (204c)) (Merlan 1994: 232–234). In other words, while the criterion of clear delineation from other modifiers is not met (because all modifiers are flexible), the edge criterion is fulfilled. In other words, the analysis of a determiner slot depends on whether the criterion of edge position is considered to be strong enough by itself (see section 2). If we were to identify a determiner slot despite the lack of clear delineation, there are two analytical options, viz. type 2 (determiner – head – modifier) or a variant of type 3 (determiner – modifier – head – modifier – determiner). In a type 2 analysis, the post-head demonstrative and possessive pronoun have a non-determiner function, while in a type 3 analysis they have a determiner function.[133]

(204) Wardaman (Merlan 1994: 227–234, 388; own glossing for b-c)
    a. Template (W+E): dem/poss – A – N – A;
                      interr – N;
                      N – dem/poss;
                      num – N or N – num
    b. *nana*   *yijad*   *wurren*
       that.ABS big.ABS child.ABS
       'the big child'

---

[133] This is in fact a more general problem: when can we analyse post-head use of demonstratives (or other elements) as having a non-determiner function, and when can we posit a second, post-head determiner slot? This of course depends on the exact function of the modifiers in post-head position, which can only be decided for each language individually, following a detailed study of NPs. For some languages, it seems that the function of the post-head demonstrative is still determiner-like: their use is associated with certain discourse contexts, which points to a function similar to the 'topic determiners' Stirling & Baker (2007) described (cf. chapter 5, section 1). In Wardaman, for instance, the post-head demonstrative is associated with a shift in participants (Merlan 1994: 245). Other possible reasons to posit a second determiner slot could be a clear, systematic distribution between both determiner positions in terms of use (as argued for Umpila/Kuuku Ya'u by Hill [2018]), or a functional similarity between the two slots.

c. *nana   wurren   yijad*
   that.ABS child.ABS big.ABS
   'the big child'
d. ***mernden nana***   *dimana-warra-yi*   *ø-we-ndi*
   white.ABS that.ABS horse-having-ADV 3SG-fall-PST
   'that whitefella fell down with his horse'

4.2 Languages without a determiner slot

There is a group of 25 languages that do show at least some evidence against a determiner slot: in other words, they have negative evidence on one of the criteria, and no information or negative evidence on the other criterion. An overview is given in table 19 (Appendix); see also map 13 above. These languages are mainly situated in the north-west of Australia (including several Ngumpin-Yapa, Mindi and Gunwinyguan languages – though not all) and in New South Wales. The group mostly consists of languages where all types of modifiers can occur on either side of the head, i.e. where the delineation criterion is not met. Note that the descriptions of these languages have generally not focused on functional roles in the NP, or meaning changes between different positions, so there is a good chance that some languages may change categories should such detailed studies be carried out.

In six of these languages, modifiers with determining functions (such as demonstratives) are not clearly delineated from other modifiers and do not necessarily occur at the edge, i.e. they violate both of the syntagmatic criteria discussed in section 2. In other words, while there may be elements that mark identifiability, they do not coalesce into a single morphosyntactic slot or category. An example is Jaminjung (Schultze-Berndt 2000: 44–45; Schultze-Berndt & Simard 2012: 7), where the co-occurrence of a demonstrative and adjective on the same side of the head can involve either order of modifiers (205a-b).[134] A similar example was given in (162) above for Ngan'gityemerri/Ngan'gikurunggurr.

---

[134] However, note that determining elements always occur to the left of other modifiers (even though both types of modifiers have flexible positions). This is why Schultze-Berndt (2000: 44–45) actually argues in favour of a determiner slot for Jaminjung. In my analysis, I do not judge this to be a sufficient fulfilment of the criterion of delineation. However, suppose we do allow this as a valid argument, then the language is still potentially problematic in terms of the edge criterion. Now if the edge criterion is discarded (see section 2 on the relative strength), then Jaminjung would be the only language of the sample showing evidence for a clear non-edge determiner slot.

(205) Jaminjung (Schultze-Berndt 2000: 45)
   a. A: ***thanthu*=gun mangurrb-bari wirib**,
        DEM=CONTR   black-QUAL   dog
     B: *Ngayin*   *burrb gani-bida*...
        meat/animal finish 3SG>3SG-FUT:eat
     'A: that black dog – B: -it will eat up the meat'
   b. *ngayin*=gun thanthu burrb gani-bida   ngarrgina\
     meat=CONTR DEM   finish 3SG>3SG-FUT:eat 1SG.POSS
    ...***wirib thanthu mangurrb-bari***[135]
     dog   DEM   black-QUAL
     'it will eat up that meat of mine ... that black dog'

The other 19 languages in this group also show flexible word order for all modifiers, but there is limited or no information on multiple-word NPs (and consequently also on the edge criterion).[136] In Garrwa, for instance, all types of modifiers are flexible with respect to the head (Mushin 2012: 103–104, 256–257, examples; see also the discussion in chapter 6, section 3.1.3). Apart from a few examples, no information is available on the relative order of modifiers. There is, however, a clear preference for demonstratives and possessive pronouns to occur in initial position, but this is analysed as a pragmatic tendency rather than a syntactic one (Mushin p.c.). An alternative analysis, viz. that there is an initial determiner slot and that its typical fillers can occasionally occur in another modifier position, also seems plausible, but needs more evidence.

5 Conclusion

This study has identified a determiner slot or zone in at most 50 Australian languages (with less evidence for 22) out of my total sample of 100 languages. This determiner slot/zone is manifested in four different ways, each showing edge

---

135 Note that Jaminjung in this case still follows Greenberg's universal 20 (1966: 87; see also Dryer's discussion on this universal [2007b: 111–113]). This universal states that when a demonstrative and an adjective both precede the head, the demonstrative always comes first; when they both follow the nominal head, the demonstrative usually comes last, but it can also come between the head and the adjective. In other words, the word order N-dem-A is not unexpected cross-linguistically.

136 For some languages, a few examples of multiple-word NPs are attested, showing the demonstrative further from the head than the adjective, or a combination of a demonstrative and a possessive pronoun as modifiers, but the evidence is too limited to properly identify a determiner slot.

position, and (mostly) clear delimitation from other modifiers. We speak of a 'determiner zone' when determiners co-occur, which creates determiner complexes. In most languages, this determiner slot or zone is optional, in the sense that bare nouns can be used for all values in the system (e.g. definite or indefinite, specific or non-specific).

The function of the elements occurring in the determiner slot can broadly be described as 'marking the identifiability status of the referent'. There are a few elements in the sample which seem to encode only that, and are specialised in this slot, such as the article in Marra. Most other elements, however, encode other things as well. Accordingly, they can occur either as determiner or as another type modifier (or even as head), thus profiling or backgrounding the feature of identifiability. Preferences vary: some elements, such as demonstratives or personal pronouns, are more typically used as determiners, with an inherently more prominent feature of 'identifiability', while other elements, such as quantifiers, are typically used as non-determiner modifiers, highlighting another feature that is more prominent (such as quantity or quality). Other elements hover in between these two, having more equally distributed features of 'identifiability' and description in their semantics. In any case, what this shows is that in the majority of cases examined in this study, there is no necessary link between categories or parts of speech and determiner slots.

As mentioned in chapter 5, section 1, this many-to-many relation between word classes and functional roles has also been amply demonstrated for other languages, including 'classic' determiner languages like Spanish, English and Swedish (see chapter 5, section 1 for examples). What this analysis has added, however, is a systematic overview of the degree and distribution of flexibility across languages. This overview also included some less typical cases like quantifiers and numerals, which suggests proposals for a general link between determination and quantification (like Davidse 2004) may also be relevant cross-linguistically.

8 Conclusion

In this book, I have studied NP structures in Australian languages, based on data from a sample of 100 languages. I have analysed these structures from two different perspectives, each with its own aims and focus: a general survey in Part I, and a more in-depth analysis in Part II.

Part I offered a general survey of NP features, using the Australianist and the general typological literature, as well as data from the grammars of the sample, in order to develop a consolidated account of the literature. My hope is that this survey can serve as a basis for further research for both fieldworkers and typologists. The survey was organised in terms of five basic functional domains, viz. classification, qualification, quantification, determination, and the overall question of NP constituency. For each of the five domains, the survey tried to situate the Australian material in a broader typological context, bring out the main lines of research in the available literature, and highlight the most important questions that remain. The survey of classification was the most extensive, as this is the aspect of NP structure that has been studied most intensively in the Australian literature. Even here, however, there are a few questions that remain, most prominently the syntactic analysis of generic-specific constructions, and the role of class variation and perspectivisation in noun class systems. The surveys of qualification and quantification were somewhat less extensive, focusing mainly on the question of word class status for qualification, and number marking for quantification, the two issues that have received most attention in the literature. Some of the questions to come out of these surveys include the relative weight of the various criteria used to posit a separate class of adjectives, the delimitation between syntactic qualification and compounding, and the relative lack of attention to semantically more specific means of quantification, like quantifiers and numerals. The surveys of determination and NP constituency were the briefest, bringing to light the largest gaps in the literature. Determination is only rarely discussed in the Australianist literature, especially as concerns the syntactic status of determiners, and NP constituency, while frequently mentioned, has not really been tested beyond a handful of languages.

There is one more general issue that recurred in several parts of the discussion: many Australian languages seem to have a relatively flexible relation between category and functional structure in the nominal domain. This flexibility is reflected in two ways. On the one hand, Australian languages commonly have structurally defined categories, i.e. categories that are only distinct in terms of their syntactic distribution, but not in terms of morphological properties. This is the case for the adjective-noun distinction in a fair number of the languages, where an adjectival subclass of nominals can only be distinguished in terms of distinct syntactic behaviour. Another good example is nominal classifiers, which are in most (if not all) languages not a separate category, but are rather defined in terms of the particular position they hold in a classifying construction (cf. Wilkins 2000). On the other hand, quite a few Australian languages also have underdetermined categories, which can be used in different functional roles in the same language. For instance, in several languages, modifiers like quantifiers, possessive pronouns, demonstratives and even third person pronouns are flexible between functional roles as determiners and as modifiers (see chapter 7). Also, about one third of the languages has a flexible 'nominal' class, whose members can function both referentially and attributively (see chapter 3). In both situations, viz. distributionally defined categories and underdetermined categories, functional structure plays a vital role. Of course, there are also examples of specialised categories: some languages have a clearly separate adjective class, a few languages have a specialised article, and most languages have ignoratives, demonstratives and third person pronouns that are specialised in a determiner functional role (when used in the NP). In several languages, category and functional structure do seem to overlap quite neatly in the NP overall (e.g. Kuuk Thaayorre, Umpithamu, Umpila), but it is the flexible relation between the two in many other languages that has drawn most attention in the literature. The extent to which similar flexibility is attested cross-linguistically is unclear, but it could shed more light on where Australian languages stand and how different they really are from other languages around the world.

Part II presented a more in-depth analysis of the two major questions to come out of the survey. Chapter 6 took up the question of (the lack of) NP constituency, which has featured prominently in both the theoretical and typological literature, especially in relation to Australian languages. I used a set of concrete criteria for constituency, like word order, locus of case marking, diagnostic slots and prosody, to show that there is no strong evidence against NP constituency in my sample. In fact, about two thirds of the language show clear evidence in favour of NP constituency, with particular 'hotbeds' in central Australia and Cape York (and nearby languages in the Gulf of Carpentaria). More interestingly, the results also show that the other languages, which have flexible order of nominal elements and thus seem to conform to received ideas about absence of NPs, do not in fact lack NP constituents completely. Most of these languages do allow construal as NP, for instance when occurring in diagnostic slots, with phrasal marking, or in other specific cases (e.g. with particular determiners). These results led to the conclusion that it may be more interesting to investigate where and how languages allow NP construal, than to categorise entire languages according to a simple yes-no distinction. This idea was also applied to the analysis of discontinuous structures, which I argued are a separate construction type, in addition to other types of construal a language may have available (i.e. the structural possibilities for elements that jointly establish reference). Chapter 7, finally, investigated the syntactic status of determining elements. I used a combination of syntagmatic and paradigmatic parameters to show that a determiner slot can be identified in about half of the languages of the sample, across the continent (manifested in four ways), while there is evidence against the presence of a determiner slot in about a quarter of the languages. For the languages that have determiner slots, I also surveyed the types of elements that can occur in such a slot. These elements are often not specialised, but tend to occur both as determiner and as other type of modifier (e.g. a qualifier or number marker). This can be linked to their semantics: they often encode not only a feature of identifiability, but other features as well, like number, possession or deictic information. Each of these features can be highlighted when occurring in a particular slot. This part of the analysis also brought to attention some elements that are somewhat under-studied as determiners, like personal pronouns, or less expected in determiner uses, like quantifiers.

The analysis in this study has also raised a number of questions for further research. A first question concerns the expansion of the dataset to include complex NPs. The analysis in this study was limited to simple NPs, but complex NPs invite a whole range of new questions, like what the semantic range of embedded NPs is, how to delimit these from apparently similar constructions (like secondary predication), and especially also what this tells us about the status of NPs. I briefly commented on adjective and quantifier phrases in chapters 3 and 4, but other types of complex NPs are also attested in Australian languages, e.g. embedded NPs with adnominal case-marking (see e.g. Dench & Evans 1988), different types of complex possessive structures, and inclusory constructions (Singer 2001). The availability of complex NPs can also be used in extending arguments about NP constituency (see chapter 6).

Another question that has not been touched upon yet concerns the link between patterns of determination and patterns of constituency. There are several suggestions in the literature that there is such a connection, from different theoretical traditions. From a generative perspective, for instance, Gil (1987) argues that 'configurational' languages (e.g. with a fixed NP-internal word order) have obligatory marking of definiteness, while 'non-configurational' languages (e.g. with flexible NP-internal word order) do not have such obligatory marking (see also Lyons [1999: 154–156] for a comment on this). From a constructional and diachronic perspective, Himmelmann (1997: 156) argues that languages with NPs with looser internal structures do not have strongly grammaticalised determiners ("D-elements"), but not the other way round – i.e. languages with clearly structured NPs do not necessarily have grammaticalised determiners. Building on these ideas, Schultze-Berndt & Simard (2012: 1025) also link the absence of obligatory determiners (especially definite articles) in a particular language to the availability of discontinuous structures in the same language. Focusing on Himmelmann's hypothesis, a quick comparison between the results of chapters 6 and 7 shows that it does seem to largely hold for the languages of the sample. For most languages with some evidence against NP constituency (i.e. with flexible word order, especially in the north and northwest of Australia), no determiner slot (and accordingly no specialised determiners) could be identified, whereas languages with clear evidence in favour of NP constituency include both languages with a clear determiner slot and languages without one. Obviously, as amply demonstrated in chapter 7, the presence of a determiner slot in a particular language does not necessarily imply that this language has specialised determiners (i.e. there is no one-on-one relation between function and class). On the basis of my data, I can only point out some cases of specialised, and thus more grammaticalised, determiners. Personal pronouns in adnominal use, for instance, are almost always specialised in the determiner slot in languages which have one. In some languages, such pronouns even show further signs of grammaticalisation, like semantic bleaching (originally '3SG' forms are used for different number values), semantic generalisation (both animate and inanimate referents are allowed), and/or paradigmatisation (the use of the pronominal determiner is obligatory in specific contexts, and its absence is a paradigmatic choice) (Louagie & Verstraete [2015: 178–183]; see chapter 7, sections 2.5 and 3.1 for an example from Arrernte). Having said this, there are also some interesting cases which at first sight seem to contradict Himmelmann's hypothesis. Some languages with good evidence against NP constituency (viz. flexible order in the NE) do seem to have determiners which are grammaticalised to some extent, in that they are the only elements to have a fixed position in the NE: these cases include the article in Marra (see chapter 7, sections 3.1 and 4.1), the third person pronoun in Wambaya (see table 18), the indefinite 'one' in Bininj Kunwok (see chapter 7, sections 3.6 and 4.1) and five more (see table 18). Note that these eight languages are unrelated, but all situated in the north(-west) of the country, with four in the Top End. In my analysis, however, these are not really exceptions to the hypothesis. It is important to keep in mind that NP constituency is not an all-or-nothing phenomenon, and interestingly, this seems to be true for determiner slots as well: a language like Bininj Kunwok was analysed as allowing the structural possibility of NP units only in marginal ways, one of which involves precisely a determiner slot (viz. with an indefinite 'one'). These are of course only first impressions, and this is a question that needs much more work.

In addition to typological questions, the analysis also raises a number of questions that require other methods, specifically discourse-based studies of individual languages. This is especially the case for further study of determination and NP constituency. First, as already mentioned, my analysis of NP constituency led to the idea that it may be more interesting to typologise languages on the basis of where and how they allow NP construal, than on the basis of its mere presence or absence. In this analysis, I proposed a rough typology of three types (simply called A-B-C, see chapter 6): two extremes, one with default NP construal and one with no or only marginal NP construal, and a third type in the middle. This is of course just a starting point, based on secondary sources (grammars) rather than a direct analysis of primary materials (texts). In order to develop a more fine-grained typology, the focus would need to be on individual languages, and we would need to make inventories of available construals in the nominal domain and analyse corpora of texts to determine how and where each construal is used, and then bring together the results across languages. I have already hinted at a range of potential construals (i.e. structural possibilities) in chapters 6 and 7, such as classic NP constructions, specific determiner constructions, discontinuous structures, and motivated alternations between phrasal and word marking. Other relevant construals include motivated alternations between word orders, dislocated nominal expressions, repetitions, and ellipsis. In addition, structures with different types of heads also need to be taken into account: compare, for instance, Hill's (2018: 139) suggestion that different types of heads prefer different types of modifiers in Umpila. Not all languages will have the same range of construals available, and even if they do, they may be implemented quite differently in discourse. By exploring these questions, we could develop a more fine-grained typology of NP structures, based on what construals languages have available and how these carve up the nominal domain.

A second question that requires further discourse work concerns the semantics of determiners. So far, I have defined this quite broadly as 'marking the identifiability status of the referent' (following the general literature on this topic), and I have presented some general ideas about the semantics of individual determining elements, and how this affects their use as a determiner or as another type of modifier. Individual grammars provide a range of semantic descriptions, however, and there are also some general ideas about semantically distinct classes of determiners (like Stirling & Baker's [2008] 'topic determiner'). Discourse-based work is required to pinpoint the precise semantics of determiners in individual languages, and to determine how this fits in with larger categories of determines. This type of work has been done for a number of languages, as mentioned in chapter 7, but for many others it has not, and it would be interesting to see whether the analyses that are available in the literature are more broadly applicable across the sample.

Finally, there is also the question in how far my findings in the domains of NP constituency and determination can be extrapolated outside Australia. For the question of constituency, as mentioned in chapter 6, I believe that an alternative typology, based on types and uses of nominal construal rather than its simple presence or absence, can (and should) also be applied to languages outside Australia. There are some indications that this may be a good way to go. For instance, the idea that certain types of modifiers tend to be more tightly 'integrated' in the NP than others has been established for a range of languages, either depending on the type of modifier (as in several South-American languages [Krasnoukhova 2012: 177–181], see chapter 5, section 2), or on its position relative to its semantic head (as in Dutch, where post-head modifiers are argued to be syntactically independent [Van de Velde 2009: 51–129]). Another relevant point is the specific functional motivation of discontinuous structures, which has been demonstrated for several languages around the world (e.g. Polish [Siewierska 1984], see chapter 5, section 2; Fox [Dahlstrom 1987], Swampy Cree [Reinholtz 1999: 208], and Croatian [Fanselow & Ćavar 2002], all cited in [Schultze-Berndt & Simard 2012: 1038]; see also [Rijkhoff 2002: 258–259] for more references). In chapter 7, I discussed the absence of a one-to-one relation between word class and functional role in the domain of determiners. Again, this is cross-linguistically quite common. Possessives are a particularly well-known case; they can have qualifier, determiner or (sub)classifier functions in different languages (see chapter 5, section 1). There are other examples as well, like certain types of adjectives that have (or have acquired) determiner functions (e.g. Davidse et al. 2008; Van de Velde 2010). Given that languages differ quite widely in terms of the organisation of word classes (see Hengeveld et al. [2004] and Hengeveld & Rijkhoff [2005]; see chapter 3, section 1), the extent to which they allow flexibility of word classes across different functions in the NP presumably also differs quite widely. From a more theoretical perspective, this also ties in with general questions about the relation between constructions and word classes, as discussed in various types of construction grammar (for instance Croft 2001).

Appendix

As mentioned in the introduction to Part II, decisions about each individual language are brought together in tables (one for each parameter studied), with reference to the precise part of the sources on which the analysis is based. All of the tables are put together here, so as not to interrupt the flow of the text too much.

1 Tables relating to chapter 6

Table 10: Word order in the NE. Languages analysed in terms of functional classes in the grammatical descriptions are marked with * after the language name.

Fixed order (21 languages)	
Alyawarra	(Yallop 1977: 116–117; no information about longer NEs)
	<u>note</u>: Reverse order of dem possible (Yallop 1977: 112), but no examples found in grammar
Anguthimri	(Crowley 1981: 162, 178; limited information about longer NEs)
	<u>note</u>: Reverse order of dem in one example (Crowley 1981: 177)
Arrernte	(Wilkins 1989: 102–103)
	<u>note</u>: Some modifiers "more fluid" with respect to each other, but no examples found in grammar
Dalabon*	(Cutfield 2011: 50–58, 90–96, 113, 122–123, examples)
Dyirbal	(Dixon 1972: 60–61)
Gaagudju*	(Harvey 2002: 315–320)
Gooniyandi*	(McGregor 1990: 253)
Kayardild*	(Evans 1995a: 235; Round 2013: 133–135)
Kuuk Thaayorre	(Gaby 2017: 195–197)
	<u>note</u>: Third person pronouns are flexible at either edge (but are more commonly found at the left edge) (Gaby 2017: 213). Gaby (2017: 216) analyses these pronouns as being syntactically apposed to the NP, but also shows evidence for a grammaticalisation pathway towards integration in the NP as determiners (see also chapter 7, section 2.4).
Lardil	(Klokeid 1976: 11, (few) examples)
Limilngan*	(Harvey 2001: 112)
Marrithiyel	(Green 1989: 48; Green 1997: 246)
	<u>note</u>: Num and dem/pron flexible with respect to each other
Martuthunira*	(Dench 1994: 189–198)
Ngarrindjeri	(Yallop 1975: 28; Bannister 2004: 66; no information about longer NEs)

Table 10 (continued)

Nyulnyul*	(McGregor 2011: 400–405)
Nyungar*	(Douglas 1976: 44–45)
Panyjima*	(Dench 1991: 186)
Tiwi*	(Lee 1987: 221–230)
Umbuygamu	(Sommer 1998: 22, 28; Ogilvie 1994: 39; examples throughout both sources; no information about longer NEs or about the position of adnominal demonstratives)
Umpithamu*	(Verstraete 2010)
Uradhi	(Crowley 1983: 371)

Restricted flexibility (44 languages)

Limited in frequency (19 languages)

Atynyamathanha	(Schebeck 1974: 61, examples; no information about longer NEs or about the position of adnominal demonstratives)
Biri	(Terrill 1998: 29, 45–47; no information about longer NEs)
Bundjalung	(Sharpe 2005: 98, examples)
Dhuwal (at least Djapu)	(Morphy 1983: 83–87 for Djapu) note: Wilkinson (1991: 124) only mentions a "lack of strict ordering conventions" for Djambarrpuyngu and further refers to Morphy (1983).
Kala Lagaw Ya	(Ford & Ober 1987: 10; Ford & Ober 1991: 124–126, 130; Stirling 2008: 177; examples throughout all sources)
Karajarri	(Sands 1989: 65–66; no information about longer NEs or about the position of adnominal demonstratives)
Kugu Nganhcara	(Smith & Johnson 2000: 419–420)
Malakmalak	(Birk 1976: 146–148, Hoffmann p.c.; limited information about longer NEs)
Mathi-Mathi/ Letyi-Letyi/ Wati-Wati	(Blake et al. 2011: 79, examples; no information about longer NEs)
Ndjébbana	(McKay 2000: 293–294)
Ngiyambaa	(Donaldson 1980: examples)
Oykangand	(Hamilton 1996: 2, 6; Sommer 1970: examples)
Pitta-Pitta	(Blake 1979b: 214, p.c.; limited information about longer NEs and about the position of qualifying modifiers)
Rimanggudinhma	(Godman 1993: 78; no information about longer NEs)
Warray	(Harvey 1986: 59, 246)
Yanyuwa	(Kirton 1971: 10, examples; Kirton & Charlie 1996: examples)
Yawuru	(Hosokawa 1991: 80–81, 443, 472, 491, 740)
Yidiny	(Dixon 1977: 247–249)
Yingkarta*	(Dench 1998: 50–51)

Table 10 (continued)

Flexibility of determining elements at the edges (17 languages)	
Alawa	(Sharpe 1972: 2, examples)
	note: Variable order, partly based on emphasis and length of nominal expression according to Sharpe (1972: 2), but clear tendencies from examples
Arabana / Wangkangurru	(Hercus 1994: 284, examples)
Diyari	(Austin 2011: 100, examples)
Djabugay	(Patz 1991: examples)
Duungidjawu	(Kite & Wurm 2004: 95–96, examples; limited information about longer NEs)
Emmi	(Ford 1998: 103, 138, 148, examples; no information about longer NEs)
Guugu Yimidhirr	(Haviland 1979: 104, examples)
Kuku Yalanji	(Patz 2002: 119–121, 202, examples)
Matngele	(Zandvoort 1999: (few) examples)
Paakantyi	(Hercus 1982: 98–101, examples)
Tharrgari	(Klokeid 1969: examples; no information about longer NEs or position of qualifying modifiers)
Umpila/Kuuku Ya'u *	(Hill 2018: 123)
Worrorra	(Clendon 2000, 2014: examples)
Yalarnnga	(Breen & Blake 2007: 57–58, examples; no information about longer NEs and limited information about the position of qualifying modifiers)
Yandruwandha	(Breen 2004a: 47, examples)
Yankunytjatjara	(Goddard 1985: 47, 49, 55–56, 60)
	note: The demonstrative can also occur immediately following the generic noun, where it has a 'restrictive' sense (next to initial or final position, where it has a 'non-restrictive' sense). This analysis differs from Bowe's (1990: 30–36), who mentions the same ordering possibilities for Pitjantjatjara, but associates initial demonstratives with contrast and demonstratives immediately following the head noun with 'emphatic' demonstrative semantics. Final demonstratives are considered to be in apposition, and to express simple definiteness.
Yir Yoront	(Alpher 1973: 281–289)

Flexibility of adjective-like modifiers; determining elements fixed at one edge (8 languages)	
Gathang	(Lissarrague 2010: 48, 103–104, examples; no information about longer NEs)
	Note: Reverse order of dem in one example (Lissarrague 2010: 121)

Table 10 (continued)

Mangarrayi	(Merlan 1989: 29, 51, examples; limited information about longer NEs)
Mawng*	(Forrester 2015: 45)
Mayi	(Breen 1981b: 63)
Nhanda	(Blevins 2001: examples; no information about longer NEs)
Wadjiginy	(Ford 1990: 88, examples; Tryon 1974: 209; no information about longer NEs)
	note: According to Tryon (1974: 208), adjectives have a fixed position, but I rely on the most recent source for my categorisation
Wajarri	(Douglas 1981: 240–244)
	note: Only the quantifying adjective is flexible, the rest of the modifiers has a fixed order. Also, younger speakers often switch to A-N order instead of the regular N-A.
Yindjibarndi	(Wordick 1982: 160, examples)
	note: Wordick (1982: 160) claims that the adnominal demonstrative is flexible but tends to come in initial position, but I have found only one example in final position

Flexibility (30 languages)

Anindilyakwa	(van Egmond 2012: 303)
Bardi	(Bowern 2012: 331–336, p.c.)
Bilinarra	(Meakins & Nordlinger 2014: 103–104)
Bininj Kunwok	(Evans 2003a: 243–244, examples)
Burarra	(Green 1987: (few) examples; Carew p.c.)
Dharrawal/ Dharumba/ Dhurga/Djirringanj	(Besold 2012: 287–289; no information about longer NEs)
Djinang	(Waters 1989: 195–196)
Garrwa	(Mushin 2012: 103–104, 256–257, examples)
Giimbiyu	(Campbell 2006: (some) examples; no information about longer NEs)
Gumbaynggir	(Eades 1979: 313, examples)
Jaminjung	(Schultze-Berndt 2000: 44–45; Schultze-Berndt & Simard 2012: 7)
Jaru	(Tsunoda 1981: 95, p.c.)
Jingulu	(Pensalfini 2003: examples)
Marra	(Heath 1981: 64, 290)
Miriwung	(Kofod 1978: 52, examples)
Muruwari	(Oates 1988: 51, 55, 82, 87–88, examples; limited information on longer NEs)
Ngan'gityemerri/ Ngan'gikurunggurr	(Reid 1997: 267)
	note: Fixed head first, which could also be seen as an edge-preserving type of flexibility
Nyangumarta	(Sharp 2004: 301–313)

Table 10 (continued)

Rembarrnga	(Saulwick 2003: 81; McKay 1975: 67–70)
Ritharngu	(Heath 1980: examples; no information about longer NEs or about the position of attributive modifiers)
Ungarinyin	(Rumsey 1982: 58, 138; Spronck 2015: 37–38, 166, p.c.)
Walmajarri	(Richards 1979: 99, examples; Hudson 1978: examples; no information about longer NEs)
Wambaya	(Nordlinger 1998a: 130–136)
Wangkajunga	(Jones 2011: 232, 235–240; no information about longer NEs)
Wardaman	(Merlan 1994: 228–235)
Warlpiri	(Hale et al. 1995: 1435)
Warrongo	(Tsunoda 2011: 347–352)
Warumungu	(Simpson 2002: 42, examples; no information about longer NEs)
Wirangu	(Hercus 1999: 81, examples; no information about longer NEs)
Yuwaalaraay	(Williams 1980: 96–97; Giacon 2017: 364–369)

Unknown (5 languages)
Grammar does not allow us to make generalisations concerning word order

Bunganditj	(Blake 2003: 52, examples)
Dharumbal	(Terrill 2002: 48, examples)
Margany/ Gunya	(Breen 1981a: 335, examples)
Wathawurrung	(Blake 1998 ed.: 84, examples)
Yorta Yorta	(Bowe & Morey 1999: 106, examples)

Table 11: Locus of case marking (in simple nominal expressions; core case markers).

Only phrasal case marking (18 languages)

Arrernte	(Wilkins 1989: 102)	right edge
Atynyamathanha	(Schebeck 1974: examples)	right edge
Bardi	(Bowern 2012: 169–170)	left edge
Dalabon	(Cutfield 2011: 42, 84)	head
Kala Lagaw Ya	(Ford & Ober 1987: examples; Ford & Ober 1991: examples; Stirling 2008: examples)	right edge note: Unclear if word marking is also possible
Kugu Nganhcara	(Smith & Johnson 2000: 385)	right edge
Kuuk Thaayorre	(Gaby 2017: 195)	right edge note: No marking on adnominal demonstratives
Malakmalak	(Birk 1976: 147–148)	right edge
Marrithiyel	(Green 1989: 2, 48)	right edge

Table 11 (continued)

Ngan'gityemerri/ Ngan'gikurunggurr	(Reid 1990: 326, examples)	right edge note: Unclear if word marking is also possible
Nyungar	(Douglas 1976: 44)	right edge
Umbuygamu	(Ogilvie:1994 63; Sommer 1998: 22)	right edge; sometimes head (initial)
Umpila / Kuuku Ya'u	(Hill 2018: 125)	right edge note: Demonstratives cannot inflect for case
Umpithamu	(Verstraete 2010)	right edge note: Unclear if demonstratives can inflect for case
Wadjiginy	(Ford 1990: 90, 91)	right edge note: Also example of left-edge marking
Yankunytjatjara	(Goddard 1985: 47)	right edge
Yawuru	(Hosokawa 1991: 81)	left edge

Phrasal and word marking (39 languages)

Phrasal marking as main option (18 languages)

Alyawarra	(Yallop 1977: 116–118)	(i) right edge ("normally") (ii) each element ("not ungrammatical")
Anguthimri	(Crowley 1981: 178, examples)	(i) head (= left edge) (ii) each element
Arabana / Wangkangurru	(Hercus 1994: 114, 282–284)	(i) right edge (ii) last two or all elements (emphatic)
Diyari	(Austin 2011: 97–99)	(i) right edge (ii) each element ("special emphasis or contrast")
Djinang	(Waters 1989: 196)	(i) one element (unclear which one) (ii) each element (most frequently when two elements; likelihood depending on case marker: PERL, ALL, ABL, LOC > ERG, INSTR, GEN > DAT, OR > ACC)
Gooniyandi	(McGregor 1990: 173–174, 276–284; McGregor 1989)	(i) one element (ii) each element (avoiding ambiguity, emphasis, contrast; usually two-word NPs, clause-initial or clause-final, once per clause)

Table 11 (continued)

Mathi-Mathi / Letyi-Letyi/ Wati-Wati	(Blake et al. 2011: 112)	(i) right edge (ii) each element (Dem-N)
Ngarrindjeri	(Yallop 1975: 29)	(i) only on modifier (dropped from head N) ("frequently") (ii) each element
Nyulnyul	(McGregor 2011: 398, 419)	(i) left edge (ii) each element (prominence to each element)
Oykangand	(Hamilton 1996: 19–20; Sommer 1970: 17)	(i) right edge (ii) also left edge or each element (Dem)
Paakantyi	(Hercus 1982: 100)	(i) right edge (ii) each element (when Dem/Interr-N)
Rembarrnga	(McKay 1975: 71)	(i) prefixes left edge, suffixes right edge ("normally") (ii) any or all elements <u>note:</u> Author only tested this for N+A sequences
Tharrgari	(Klokeid 1969: 13)	(i) only one noun ("generally"; unclear which one) (ii) each element (examples)
Uradhi	(Crowley 1983: 334, 371–372)	(i) head (ii) each element (but A "rarely" take case)
Wajarri	(Douglas 1981: 241; Marmion 1996: 33)	(i) right edge ("very common") (ii) each element
Warray	(Harvey 1986: 252–253)	(i) right edge (ii) also each element or left edge (for LOC and GEN)
Wirangu	(Hercus 1999: 48)	(i) right edge (ii) each element ("emphatic or stilted")
Yandruwandha	(Breen 2004a: 101)	(i) right edge (ii) one element other than right edge or each element ("much less commonly")
Yir Yoront	(Alpher 1973: 291–292; Alpher 1991: 67–69)	(i) right edge (case postpositions only option; suffixes main option) (ii) each element (suffixes minor option) (with the exception of pronouns)

Table 11 (continued)

Phrasal marking as minor option (11 languages)

Bilinarra	(Meakins & Nordlinger 2014: 106)	(i) each element (ii) head (rare, analysed as language shift phenomenon)
Djabugay	(Patz 1991: 290)	(i) each element (ii) right edge (casual speech)
Duungidjawu	(Kite & Wurm 2004: 27–28, 37, 96, examples)	(i) each element (ii) right edge (COM) note: According to Kite & Wurm (2004: 96), case is marked "only to head of NP or optionally to other elements"; analysis above based on examples
Garrwa	(Mushin 2012: 55)	(i) each element ("greatly prefer [red]") (ii) one element (unclear which one)
Kuku Yalanji	(Patz 2002: 119)	(i) each element (ii) right edge ("occasionally" but corrected by speakers when editing their own narratives)
Margany/ Gunya	(Breen 1981a: 337)	(i) each element: "usual practice" (ii) but "not obligatory" note: Unclear which element is marked when there is phrasal marking
Ngiyambaa	(Donaldson 1980: 232)	(i) each element (ii) one element (two-word nominal expressions; "WHICH one seems to be a matter of taste." (Donaldson 1980: 232))
Walmajarri	(Hudson 1978: 17; Richards 1979: 95)	(i) each element (ii) one element (fast or conversational speech; unclear which one)
Warumungu	(Simpson 2002: 87–88; Simpson & Heath ms: §4.3)	(i) each element (ii) right edge ("occasionally")
Yindjibarndi	(Wordick 1982: 142)	(i) each element (ii) one element (unclear which one)
Yingkarta	(Dench 1998: 52)	(i) each element (ii) right edge (rare, two-word NEs)

Table 11 (continued)

Phrasal marking as one of the options (unclear or strictly depending on word class)
(10 languages)

Dharrawal/ Dharumba/ Dhurga/ Djirringanj	(Besold 2012: 157)	(i) first or last element (ii) each element note: Unclear what main option is
Guugu Yimidhirr	(Haviland 1979: 102–104)	(i) right edge ("often") (ii) each element
Jaminjung	(Schultze-Berndt 2000: 43)	(i) any one element (ii) more than one element note: Probably conditioned by differences in information structure
Jingulu	(Pensalfini 2003: 176)	(i) right edge (ii) left edge (dem attracts case marking) (iii) each element
Karajarri	(Sands 1989: 69)	(i) left edge (ii) each element note: Unclear what main option is
Mayi	(Breen 1981b: 63–64)	(i) any one element (ii) more elements note: Personal pronouns and numerals unmarked in two-word nominal expressions
Muruwari	(Oates 1988: 7, 55, 62, 67, 68, 82)	(i) right edge (N-A; dem-N (ERG); A-N (ERG); LOC, ALL/DAT) (ii) left edge (LOC, ALL/DAT) (iii) each element (Num+N (ERG); N+N (ERG); dem-N(ERG) minor; A-N (ERG) minor; LOC, ALL/DAT (emphasis)) note: Depends on kind of modifier and case marker note: Unclear for longer NEs
Nhanda	(Blevins 2001: 129)	(i) one element (usually but not always right edge) (ii) each element
Ritharngu	(Heath 1980: examples)	(i) right edge (ii) each element
Warlpiri	(Hale et al. 1995: 1434; Nash 1986: 159–160)	(i) right edge (ii) each element

Table 11 (continued)

Only word marking (26 languages)		
Alawa	(Sharpe 1972: 70)	
Biri	(Terrill 1998: 14, examples)	note: Adjective and possessive pronoun remain unmarked
Bundjalung	(Sharpe 2005: examples)	
Dhuwal	(Morphy 1983: 47, 85–86; Wilkinson 1991: 124)	note: Optional marking of quantifying nominals (often unmarked), hypothetical and indefinite determiners (usually marked), dual and plural pronoun number markers
Dyirbal	(Dixon 1972: 106, examples)	
Gathang	(Lissarrague 2010: 102)	
Gumbaynggir	(Eades 1979: examples)	note: Demonstratives cannot inflect for case
Jaru	(Tsunoda 1981: 94–95, p.c.)	note: Ergative marking on demonstratives *yala/yalu* and *murla/murlu* can be left out.
Kayardild	(Evans 1995a: 233)	
Lardil	(Klokeid 1976: 11)	
Mangarrayi	(Merlan 1989: 51)	
Marra	(Heath 1981: 64)	note: Article cannot take case inflections; demonstratives only optionally inflect for case
Martuthunira	(Dench 1994: 60, 189)	note: Complementising case shows head marking
Nyangumarta	(Sharp 2004: 302–303)	
Panyjima	(Dench 1991: 125)	
Pitta-Pitta	(Blake 1979b: examples, p.c.)	
Wambaya	(Nordlinger 1998a: 131–132)	note: Possessive phrase unmarked
Wangkajunga	(Jones 2011: 10)	
Wardaman	(Merlan 1994: 105)	
Warrongo	(Tsunoda 2011: 342, 361)	note: Possessive pronoun unmarked
Wathawurrung	(Blake 1998 ed.: 84)	
Yalarnnga	(Breen & Blake 2007: examples)	
Yanyuwa	(Kirton & Charlie 1996: 10; Kirton 1971: 10)	
Yidiny	(Dixon 1977: 247)	
Yorta Yorta	(Bowe & Morey 1999: 82)	
Yuwaalaraay	(Giacon 2017: 364, p.c.)	note: Possessive phrase unmarked

Table 11 (continued)

No case marking for core cases (phrasal or word for other cases; options discussed in third column) (13 languages)

Anindilyakwa	(van Egmond 2012: 1, 302–304)	for LOC, ABL, ALL, INS: – modifier, or if no modifiers on head – all elements (no further comment)
Bininj Kunwok	(Evans 2003a: 230)	optionally on any one element for "non-core cases" note: Some dialects use ABL or INS as an optional ergative marker.
Burarra	(Green 1987: 16–18, examples)	LOC/INS prefix (Green 1987: 17–18), marked on all elements of the NE
Emmi	(Ford 1998: 103)	right edge for INS, DAT/ALL, ABL/CAUS, COM, LOC
Gaagudju	(Harvey 2002: 263)	unknown for DAT/LOC clitics
Giimbiyu	(Campbell 2006: 36, 58)	right edge for LOC and INS
Limilngan	(Harvey 2001: 71, 113)	optionally on right edge for OBL, LOC, SOURCE, COM and PRIV note: Unclear if word marking is also possible; based on very limited data (Harvey 2001: 113)
Matngele	(Zandvoort 1999: 42)	unknown note: INS is (rarely) used as an agentive marker
Mawng	(Singer 2006: ch. 4, 83)	left edge for LOC (preposition)
Ndjébbana	(McKay 2000: 155)	unknown for ABL, PURP, object of hunt
Tiwi	(Lee 1987: 100, 235–236)	left edge for LOC (preposition)
Ungarinyin	(Rumsey 1982: 58, 61; Spronck 40, p.c.)	right edge for "non-grammatical cases"; sometimes other element or each element
Worrorra	(Clendon 2014: 18, 256–272, examples)	unknown for LOC

Unknown / other (4 languages)

Bunganditj		
Dharumbal		note: Only one example of multi-word nominal expression; it shows right edge marking
Miriwung		
Rimanggudinhma		

Table 12: Diagnostic slots.

Diagnostic slots		
Bilinarra	(Meakins & Nordlinger 2014: 102)	bound pronouns following the first constituent note: Bound pronouns can also have other positions, but only in marked cases (Meakins & Nordlinger 2014: 4)
Bunganditj	(Blake 2003: 38)	subject pronominal clitic following initial interrogative (or verb) note: Unclear if these pronouns also follow NEs apart from interrogatives
Garrwa	(Mushin 2012: 6–7, 36–37; Simpson & Mushin 2008; Mushin p.c.)	pronominal cluster in 2nd position, but usually verb-initial basic word order
Jaru	(Tsunoda 1981: 107)	catalyst *nga-* plus enclitic pronouns in 2nd position
Kuuk Thaayorre	(Gaby 2017: 154, examples)	pronominal clitics following the first constituent (or the verb/auxiliary) (emergent)
Lardil	(Klokeid 1976: 261)	clitics following the first constituent, e.g. *thada* 'meanwhile', *tha* 'now, then, after that'
Ngarrindjeri	(Bannister 2004: 64)	reduced pronouns attached to first element of clause note: No examples following a multiple-word NE
Ngiyambaa	(Donaldson 1980: 130, 236, 237)	pronominal or particle enclitics attached to topic of sentence, which is always at the left of the clause
Ritharngu	(Heath 1980: 43, 90)	pronominal enclitics, attached to first constituent of clause
Wajarri	(Marmion 1996: 66)	pronominal clitics following first element note: No examples following a multiple-word NE
Walmajarri	(Hudson 1978: 18)	verbal auxiliary "as second word"; both examples where it follows the first word of a multiple-word NE (e.g. Hudson 1978: 89, sentence 44) and where it follows the whole multiple-word NE (e.g. Richards 1979: 97, example 4)
Wambaya	(Nordlinger 1998a: 131)	auxiliary following first constituent

Table 12 (continued)

Wangkajunga	(Jones 2011: 9, 233–235, 245–246)	pronominal clitics following first constituent; sometimes in third position: (i) when the sentence starts with a conjunction followed by a pause (and then another constituent + clitics), (ii) when the clitics follow a verb which is not in first position (this may reflect English word order)
Warlpiri	(Hale et al. 1995: 1431; Simpson 2007)	auxiliary following first constituent, or sometimes second constituent (in specific discourse contexts [Simpson 2007]) <u>note</u>: Exceptionally, the auxiliary can appear in first position (see Laughren et al. 2005, referred to in Simpson 2007: 492).
Warumungu	(Simpson 1998: 725; Simpson 2002: 80)	pronominal cluster following first constituent
Wathawurrung	(Blake 1998 ed.: 77, 82)	subject pronominal clitic following first element, but usually verb-initial word order <u>note</u>: Unclear if first word or first constituent
Yankunytjatjara	(Goddard 1985: 37, 61)	optional pronominal clitics following first constituent; particles *puṯa* 'what do you say' and *kunyu* quotative
Yingkarta	(Dench 1998: 5)	optional bound pronouns following the first constituent
Yir Yoront	(Alpher 1991: 38)	pronouns enclitic to first constituent of clause <u>note</u>: No examples following a multiple-word NE

Table 13: Prosody.

Prosody		
Atynyamathanha	(Schebeck 1974: 61)	intonation distinguishes between one or more NPs (no further comment)
Bilinarra	(Meakins & Nordlinger 2014: 102–103)	- absence of pause - same intonational phrase
Dalabon	(Cutfield 2011: 56, 133)	pause for apposition
Dhuwal (only Djapu)	(Morphy 1983: 140)	pause for apposition
Djinang	(Waters 1989: 196)	pause for apposition

Table 13 (continued)

Gaagudju	(Harvey 2002: 316, 319)	same intonation phrase
Garrwa	(Mushin 2012: 255)	prosodic unithood note: Members of a nominal group may also occur across intonation boundaries
Gooniyandi	(McGregor 1990: 284)	same intonation or tone unit
Jaminjung	(Schultze-Berndt & Simard 2012: 1021–1025)	NP coincides with prosodic phrase
Kuuk Thaayorre	(Gaby 2017: 196)	- absence of pause - single intonation contour - primary stress peak
Limilngan	(Harvey 2001: 112)	single intonation unit
Marra	(Heath 1981: 64)	pause for apposition
Martuthunira	(Dench 1994: 189)	single intonation contour
Paakantyi	(Hercus 1982: 99)	pause for apposition
Umpila/ Kuuku Ya'u	(Hill 2018: 126)	- single intonation contour - absence of pause
Wajarri	(Douglas 1981: 243)	apposition: "after a non-final intonational juncture (rising pitch)"
Wangkajunga	(Jones 2011: 233)	- absence of pause - single intonation pattern
Wardaman	(Merlan 1994: 225–226)	single tone unit
Warray	(Harvey 1986: 252)	same intonation unit

2 Tables relating to chapter 7

Table 14: Determiners: languages of type 1.

Type 1: determiner(s) – HEAD – modifier(s)		
language	possible fillers of determiner slot/ zone	reference
clear evidence		
Dalabon*	pron, dem, log	(Cutfield 2011: 50–58, 91–96, 113, 122–123, examples)
Dyirbal	dem, poss co-occurrence (example): poss – dem	(Dixon 1972: 60–61, examples)
Gaagudju*	interr-indef, dem, (poss)pron, num 'one', log co-occurrence: dem – log	(Harvey 2002: 316–320)

Table 14 (continued)

Limilngan*	interr(-indef), dem, poss, ?num, log	(Harvey 2001: 112–113, examples)
Uradhi	pron, dem, poss/possNP, log *competition & co-occurrence: pron/ dem – poss/possNP*	(Crowley 1983: 371, 377, examples)
mixed evidence		
Dhuwal (at least Djapu)	indef, pron, dem, poss, inal.poss, ?num/ quant, ?log, ?loc *co-occurrence: pron – dem*	(Morphy 1983: 83–87, examples)
Ndjébbana	interr, pron, dem, ?num, log	(McKay 2000: 293–294, examples)

Table 15: Determiners: languages of type 2.

Type 2: determiner(s) – modifier(s) – HEAD – modifier(s)		
language	possible fillers of determiner slot/zone	reference
clear evidence		
Gooniyandi*	indef, pron, dem, poss/possNP, num, indef-log, NP-ABL *co-occurrence: any – indef-log*	(McGregor 1990: 253–276)
Martuthunira*	?interr-indef, dem, poss, log	(Dench 1994: 189–193, examples)
Mawng*	?interr, pron, dem *co-occurrence: pron – dem or reverse*	(Forrester 2015: 45)
Mayi	interr, pron, dem *competition: pron / dem / interr*	(Breen 1981b: 63)
Nyulnyul*	interr, pron, dem, poss, log *co-occurrence: pron or dem – log*	(McGregor 2011: 399–413)
Panyjima*	dem, ?num, ?log *co-occurrence: dem – num or log* *(unclear if separate quantifier slot)*	(Dench 1991: 186)
Tiwi*	pron, dem, poss/possNP, ?quant/num, log, 'definites' *co-occurrence: log – def – dem – quant/num/log* *(cut-off point det vs. mod unknown)*	(Lee 1987: 221–230)

Table 15 (continued)

more limited or mixed evidence		
Biri	interr, dem, ?poss	(Terrill 1998: 29, 45–46, examples)
Bundjalung	dem, poss, ?num, log *co-occurrence: dem(VIS) – dem (NVIS); dem – poss (ambiguous example of reverse order)* *(unclear if separate quantifier slot)*	(Sharpe 2005: 98, examples)
Gathang	pron, dem, poss	(Lissarrague 2010: 39, 103–105, examples)
Mangarrayi	interr-indef, dem, poss (but rarely used)	(Merlan 1989: 29–30, 51, examples)
Nhanda	dem, ?poss	(Blevins 2001: 77, 83, examples)
Wadjiginy	indef, pron, dem	(Tryon 1974: 209; Ford 1990: examples)
Yanyuwa	interr, pron, dem, ?poss, log *co-occurrence: dem – log – poss;* *competition: dem / poss*	(Kirton 1971: 10, examples; Kirton & Charlie 1996: examples)
Yindjibarndi	interr(-indef), dem, num	(Wordick 1982: 160, examples)

Table 16: Determiners: languages of type 3.

Type 3: determiner(s) – HEAD – modifier(s) – determiner(s)		
language	**possible fillers of determiner slot/zone**	**reference**
clear evidence		
Arabana/ Wangkangurru	interr(-indef?) (only initial), pron, dem, poss	(Hercus 1994: 284, examples)
Diyari	interr-indef (only initial), pron(-deictic), poss/possNP, loc *co-occurrence (initial): pron(-deictic) – poss/possNP*	(Austin 2011: 100, examples)
Djabugay	dem, poss	(Patz 1991: examples)
Guugu Yimidhirr	pron, dem, poss, quant, log *co-occurrence (initial): pron – any*	(Haviland 1979: 104, examples)

Table 16 (continued)

Language	Description	Source
Kuku Yalanji	interr-indef, pron (only initial), dem, poss, ?quant/num	(Patz 2002: 119–121, 202, examples)
Matngele	dem *(note: position poss unknown)*	(Zandvoort 1999: examples)
Paakantyi	interr-indef (only initial), dem, poss ! *modifiers pre-head: determiner(s) – modifier(s) – head – determiner(s)*	(Hercus 1982: 98–101, examples)
Umpila / Kuuku Ya'u*	?interr-indef, pron, dem, poss, quant, log *co-occurrence (initial): pron – dem – quant; competition: poss / rest*	(Hill 2018: 126–140)
Worrorra	pron, dem, poss *co-occurrence (examples): dem & poss: one in each slot (either way), ana dem – def dem – head, def dem – head – contextual dem*	(Clendon 2000, 2014: examples)
Yandruwandha	interr(-indef) (only initial), pron(-deictic), poss	(Breen 2004a: 47, 67–68, examples)
Yir Yoront	pron, dem *most common co-occurrence: head – dem – pron*	(Alpher 1973: 281–289, examples)

more limited or mixed evidence

Language	Description	Source
Alawa	dem, poss (only final) ! *modifiers pre-head*	(Sharpe 1972: examples)
Anguthimri	pron (only initial), dem *co-occurrence (examples): pron – dem – head, pron – head – dem*	(Crowley 1981: 162, 178, examples)
Duungidjawu	interr-indef (only initial), pron (only initial), dem, poss, ?num *co-occurrence (examples): head – dem – poss, 'one' – dem – head*	(Kite & Wurm 2004: 95–96, examples)
Emmi	interr (only initial), dem, ?compound modifier containing numeral	(Ford 1998: 138, 148, examples)
Nyungar*	dem(=pron) (only final), poss (only initial)	(Douglas 1976: 44–45)
Wajarri	?pron (only initial), dem (only final), poss,[1] possNP (only initial), ?quant *co-occurrence: poss – quant (initial), quant – dem (final)*	(Douglas 1981: 240–244, examples)

Table 16 (continued)

Yalarnnga	interr (only initial), pron (only initial), dem, poss, num (only initial) *co-occurrence (examples): dem – poss – head, dem – num – head* <u>note:</u> position of A uncertain; only one example of adnominal use, Blake p.c.	(Breen & Blake 2007: 57–58, examples)

[1]The status of the possessive pronoun is not entirely clear: the NP template in Douglas (1981: 241) suggests that the possessive only occurs in initial position and together with the head noun forms the head of the NP. However, some examples have also been found of a possessive pronoun following the head noun. The categorisation of Wajarri as a type 3 language depends on how the possessive pronoun is analysed: if it has a determiner function, we have an initial determiner slot (which can, incidentally, also include a quantifier), in addition to a final slot containing a demonstrative and possibly also a possessive pronoun.

Table 17: Determiners: languages of type 4.

Type 4: HEAD – modifier(s) … determiner(s) OR determiner(s) … modifier(s) – HEAD			
language	position head	possible fillers of determiner slot/zone	reference
clear evidence			
Arrernte	initial	?interr, pron, dem, ? quant, ?indef 'one' *co-occurrence: ?quant – dem – pron* *(cut-off point mod vs. det unknown)*	(Wilkins 1989: 102–103)
Kayardild*	final[2]	interr, indef, pron, dem, poss/possNP, log, compass *co-occurrence: dem – compass, 'same'*	(Evans 1995a: 235–241; Round 2013: 133–135)
Lardil	final	?interr, ?pron, dem, ? quant *(cut-off point mod vs. det unknown)*	(Klokeid 1976: 11, examples)

Table 17 (continued)

Marrithiyel	initial	dem, poss, ?num competition & co-occurrence: num – dem/poss or reverse	(Green 1997: 246)
Umpithamu*	initial	pron, poss competition & co-occurrence: num – poss/pron (cut-off point mod vs. det unknown; position dem unknown)	(Verstraete 2010)

more limited or mixed evidence

Kala Lagaw Ya	final (usually)	pron, dem, poss, ?num co-occurrence: pron – dem or reverse, dem – poss – ?num (cut-off point mod vs. det unknown)	(Ford & Ober 1987: 10; Ford & Ober 1991: 124–126; Stirling 2008: 177; examples throughout all sources)
Kugu Nganhcara	initial	?interr-indef, ?pron, dem, ?poss, ?poss/COM/PRIV.NP, ?quant co-occurrence: quant – poss/COM/PRIVNP- dem (cut-off point mod vs. det unknown)	(Smith & Johnson 2000: 419–421, examples)
Kuuk Thaayorre	initial	interr-indef, ?pron, dem (pron or adnom), ?poss, ?quant co-occurrence: poss – quant – dem.pron – interr-indef – adnom. dem (cut-off point mod vs. det unknown)	(Gaby 2017: 195, 209–216)
Oykangand	initial	?pron, dem, poss	(Hamilton 1996: 2, 6; Sommer 1970: examples)
Yingkarta*	final (usually)	pron, dem, poss	(Dench 1998: 50–51)

[2]Round (2013: 133–135) and Evans (1995a: 235) differ in their analysis of the Kayardild NP. Evans proposes a post-head modifier, which Round (2013: 135) discards because it "fails to restrict the function of the nominal word which fills it." In both analyses, there is a clear initial determiner slot.

Table 18: Determiners: languages with mixed evidence.

Fixed determiner slot for one element			
Bininj Kunwok	indef 'one' (cf. also table 19 below)	initial	(Evans 2003a: 243–244, examples)
Burarra	interr, pron	initial	(Green 1987: 22, examples; Carew p.c.)
Djinang	pron note: Possibly also the demonstrative, as it has a tendency to precede the head	initial	(Waters 1989: 195–196)
Giimbiyu	interr	initial	(Campbell 2006: 53, examples)
Jaru	interr note: Possibly also dem and pron, as they prefer to precede the head	initial	(Tsunoda 1981: 95, p.c.)
Marra	article	initial	(Heath 1981: 64, 290)
Ungarinyin	interr, anaphoric pron note: The anaphoric pronoun rarely precedes the head noun; this occurs with a highlighting function (Spronck 2015: 175). Spronck (2015: 167–168; 175–176) also identifies certain 'determiner constructions', which are combinations of determining elements that together have specific discourse functions	final	(Rumsey 1982: 58, 138; Spronck 2015: 37–38, 166–168, 175–176, examples, p.c.)
Wambaya	interr-indef, pron note: The personal pronoun can also switch position with the initial demonstrative. The other modifiers can precede or follow the head. When they precede the head, they have a fixed order: dem– poss. pron – num – A, which reminds us of the languages of type 4 (i.e. with an initial determiner slot). It is unclear how to analyse the post-head modifier if we would want to maintain the type 4 analysis.	initial	(Nordlinger 1998a: 130–136, examples)

Table 18 (continued)

Other mixed evidence		
Pitta-Pitta	Template (W+E): head – attributive; poss – head (or head – poss); head – pron (or pron – head)[3] Potential determiner slot: Type 3 with poss and pron as fillers (each having a preferred position) – Evidence in favour of determiner slot: Delimited from attributive modifiers in the sense that they are flexible, while attributives (possibly) have a fixed order. – Evidence against determiner slot: No information about edge position; limited information on position of attributive modifiers (possibly also flexible)	(Blake 1979: 214, p.c.)
Wardaman	Template (W+E): dem/poss – A – N – A; N – dem/poss; interr – N; num – N or N – num Potential determiner slot: Variant on type 3 with dem and poss as fillers – Evidence in favour of determiner slot: Edge position for dem / poss – Evidence against determiner slot: All types of modifiers flexible (i.e. no clear delineation)	(Merlan 1994: 227–234, examples)

Table 18 (continued)

Yankunytjatjara	Template (W+E): dem – generic – dem – specific – descriptive A(s) – quant – def – dem; poss – N or N – poss; non-attributive modifier – N ('syntactic compound'); def – pron(head); N – interr Potential determiner slot: Type 3 with dem, poss and def (pron) as fillers – Evidence in favour of determiner slot: Edge position; clear delineation from other modifiers – Evidence against determiner slot: Dem can also occur immediately following the generic noun (but there is a functional difference, see table 10)	(Goddard 1985: 47, 49, 55–56, 60, examples; see also Bowe 1990: 30–36 on Pitjantjatjara)
Yawuru	Template (W+E): pers.pron – N ("always") dem – N ("usually") N – poss.pron ("almost always") attr.mod. – head or head – attr.mod. interr – N Potential determiner slot: Type 2 (with pron, dem and rarely poss as fillers, and post-head elements as qualifiers) OR variant on type 3 (with pron, dem and poss as fillers, having different preferences for a particular determiner slot) – Evidence in favour of determiner slot: Determining elements seem to be generally more fixed than attributive modifiers (i.e. there is some delineation) – Evidence against determiner slot: Most types of modifiers flexible; no information on edge position	(Hosokawa 1991: 80, 443, 472, 491, 740, examples)

Table 18 (continued)

Yidiny	<u>Template (W):</u> interr-indef – N; poss – N *(almost always)*; dem – N or N – dem or "sometimes between other elements"; N – A/num/log (or num – N *(rare)*) <u>Potential determiner slot:</u> Type 1 or type 3 (both with interr-indef, poss, dem and possibly num as fillers) – <u>Evidence in favour of determiner slot:</u> Determining elements delimited from other elements (one can precede the head, the other cannot) – <u>Evidence against determiner slot:</u> No information on edge position, and demonstrative can also occur between other elements	(Dixon 1977: 247–249)

[3]Note that pronouns almost always include a deictic suffix. One of these seems to have grammaticised in that it is used as the unmarked form when used adnominally (Blake 1979: 193–194; see also Louagie & Verstraete 2015: 163, 184).

Table 19: Determiners: languages with (some) evidence against a determiner slot.

Potential determiners can occur between the head and other modifiers	
Bardi	(Bowern 2012: 327–336, 768, p.c.) <u>note:</u> Poss always at one of the edges; post-head modifier is non-restrictive or contrastive; poss, dem and pron seem to be in complementary distribution
Bininj Kunwok	(Evans 2003a: 243–244, examples) *(cf. also table 18)*
Jaminjung	(Schultze-Berndt 2000: 44–45; Schultze-Berndt & Simard 2012: 7) <u>note:</u> Dem always precedes other modifiers, most commonly dem – mod – head – mod or head – dem – mod
Muruwari	(Oates 1988: 51, 55, 82, 87–88, examples) <u>note:</u> Poss always follows the head noun
Ngan'gityemerri/ Ngan'gikurunggurr	(Reid 1997: 267)
Warrongo	(Tsunoda 2011: 347–352)

Table 19 (continued)

All types of modifiers have a flexible position with respect to the head, but there is no or limited information on the relative order modifiers	
Anindilyakwa	(van Egmond 212: 303)
Bilinarra	(Meakins & Nordlinger 2014: 103–104)
	note: Dem and poss tend to precede the head
Dharrawal / Dharumba / Dhurga / Djirringanj	(Besold 2012: 287–289)
Garrwa	(Mushin 2012: 103–104, 256–257, examples)
	note: Dem and poss tend to occur in pre-head position (Mushin 2012: 256–257), and there are some examples showing a dem-A-head, dem-poss-head or poss-dem-head order. All these preferences in word order are not grammatical but pragmatic (Mushin p.c.).
Gumbaynggir	(Eades 1979: 313, examples)
	note: The examples seem to show a tendency for dem, pron and poss to precede the head, and for other modifiers to follow the head
Jingulu	(Pensalfini 2003: examples)
Mathi-Mathi/ Letyi-Letyi / Wati-Wati	(Blake et al. 2011: 79, examples)
	note: The examples show a strong tendency for dem to occur in pre-head position
Miriwung	(Kofod 1978: 52, examples)
	note: There is a tendency for dem (examples) and poss (Kofod 1978: 52) to precede the head
Ngiyambaa	(Donaldson 1980: examples)
	note: Almost all examples show a head-final word order
Nyangumarta	(Sharp 2004: 301–313)
	note: A functional analysis is made (Sharp 2004: 304–313), but it is not entirely clear whether the functions are associated with a certain modifier slot, as Sharp also mentions that "[i]n this arrangement ordering is not fixed" (2004: 304). In any case, dem usually occur initially, num tend to precede the head, adj and poss tend to follow the head (Sharp 2004: 301, 304), and it is unknown whether pron show a preference for a particular position
Rembarrnga	(Saulwick 2003: 81; McKay 1975: 67–70)
	note: Tendency for dem to precede head (McKay 1975: 67)
Rimanggudinhma	(Godman 1993: 78)
Walmajarri	(Richards 1979: 99, examples; Hudson 1978: examples)
Wangkajunga	(Jones 2011: 232, 235–240)
Warlpiri	(Hale et al. 1995: 1435)
Warray	(Harvey 1986: 59, 246)

Table 19 (continued)

Warumungu	(Simpson 2002: 42, examples)
Wirangu	(Hercus 1999: 81, examples)
	<u>note:</u> There is a very strong tendency for pron to follow the head (Hercus 1999: 81)
Yuwaalaraay	(Williams 1980: 96–97; Giacon 2017: 364–369)

Table 20: Determiners: identification of determiner slot unknown.

Identification of determiner slot unknown	
Alyawarra	(Yallop 1977: 116–117)
Atynyamathanha	(Schebeck 1974: 61, examples)
Bunganditj	(Blake 2003: 52, examples)
Dharumbal	(Terrill 2002: 48, examples)
Karajarri	(Sands 1989: 65–66)
Malakmalak	(Birk 1976: 146–148; Hoffmann p.c.)
Margany/ Gunya	(Breen 1981a: 335, examples)
Ngarrindjeri	(Yallop 1975: 28; Bannister 2004: 66)
Ritharngu	(Heath 1980: examples)
Tharrgari	(Klokeid 1969: examples)
Umbuygamu	(Sommer 1998: 22, 28; Ogilvie 1994: 39; examples throughout both sources)
Wathawurrung	(Blake 1998 ed.: 84, examples)
Yorta Yorta	(Bowe & Morey 1999: 106, examples)

References

Adamson, Sylvia. 2000. A lovely little example: Word order options and category shift in the premodifying string. In Olga Fischer, Anette Rosenbach & Dieter Stein (eds.), *Pathways of change: Grammaticalization in English*, 39–66. Amsterdam & Philadelphia: John Benjamins Publishing Company.

Aikhenvald, Alexandra Y. 2003. *Classifiers: A typology of noun categorization devices*. Oxford: Oxford University Press.

Allan, Keith. 1977. Classifiers. *Language* 53. 283–310.

Alpher, Barry. 1973. Son of ergative: The Yir Yoront language of northeast Australia. Ithaca, NY: Cornell University doctoral dissertation.

Alpher, Barry. 1987. Feminine as the unmarked gender: Buffalo girls are no fools. *Australian Journal of Linguistics* 7(2). 169–187.

Alpher, Barry. 1991. *Yir-Yoront lexicon: Sketch and dictionary of an Australian language*. Berlin & New York: Mouton de Gruyter.

Alpher, Barry. 2001. We came here on different boats: observations on distributivity as marked in two widely separated Australian languages, with thoughts on the number 1. In Robert Pensalfini & Norvin Richards (eds.), *MIT Working Papers on Endangered and Less-Familiar Languages* 2, 9–28.

Austin, Peter. 1981. *A grammar of Diyari, South Australia*. Cambridge: Cambridge University Press.

Austin, Peter. 2011. *A grammar of Diyari, South Australia*. 2nd edition. http://www.academia.edu/2491078/A_Grammar_of_Diyari_South_Australia (accessed 7 October 2013).

Austin, Peter & Joan Bresnan. 1996. Non-configurationality in Australian Aboriginal languages. *Natural Language and Linguistic Theory* 14. 215–268.

AUSTLANG: Australian Indigenous Languages Database. Available online at https://collection.aiatsis.gov.au/austlang/about (accessed 25 June 2019).

Bach, Emmon, Eloise Jelinek, Angelika Kratzer & Barbara H. Partee (eds.). 1995. *Quantification in natural languages*. Dordrecht: Springer.

Bache, Carl. 1978. *The order of premodifying adjectives in Present-Day English*. Odense: Odense University Press.

Bache, Carl. 2000. *Essentials of mastering English: A concise grammar*. Berlin & New York: Mouton de Gruyter.

Baker, Brett. 2002. How referential is agreement? The interpretation of polysynthetic disagreement morphology in Ngalakgan. In Nicholas Evans & Hans-Jürgen Sasse (eds.), *Problems of polysynthesis*, 51–86. Berlin: Akademie Verlag.

Baker, Brett. 2008. The interpretation of complex nominal expressions in Southeast Arnhem Land languages. In Ilana Mushin & Brett Baker (eds.), *Discourse and grammar in Australian languages*, 135–166. Amsterdam & Philadelphia: John Benjamins Publishing Company.

Baker, Mark. 2001. The natures of nonconfigurationality. In Mark Baltin & Chris Collins (eds.), *Handbook of contemporary syntactic theory*, 407–438. Oxford: Blackwell.

Bani, Ephraim & Barry Alpher. 1987. Garka a ipika: Masculine and feminine grammatical gender in Kala Lagaw Ya. *Australian Journal of Linguistics* 7(2). 189–201.

Bannister, Corinne. 2004. A longitudinal study of Ngarrindjeri. Sydney: University of Sydney BA Hons thesis.

Behaghel, Otto. 1932. *Deutsche Syntax: Eine geschichtliche Darstellung, vol. IV: Wortstellung-Periodenbau*. Heidelberg: Carl Winter.
Besold, Jutta. 2012. Language recovery of the New South Wales south coast Aboriginal languages. Part A: Analysis and philology. Canberra: Australian National University doctoral dissertation.
Bickel, Balthasar & Johanna Nichols. 2007. Inflectional morphology. In Timothy Shopen (ed.), *Linguistic typology and syntactic description. Volume III: Grammatical categories and the lexicon*, 169–240. 2nd edition. Cambridge: Cambridge University Press.
Birk, David. 1976. *The Malakmalak language, Daly River (Western Arnhem Land)*. Canberra: Pacific Linguistics.
Bittner, Maria & Ken Hale. 1995. Remarks on definiteness in Warlpiri. In Emmon Bach, Eloise Jelinek, Angelika Kratzer & Barbara H. Partee (eds.), *Quantification in Natural Languages*, 81–106. Dordrecht: Springer.
Blake, Barry. 1979a. *A Kalkatungu grammar*. Canberra: Pacific Linguistics.
Blake, Barry. 1979b. Pitta-Pitta. In R. M. W. Dixon & Barry Blake (eds.), *Handbook of Australian Languages. Volume 1*, 182–242. Canberra: Australian National University Press.
Blake, Barry. 1987. *Australian Aboriginal grammar*. London: Croom Helm.
Blake, Barry (ed.). 1998. *Wathawurrung and the Colac language of southern Victoria*. Canberra: Pacific Linguistics.
Blake, Barry. 2001. The noun phrase in Australian languages. In Jane Simpson, David Nash, Peter Austin & Barry Alpher (eds.), *Forty years on: Ken Hale and Australian languages*, 415–425. Canberra: Pacific Linguistics.
Blake, Barry. 2003. *The Bunganditj (Buwandik) language of the Mount Gambier region*. Canberra: Pacific Linguistics.
Blake, Barry, Luise Hercus, Stephen Morey & Edward Ryan. 2011. *The Mathi group of languages*. Canberra: Pacific Linguistics.
Blake, Barry J. 1983. Structure and word order in Kalkatungu: The anatomy of a flat language. *Australian Journal of Linguistics* 3. 143–175.
Blankenship, Barbara. 1997. Classificatory verbs in Cherokee. *Anthropological Linguistics* 39. 92–110.
Blevins, Juliette. 2001. *Nhanda: An Aboriginal language of Western Australia*. Honolulu: University of Hawai'i Press.
Bolinger, Dwight L. 1967. Adjectives in English: Attribution and predication. *Lingua* 18. 1–34.
Börjars, Kersti. 1998. *Feature distribution in Swedish noun phrases*. Oxford & Boston: Blackwell publishers.
Bowe, Heather. 1990. *Categories, constituents and constituent order in Pitjantjatjara: An Aboriginal language of Australia*. London; New York: Routledge.
Bowe, Heather & Stephen Morey. 1999. *The Yorta Yorta (Bangerang) language of the Murray Goulburn including Yabula Yabula*. Canberra: Pacific Linguistics.
Bowern, Claire. 2011. Centroid coordinates for Australian languages v2.0. Google Earth .kmz file, available from http://pantheon.yale.edu/~clb3/ (accessed 2 January 2017).
Bowern, Claire. 2012. *A grammar of Bardi*. Berlin & New York: Mouton de Gruyter.
Bowern, Claire & Quentin Atkinson. 2012. Computational phylogenetics and the internal structure of Pama-Nyungan. *Language* 88(4). 817–845.
Bowern, Claire & Jason Zentz. 2012. Diversity in the numeral systems of Australian languages. *Anthropological Linguistics* 54(2). 133–160.

Bowler, Margit. 2017. Quantification in Warlpiri. In Denis Paperno & Edward Keenan (eds.), *Handbook of Quantifiers in Natural Language: Volume II*, 963–994. Dordrecht: Springer.
Bradley, John, Jean Kirton & the Yanyuwa community. 1992. Yanyuwa Wuka: Language from Yanyuwa country – A Yanyuwa dictionary and cultural resource. https://espace.library.uq.edu.au/view/UQ:11306 (accessed 25 June 2019).
Breban, Tine. 2002. The grammaticalization of adjectives of identity and difference in English and Dutch. *Languages in Contrast* 4(1). 165–199.
Breban, Tine. 2010. *English adjectives of comparison: Lexical and grammatical uses*. Berlin & New York: Mouton de Gruyter.
Breban, Tine & Kristin Davidse. 2003. Adjectives of comparison: The grammaticalization of their attribute uses into postdeterminer and classifier uses. *Folia Linguistica* 37(3–4). 269–317.
Breen, Gavan. 1981a. Margany and Gunya. In R. M. W. Dixon & Barry Blake (eds.), *Handbook of Australian languages. Volume 2*, 274–393. Canberra: Australian National University Press.
Breen, Gavan. 1981b. *The Mayi languages of the Queensland Gulf Country*. Canberra: Australian Institute of Aboriginal Studies.
Breen, Gavan. 2004a. *Innamincka talk: A grammar of the Innamincka dialect of Yandruwandha with notes on other dialects*. Canberra: Pacific Linguistics.
Breen, Gavan. 2004b. *Innamincka words: Yandruwandha dictionary and stories*. Canberra: Pacific Linguistics.
Breen, Gavan & Barry Blake. 2007. *The grammar of Yalarnnga: A language of Western Queensland*. Canberra: Pacific Linguistics.
Bresnan, Joan (Ed.). 1982. *The mental representation of grammatical relations*. Cambridge MA: The MIT Press.
Burling, Robbins. 1961. *A Garo grammar*. Poona: Deccan College.
Campbell, Lauren. 2006. A sketch grammar of Urningangk, Erre and Mengerrdji: The Giimbiyu languages of Western Arnhem Land. Melbourne: University of Melbourne Honours thesis.
Capell, Arthur. 1953. Notes on the Waramunga language of western Australia. *Oceania* 23(4). 297–311.
Carrington, Lois & Geraldine Triffitt. 1999. *OZBIB: A linguistic bibliography of Aboriginal Australia and the Torres Strait Islands*. Canberra: Research School of Pacific and Asian Studies.
Carto. Available online at https://carto.com (accessed on25 June 2019).
Clendon, Mark. 2000. Topics in Worora grammar. Adelaide: University of Adelaide dissertation.
Clendon, Mark. 2014. *Worrorra: A language of the north-west Kimberley coast*. Adelaide: University of Adelaide Press.
Comrie, Bernard. 2013. Numeral bases. In Matthew S. Dryer & Martin Haspelmath (eds.), *The World Atlas of Language Structures Online*. Leipzig: Max Planck Institute for Evolutionary Anthropology. Available online at http://wals.info/chapter/131 (accessed on 25 June 2019).
Comrie, Bernard, Martin Haspelmath & Balthasar Bickel. 2015. Leipzig Glossing Rules. Available online at https://www.eva.mpg.de/lingua/pdf/Glossing-Rules.pdf (accessed on 25 June 2019).
Corbett, Greville G. 1991. *Gender*. Cambridge: Cambridge University Press.
Corbett, Greville G. 2000. *Number*. Cambridge: Cambridge University Press.
Corbett, Greville G. 2007. Gender and noun classes. In Timothy Shopen (ed.), *Language typology and syntactic description. Volume III: Grammatical categories and the lexicon*, 241–279. 2nd edition. Cambridge: Cambridge University Press.

Corbett, Greville G. 2013. Number of genders. In Matthew S. Dryer & Martin Haspelmath (eds.), *The World Atlas of Language Structures Online*. Leipzig: Max Planck Institute for Evolutionary Anthropology. Available online at http://wals.info/chapter/30 (accessed on 25 June 2019).

Corbett, Greville G. 2014. Gender typology. In Greville G. Corbett (ed.), *The expression of gender*, 87–130. Berlin & New York: Mouton de Gruyter.

Corbett, Greville G. & Sebastian Fedden. 2016. Canonical gender. *Journal of Linguistics* 52. 495–531.

Craig, Colette G. 1986a. Jacaltec noun classifiers: A study in grammaticalization. *Lingua* 71. 241–284.

Craig, Colette G. 1986b. Jacaltec noun classifiers: A study in language and culture. In Colette G. Craig (ed.), *Noun classes and categorization*, 263–293. Amsterdam & Philadelphia: John Benjamins Publishing Company.

Croft, William. 2001. *Radical construction grammar: Syntactic theory in typological perspective*. Oxford: Oxford University Press.

Croft, William. 2005. Word classes, parts of speech, and syntactic argumentation. *Linguistic Typology* 9(3). 431–441.

Croft, William. 2007. Intonation units and grammatical structure in Wardaman and in cross-linguistic perspective. *Australian Journal of Linguistics* 27(1). 1–39.

Crowley, Terry. 1978. *The middle Clarence dialects of Bandjalang*. Canberra: Australian Institute of Aboriginal Studies.

Crowley, Terry. 1981. Mpakwithi dialect of Anguthimri. In R. M. W. Dixon & Barry Blake (eds.), *Handbook of Australian Languages. Volume 2*, 146–194. Canberra: Australian National University Press.

Crowley, Terry. 1983. Uradhi. In R. M. W. Dixon & Barry Blake (eds.), *Handbook of Australian Languages. Volume 3*, 306–428. Canberra: Australian National University Press.

Cunningham, M.C. 1969. A description of the Yugumbir dialect of Bandjalang. *University of Queensland Papers* 1(8). 69–122.

Cutfield, Sarah. 2011. Demonstratives in Dalabon: A language of southwestern Arnhem Land. Melbourne: Monash University doctoral dissertation.

Cysouw, Michael. 2005. Morphology in the wrong place: A survey of preposed enclitics. In Wolfang U. Dressler (ed.), *Morphology and its demarcations*, 17–37. Amsterdam & Philadelphia: John Benjamins Publishing Company.

Dahlstrom, Amy. 1987. Discontinuous constituents in Fox. In Paul Kroeber & Robert E. Moore (eds.), *Native American languages and grammatical typology*, 53–73. Bloomington: Indiana University Linguistics Club.

Davidse, Kristin. 2004. The interaction of quantification and identification in English determiners. In Michel Achard & Suzanne Kemmer (eds.), *Language, Culture and Mind*, 507–533. Stanford: CSLI Publications.

Davidse, Kristin, Tine Breban & An Van Linden. 2008. Deictification: The development of secondary deictic meanings by adjectives in the English NP. *English Language and Linguistics* 12. 475–503.

De Kuthy, Kordula. 2002. *Discontinuous NPs in German: A case study of the interaction of syntax, semantics, and pragmatics*. Stanford: CSLI Publications.

Dench, Alan. 1991. Panyjima. In R. M. W. Dixon & Barry Blake (eds.), *Handbook of Australian Languages. Volume 4*, 124–243. Oxford: Oxford University Press.

Dench, Alan. 1994. *Martuthunira: A language of the Pilbara region of Western Australia*. Canberra: Pacific Linguistics.

Dench, Alan. 1998. *Yingkarta*. München: Lincom Europa.
Dench, Alan & Nicholas Evans. 1988. Multiple case-marking in Australian languages. *Australian Journal of Linguistics* 8(1). 1–47.
Denny, Peter. 1976. What are noun classifiers good for? In Salikoko S. Carol A. Walker & Sanford B. Steever (eds.), *Papers from the twelfth regional meeting of the Chicago Linguistic Society*, 122–132. Chicago: Chicago Linguistic Society.
Derbyshire, Desmond C. 1985. *Hixkaryana and linguistic typology*. Dallas: Summer Institute of Linguistics.
Dickinson, Connie. 2002. Complex predicates in Tsafiki. Eugene, OR: University of Oregon doctoral dissertation.
Diessel, Holger. 1999. *Demonstratives: Form, function, and grammaticalization*. Amsterdam & Philadelphia: John Benjamins Publishing Company.
Dixon, R. M. W. 1972. *The Dyirbal language of North Queensland*. Cambridge: Cambridge University Press.
Dixon, R. M. W. 1977. *A grammar of Yidiny*. Cambridge: Cambridge University Press.
Dixon, R. M. W. 1980. *The languages of Australia*. Cambridge: Cambridge University Press.
Dixon, R. M. W. 1982a. Classifiers in Yidiny. *Where have all the adjectives gone? And other essays in semantics and syntax*, 185–206. Berlin & New York: Mouton de Gruyter.
Dixon, R. M. W. 1982b. Noun classes. *Where have all the adjectives gone? And other essays in semantics and syntax*, 159–184. Berlin & New York: Mouton de Gruyter.
Dixon, R. M. W. 1982c. Noun classifiers and noun classes. *Where have all the adjectives gone? And other essays in semantics and syntax*, 211–234. Berlin & New York: Mouton de Gruyter.
Dixon, R. M. W. 1982d. Where have all the adjectives gone? *Where have all the adjectives gone? And other essays in semantics and syntax*, 1–62. Berlin & New York: Mouton de Gruyter.
Dixon, R. M. W. 1982e. *Where have all the adjectives gone? And other essays in semantics and syntax*. Berlin & New York: Mouton de Gruyter.
Dixon, R. M. W. 1986. Noun classes and noun classification in typological perspective. In Colette G. Craig (ed.), *Noun classes and categorization*, 106–112. Amsterdam & Philadelphia: John Benjamins Publishing Company.
Dixon, R. M. W. 1991. *Words of our country*. St. Lucia: University of Queensland Press.
Dixon, R. M. W. 2002. *Australian languages: Their nature and development*. Cambridge: Cambridge University Press.
Dixon, R. M. W. 2004. Adjective classes in typological perspective. In R. M. W. Dixon & Alexandra Y. Aikhenvald (eds.), *Adjective classes: A cross-linguistic typology*, 1–49. Oxford: Oxford University Press.
Dixon, R. M. W. 2010. The adjective class. *Basic linguistic theory: Volume 2, Grammatical topics*, 62–114. Oxford: Oxford University Press.
Donaldson, Tamsin. 1980. *Ngiyambaa: The language of the Wangaaybuwan*. Cambridge: Cambridge University Press.
Douglas, Wilfrid. 1976. *The Aboriginal languages of the South-West of Australia*. 2nd edition. Canberra: Australian Institute of Aboriginal Studies.
Douglas, Wilfrid. 1981. Watjarri. In R. M. W. Dixon & Barry Blake (eds.), *Handbook of Australian Languages. Volume 2*, 197–272. Canberra: Australian National University Press.
Dryer, Matthew S. 2007a. Noun phrase structure. In Timothy Shopen (ed.), *Language typology and syntactic description. Volume II: Complex constructions*, 151–205. 2nd edition. Cambridge: Cambridge University Press.

Dryer, Matthew S. 2007b. Word order. In Timothy Shopen (ed.), *Language typology and syntactic description. Volume I: Clause structure*, 61–131. 2nd edition. Cambridge: Cambridge University Press.

Dryer, Matthew S. 2013a. Coding of nominal plurality. In Matthew S. Dryer & Martin Haspelmath (eds.), *The World Atlas of Language Structures Online*. Leipzig: Max Planck Institute for Evolutionary Anthropology. Available online at http://wals.info/chapter/33 (accessed on 25 June 2019).

Dryer, Matthew S. 2013b. Definite articles. In Matthew S. Dryer & Martin Haspelmath (eds.), *The World Atlas of Language Structures Online*. Leipzig: Max Planck Institute for Evolutionary Anthropology. Available online at http://wals.info/chapter/37 (accessed on 25 June 2019).

Dryer, Matthew S. 2013c. Indefinite articles. In Matthew S. Dryer & Martin Haspelmath (eds.), *The World Atlas of Language Structures Online*. Leipzig: Max Planck Institute for Evolutionary Anthropology. Available online at http://wals.info/chapter/38 (accessed on 25 June 2019).

Dryer, Matthew S. 2013d. Order of demonstrative and noun. In Matthew S. Dryer & Martin Haspelmath (eds.), *The World Atlas of Language Structures Online*. Leipzig: Max Planck Institute for Evolutionary Anthropology. Available online at http://wals.info/chapter/88 (accessed on 25 June 2019).

Eades, Diana. 1979. Gumbaynggir. In R. M. W. Dixon & Barry Blake (eds.), *Handbook of Australian Languages. Volume 1*, 244–361. Canberra: Australian National University Press.

Elbert, Samuel H. & Mary Kawena Pukui. 1979. *Hawaiian grammar*. Honolulu: University of Hawai'i Press.

Elson, Benjamín. 1960. Gramatica popoluca de la sierra. Xalapa: Universidad Veracruzana doctoral dissertation.

Epps, Patience. 2008. *A grammar of Hup*. Berlin & New York: Mouton de Gruyter.

Evans, Nicholas. 1995a. *A grammar of Kayardild with historical-comparative notes on Tangkic*. Berlin & New York: Mouton de Gruyter.

Evans, Nicholas. 1995b. A-quantifiers and scope in Mayali. In Emmon Bach, Eloise Jelinek, Angelika Kratzer & Barbara H. Partee (eds.), *Quantification in natural languages*, 206–270. Dordrecht: Springer.

Evans, Nicholas. 1997. Sign metonymies and the problem of flora–fauna polysemy in Australian linguistics. In Darrell Tryon & Michael Walsh (eds.), *Boundary rider: Essays in honour of Geoffrey O'Grady*, 133–153. Canberra: Pacific Linguistics.

Evans, Nicholas. 2002. The true status of grammatical object affixes: Evidence from Bininj Kunwok. In Nicholas Evans & Hans-Jürgen Sasse (eds.), *Problems of polysynthesis*, 15–50. Berlin: Akademie Verlag.

Evans, Nicholas. 2003a. *Bininj Gun-wok: A pan-dialectal grammar of Mayali, Kunwinjku and Kune*. Canberra: Pacific Linguistics.

Evans, Nicholas. 2003b. Introduction: Comparative non-Pama-Nyungan and Australian historical linguistics. In Nicholas Evans (ed.), *The Non-Pama-Nyungan languages of northern Australia: Comparative studies of the continent's most linguistically complex region*, 3–25. Canberra: Pacific Linguistics.

Evans, Nicholas. 2006. Dyadic constructions. In Keith Brown (ed.), *Encyclopaedia of language and linguistics*. Amsterdam: Elsevier Ltd.

Evans, Nicholas & Toshiki Osada. 2005. Mundari: The myth of a language without word classes. *Linguistic Typology* 9(3). 351–390.

Fanselow, Gisbert & Damir Ćavar. 2002. Distributed deletion. In Artemis Alexiadou (ed.), *Theoretical approaches to universals*, 65–109. Amsterdam & Philadelphia: John Benjamins Publishing Company.

Fedden, Sebastian & Greville G. Corbett. 2017. Gender and classifiers in concurrent systems: Refining the typology of nominal classification. *Glossa: a journal of general linguistics* 2(1). 1–47.

Flanagan, Paul James. 2014. A cross-linguistic investigation of the order of attributive adjectives. Ormskirk: Edge Hill University doctoral dissertation.

Floyd, Simon. 2011. Re-discovering the Quechua adjective. *Linguistic Typology* 15. 25–63.

Foley, William A. 1991. *The Yimas language of New Guinea*. Stanford: Stanford University Press.

Ford, Kevin & Dana Ober. 1987. Kalaw Kawaw Ya. Darwin: School of Australian Linguistics.

Ford, Kevin & Dana Ober. 1991. A sketch of Kalaw Kawaw Ya. In Suzanne Romaine (ed.), *Language in Australia*, 118–142. Cambridge: Cambridge University Press.

Ford, Lysbeth. 1990. The phonology and morphology of Bachamal (Wogait). Canberra: Australian National University MA thesis.

Ford, Lysbeth. 1998. A description of the Emmi language of the Northern Territory of Australia. Canberra: Australian National University doctoral dissertation.

Forrester, Katerina. 2015. The internal structure of the Mawng noun phrase. Melbourne: University of Melbourne BA Hons thesis.

Gaby, Alice Rose. 2006. A grammar of Kuuk Thaayorre. University of Melbourne doctoral dissertation.

Gaby, Alice R. 2017. *A Grammar of Kuuk Thaayorre*. Berlin & New York: Mouton de Gruyter.

Gawne, Lauren & Hiram Ring. 2016. Mapmaking for Language Documentation and Description. *Language Documentation & Conservation* 10. 188–242.

Ghesquière, Lobke. 2009. From determining to emphasizing meanings: The adjectives of specificity. *Folia Linguistica* 43(2). 311–343.

Giacon, John. 2017. *Yaluu: A recovery grammar of Yuwaalaraay and Gamilaraay: a description of two New South Wales languages based on 160 years of records*. Canberra: Asia-Pacific Linguistics.

Gil, David. 1987. Definiteness, noun phrase configurationality, and the count-mass distinction. In Eric J. Reuland & Alice G. B. ter Meulen (eds.), *The representation of (in)definiteness*, 254–269. Cambridge: MIT Press.

Gil, David. 2013. Numeral classifiers. In Matthew S. Dryer & Martin Haspelmath (eds.), *The World Atlas of Language Structures Online*. Leipzig: Max Planck Institute for Evolutionary Anthropology. Available online at http://wals.info/chapter/55 (accessed on 25 June 2019).

Gil, David. 2015. Quantifiers. In James Wright (ed.), *International Encyclopedia of the Social & Behavioral Sciences, 2nd edition, Volume 19*, 707–711. Amsterdam: Elsevier Ltd.

Glasgow, Kathy. 1994. Appendix 2: Parts of Speech (or major word classes) in Burarra – Gun-Nartpa. *Burarra-Gun-Nartpa dictionary: with English finder list*, 893–924. Darwin: Summer Institute of Linguistics.

Goddard, Cliff. 1985. *A grammar of Yankunytjatjara*. Alice Springs: Institute for Aboriginal Development.

Godman, Irene. 1993. A sketch grammar of Rimanggudinhma: A language of the Princess Charlotte Bay region of Cape York Peninsula. St. Lucia: University of Queensland BA Hons thesis.

Green, Ian. 1989. Marrithiyel: A language of the Daly River region of Australia's Northern Territory. Canberra: Australian National University doctoral dissertation.

Green, Ian. 1997. Nominal Classification in Marrithiyel. In Mark Harvey & Nicholas Reid (eds.), *Nominal Classification in Aboriginal Australia*, 229–254. Amsterdam & Philadelphia: John Benjamins Publishing Company.

Green, Rebecca. 1987. A sketch grammar of Burarra. Canberra: Australian National University BA Hons thesis.

Greenberg, Joseph. 1978. Generalizations about numeral systems. In Joseph H. Greenberg, Charles Ferguson & Edith Moravcsik (eds.), *Universals of Human Language, Volume 3: Word Structure*, 249–295. Stanford: Stanford University Press.

Greenberg, Joseph H. 1966. Some universals of grammar with particular reference to the order of meaningful elements. In Joseph H. Greenberg (ed.), *Universals of language*, 73–113. Cambridge: MIT Press.

Grinevald, Colette. 2000. A morphosyntactic typology of classifiers. In Gunter Senft (ed.), *Systems of Nominal Classification*, 50–92. New York: Cambridge University Press.

Guirardello, Raquel. 1999. Trumai reference grammar. Houston, TX: Rice University doctoral dissertation.

Gundel, Jeanette K., Nancy Hedberg & Ron Zacharski. 1993. Cognitive status and the form of referring expressions in discourse. *Language* 69(2). 274–307.

Hale, Ken. 1962. Internal relationships in Arandic of Central Australia. In Arthur Capell (ed.), *Some linguistic types in Australia*, 171–183. Sydney: Oceania.

Hale, Ken. 1975. Gaps in grammar and culture. In M. Dale Kinkade, Ken Hale & Oswald Werner (eds.), *Linguistics and anthropology: In honour of C. F. Voegelin*, 295–315. Lisse: The Peter de Ridder Press.

Hale, Ken. 1981. *On the position of Walbiri in a typology of the base.* Bloomington, IN: Indiana University Linguistics Club.

Hale, Ken. 1982. Some essential features of Warlpiri verbal clauses. In Stephen Swartz (ed.), *Papers in Warlpiri grammar: in memory of Lothar Jagst*, 217–315. Darwin: Summer Institute of Linguistics.

Hale, Ken. 1983. Warlpiri and the grammar of non-configurational languages. *Natural Language and Linguistic Theory* 1. 5–74.

Hale, Ken. 1995. *An elementary Warlpiri dictionary.* Revised edition. Alice Springs: IAD Press.

Hale, Ken, Mary Laughren & Jane Simpson. 1995. Warlpiri. In Joachim Jacobs, Arnim von Stechow, Wolfgang Sternefeld & Theo Vennemann (eds.), *Syntax: An international handbook of contemporary research*, vol. 2, 1430–1451. Berlin & New York: Mouton de Gruyter.

Halliday, M. A. K. 1985. *An introduction to Functional Grammar.* London: Edward Arnold.

Hamilton, Philip. 1996. Oykangand sketch grammar. Manuscript.

Hammarström, Harald. 2010. Rarities in numeral systems. In Jan Wohlgemuth & Michael Cysouw (eds.), *Rethinking universals: How rarities affect linguistic theory*, 11–60. Berlin & New York: Mouton de Gruyter.

Hammarström, Harald. 2014. Bibliography. Manuscript.

Hammarström, Harald, Robert Forkel & Martin Haspelmath. 2019. *Glottolog 3.4.* Jena: Max Planck Institute for the Science of Human History. Available online at http://glottolog.org (accessed on 25 June 2019).

Harvey, Mark. ms. Warray grammar. Manuscript.

Harvey, Mark. 1986. Ngoni Waray Amungal-yang: The Waray language from Adelaide River. Canberra: Australian National University MA thesis.

Harvey, Mark. 1992. The noun phrase in Australian languages: A comment. *Australian Journal of Linguistics* 12(2). 307–319.
Harvey, Mark. 1997. Nominal classification and gender in Aboriginal Australia. In Mark Harvey & Nicholas Reid (eds.), *Nominal classification in Aboriginal Australia*, 17–62. Amsterdam & Philadelphia: John Benjamins Publishing Company.
Harvey, Mark. 2001. *A grammar of Limilngan: A language of the Mary River Region, Northern Territory, Australia*. Canberra: Pacific Linguistics.
Harvey, Mark. 2002. *A grammar of Gaagudju*. Berlin & New York: Mouton de Gruyter.
Harvey, Mark & Nicholas Reid (eds.). 1997. *Nominal classification in Aboriginal Australia*. Amsterdam & Philadelphia: John Benjamins Publishing Company.
Haspelmath, Martin. 2012. How to compare major word-classes across the world's languages. *UCLA Working papers in linguistics, Theories of everything* 17(16). 109–130.
Haspelmath, Martin. 2013. Occurrence of nominal plurality. In Matthew S. Dryer & Martin Haspelmath (eds.), *The World Atlas of Language Structures Online*. Leipzig: Max Planck Institute for Evolutionary Anthropology. Available online at http://wals.info/chapter/34 (accessed on 25 June 2019).
Haviland, John. 1979. Guugu Yimidhirr. In R. M. W. Dixon & Barry Blake (eds.), *Handbook of Australian Languages. Volume 1*, 27–180. Canberra: Australian National University.
Heath, Jeffrey. 1980. *Basic materials in Ritharngu: Grammar, texts and dictionary*. Canberra: Pacific Linguistics.
Heath, Jeffrey. 1981. *Basic materials in Mara: Grammar, texts and dictionary*. Canberra: Pacific Linguistics.
Heath, Jeffrey. 1983. Referential tracking in Nunggubuyu. In Pamela Munro & John Haiman (eds.), *Switch-reference and universal grammar*, 129–149. Amsterdam & Philadelphia: John Benjamins Publishing Company.
Heath, Jeffrey. 1984. *Functional grammar of Nunggubuyu*. Canberra: Australian Institute of Aboriginal Studies.
Heath, Jeffrey. 1986. Syntactic and lexical aspects of nonconfigurationality in Nunggubuyu (Australia). *Natural Language and Linguistic Theory* 4(3). 375–408.
Hengeveld, Kees & Jan Rijkhoff. 2005. Mundari as a flexible language. *Linguistic Typology* 9(3). 406–431.
Hengeveld, Kees, Jan Rijkhoff & Anna Siewierska. 2004. Parts-of-speech systems and word order. *Journal of Linguistics* 40(3). 527–570.
Hercus, Luise. 1982. *The Baagandji language*. Canberra: Pacific Linguistics.
Hercus, Luise. 1994. *A grammar of the Arabana-Wangkangurru language, Lake Eyre basin, South Australia*. Canberra: Pacific Linguistics.
Hercus, Luise. 1999. *A grammar of the Wirangu language from the west coast of South Australia*. Canberra: Pacific Linguistics.
Hill, Clair. 2010. Noun phrases in Umpila and Kuuku Ya'u. Paper presented at the Workshop on noun phrase structure, Aarhus Universitet.
Hill, Clair. 2018. *Person reference and interaction in Umpila/Kuuku Ya'u narrative*. Nijmegen & Leuven: Radboud Universiteit Nijmegen and KU Leuven doctoral dissertation.
Himmelmann, Nikolaus. 1997. *Deiktikon, Artikel, Nominalphrase: Zur Emergenz syntaktischer Struktur*. Tübingen: Niemeyer.
Himmelmann, Nikolaus. 2001. Articles. In Martin Haspelmath (ed.), *Language typology and language universals: An international handbook.*, 831–841. Berlin & New York: Mouton de Gruyter.

Himmelmann, Nikolaus. 2013. Prosody and phrase structure. Paper presented at the NP3 workshop (Third Vigo-Newcastle-Santiago-Leuven International Workshop on The Structure of the Noun Phrase in English: Synchronic and Diachronic Explorations), KU Leuven.

Himmelmann, Nikolaus. 2014. Asymmetries in the prosodic phrasing of function words: Another look at the suffixing preference. *Language* 90(4). 927–960.

Hosokawa, Komei. 1991. The Yawuru language of West Kimberley: A meaning-based description. Canberra: Australian National University doctoral dissertation.

Hudson, Joyce. 1978. *The core of Walmatjari grammar*. Canberra: Australian Institute of Aboriginal Studies.

Hudson, Joyce & Eirlys Richards. 1984. *The Walmatjari: An introduction to the language and culture*. Darwin: Summer Institute of Linguistics – Australian Aborigines Branch.

Hundius, Harald & Ulrike Kölver. 1983. Syntax and semantics of numeral classifiers in Thai. *Studies in Language* 7(2). 164–214.

Jelinek, Eloise. 1984. Empty categories, case and configurationality. *Natural Language and Linguistic Theory* 2. 39–76.

Johnson, Steve. 1988. The status of classifiers in Kugu Nganhcara nominals. In Nicholas Evans & Steve Johnson (eds.), *Aboriginal Linguistics 1*, 198–203. Armidale: Department of Linguistics, University of New England.

Jones, Barbara. 2011. *A grammar of Wangkajunga: A language of the Great Sandy Desert of North Western Australia*. Canberra: Pacific Linguistics.

Julien, Marit. 2005. *Nominal phrases from a Scandinavian perspective*. Amsterdam & Philadelphia: John Benjamins Publishing Company.

Kapitonov, Vanya & Margit Bowler. forthcoming. Quantification in Australian languages. In Claire Bowern (ed.), *Oxford Handbook of Australian Languages*. Oxford: Oxford University Press.

Keenan, Edward & Denis Paperno (eds.). 2012. *Handbook of Quantifiers in Natural Language*. Dordrecht: Springer.

Kilham, Christine A. 1974. Compound words and close-knit phrases in Wik-Munkan. *Papers in Australian Linguistics No. 7*, 45–73. Canberra: Department of Linguistics, Australian National University.

Kirton, Jean. 1971. *Papers in Australian Linguistics No. 5*. Canberra: Pacific Linguistics.

Kirton, Jean. 1988. Men's and women's dialects. In Nicholas Evans & Steve Johnson (eds.), *Aboriginal linguistics 1*, 111–125. Armidale: Department of Linguistics, University of New England.

Kirton, Jean & Bella Charlie. 1996. *Further aspects of the grammar of Yanyuwa, northern Australia*. Canberra: Pacific Linguistics.

Kite, Suzanne & Stephen Wurm. 2004. *The Duungidjawu language of southeast Queensland: Grammar, texts and vocabulary*. Canberra: Pacific Linguistics.

Klokeid, Terry. 1969. *Thargari phonology and morphology*. Canberra: Pacific Linguistics.

Klokeid, Terry. 1976. Topics in Lardil grammar. Cambridge, MA: Massachusetts Institute of Technology doctoral dissertation.

Kofod, Frances. 1978. The Miriwung language (East Kimberley): A phonological and morphological study. Armidale: University of New England MA thesis.

Koptjevskaja-Tamm, Maria. 2003. A woman of sin, a man of duty, and a hell of a mess: Non-determiner genitives in Swedish. In Frans Plank (ed.), *Noun phrase structure in the languages of Europe*, 515–558. Berlin & New York: Mouton de Gruyter.

Krasnoukhova, Olga. 2012. The noun phrase in the languages of South America. Nijmegen: Radboud Universiteit Nijmegen doctoral dissertation.
Langacker, Ronald. 1991. *Foundations of cognitive grammar. Volume II: Descriptive application*. Stanford: Stanford University Press.
Lee, Jennifer. 1987. *Tiwi today: A study of language change in a contact situation*. Canberra: Pacific Linguistics.
Lee, Kee-dong. 1975. *Kusaiean reference grammar*. Honolulu: The University Press of Hawaii.
Leeding, Velma Joan. 1989. Anindilyakwa phonology and morphology. Sydney: University of Sydney doctoral dissertation.
Lesage, Jakob. 2014. Nominal compounds and other N-N combinations: A typological study of a sample of Pama-Nyungan languages. Leuven: KU Leuven MA thesis.
Lissarrague, Amanda. 2010. *A grammar and dictionary of Gathang: The language of the Birrbay, Guringay and Warrimay*. Nambucca Heads: Muurrbay Aboriginal Language & Culture Co-operative.
Louagie, Dana. 2017. The status of determining elements in Australian languages. *Australian Journal of Linguistics* 37(2). 182–218.
Louagie, Dana & Jean-Christophe Verstraete. 2015. Personal pronouns with determining functions in Australian languages. *Studies in Language* 39(1). 158–197.
Louagie, Dana & Jean-Christophe Verstraete. 2016. Noun phrase constituency in Australian languages: A typological study. *Linguistic Typology* 20. 25–80.
Love, J. R. B. 1934. The grammatical structure of the Worora language of north-western Australia. Adelaide: University of Adelaide MA thesis.
Lyons, Christopher. 1999. *Definiteness*. Cambridge: Cambridge University Press.
Marácz, László & Pieter Muysken (eds.). 1989. *Configurationality: the typology of asymmetries*. Dordrecht: Foris Publications.
Marmion, Douglas. 1996. A description of the morphology of Wajarri. Armidale: University of New England BA Hons thesis.
Matsumoto, Yo. 1993. Japanese numeral classifiers: A study of semantic categories and lexical organization. *Linguistics* 31. 667–713.
Matthewson, Lisa (ed.). 2008. *Quantification : a cross-linguistic perspective*. Bingley: Emerald.
McGregor, William. 1989. Phrase fracturing in Gooniyandi. In László Marácz & Pieter Muysken (eds.), *Configurationality: The typology of asymmetries*, 207–222. Dordrecht: Foris Publications.
McGregor, William. 1990. *A functional grammar of Gooniyandi*. Amsterdam & Philadelphia: John Benjamins Publishing Company.
McGregor, William. 1992. The noun phrase as a grammatical category in (some) Australian languages: A reply to Mark Harvey. *Australian Journal of Linguistics* 12(2). 315–319.
McGregor, William. 1997a. Functions of noun phrase discontinuity in Gooniyandi. *Functions of Language* 4. 83–114.
McGregor, William. 1997b. *Semiotic grammar*. Oxford: Clarendon Press.
McGregor, William. 2002. *Verb classification in Australian languages*. Berlin & New York: Mouton de Gruyter.
McGregor, William. 2004. *The languages of the Kimberley, Western Australia*. London: RoutledgeCurzon.
McGregor, William. 2005. Quantifying depictive secondary predicates in Australian languages. In Nikolaus Himmelmann & Schultze-Berndt (eds.), *Secondary predication and adverbial modification: The typology of depictives*, 173–200. Oxford: Oxford University Press.

McGregor, William. 2008. The origin of noun classes in Worrorran languages. In Claire Bowern, Bethwyn Evans & Luisa Miceli (eds.), *Morphology and language history: In honour of Harold Koch*, 185–200. Amsterdam & Philadelphia: John Benjamins Publishing Company.

McGregor, William. 2011. *The Nyulnyul language of Dampier land, Western Australia. 2 vols.* Canberra: Pacific Linguistics.

McGregor, William. 2013. Lexical categories in Gooniyandi, Kimberley, Western Australia. In Jan Rijkhoff & Eva van Lier (eds.), *Flexible word classes: typological studies of underspecified parts of speech*, 221–246. Oxford: Oxford University Press.

McGregor, William & Alan Rumsey. 2009. *Worrorran revisited: The case for genetic relations among languages of the Northern Kimberley region of Western Australia.* Canberra: Pacific Linguistics.

McKay, Graham. 1975. Rembarnga: A language of central Arnhem Land. Canberra: Australian National University Doctoral dissertation.

McKay, Graham. 2000. Ndjébbana. In R. M. W. Dixon & Barry J. Blake (eds.), *Handbook of Australian Languages. Volume 5*, 155–356. Oxford: Oxford University Press.

McKelson, Kevin. 1989. Studies in Karajarri. Manuscript.

Meakins, Felicity & Rachel Nordlinger. 2014. *A grammar of Bilinarra: An Australian Aboriginal language of the Northern Territory*. Berlin & New York: Mouton de Gruyter.

Merlan, Francesca. 1989. *Mangarayi*. London: Routledge.

Merlan, Francesca. 1994. *A grammar of Wardaman: A language of the Northern Territory of Australia*. Berlin & New York: Mouton de Gruyter.

Merlan, Francesca, Steven Powell Roberts & Alan Rumsey. 1997. New Guinea "classificatory verbs" and Australian noun classification: A typological comparison. In Mark Harvey & Nicholas Reid (eds.), *Nominal classification in Aboriginal Australia*, 63–104. Amsterdam & Philadelphia: John Benjamins Publishing Company.

Milsark, G. 1977. Toward an explanation of certain peculiarities of the existential construction in English. *Linguistic Analysis* 3(1). 1–29.

Mithun, Marianne. 1984. The evolution of noun incorporation. *Language* 60(4). 847–894.

Morphy, Frances. 1983. Djapu, a Yolngu dialect. In R. M. W. Dixon & Barry Blake (eds.), *Handbook of Australian Languages. Volume 3*, 1–304. Canberra: Australian National University Press.

Mushin, Ilana. 1995. Epistememes in Australian languages. *Australian Journal of Linguistics* 15. 1–31.

Mushin, Ilana. 2012. *A grammar of (Western) Garrwa*. Berlin & New York: Mouton de Gruyter.

Nash, David. 1986 [1980]. *Topics in Warlpiri grammar*. New York & London: Garland Publishing Inc.

Nordlinger, Rachel. 1998a. *A grammar of Wambaya, Northern Territory (Australia)*. Canberra: Pacific Linguistics.

Nordlinger, Rachel. 1998b. *Constructive Case: Evidence from Australian Languages*. Stanford: CSLI Publications.

Nordlinger, Rachel. 2014. Constituency and grammatical relations. In Harold Koch & Rachel Nordlinger (eds.), *The languages and linguistics of Australia: A comprehensive guide*, 215–262. Berlin & New York: Mouton de Gruyter.

Oates, Lynette. 1988. *The Muruwari Language*. Canberra: Research School of Pacific and Asian Studies, Australian National University.

Ogilvie, Sarah. 1994. *The Morrobalama (Umbuygamu) language of Cape York Peninsula, Australia*. Canberra: Australian National University MA thesis.
OZBIB: A linguistic bibliography of Aboriginal Australia and the Torres Strait Islands. Available online at http://ozbib.aiatsis.gov.au/ (accessed on 25 June 2019).
Paperno, Denis & Edward Keenan (eds). 2017. *Handbook of Quantifiers in Natural Language: Volume II*. Dordrecht: Springer.
Patz, Elisabeth. 1991. Djabugay. In R. M. W. Dixon & Barry Blake (eds.), *Handbook of Australian Languages. Volume 4*, 244–347. Oxford: Oxford University Press.
Patz, Elisabeth. 2002. *A grammar of the Kuku Yalanji language of north Queensland*. Canberra: Pacific Linguistics.
Pavey, Emma. 2010. *The structure of language: An introduction to grammatical analysis*. Cambridge: Cambridge University Press.
Payne, John & Rodney Huddleston. 2002. Nouns and noun phrases. In Rodney Huddleston & Geoffrey Pullum (eds.), *The Cambridge grammar of the English language*. Cambridge: Cambridge University Press.
Pensalfini, Robert. 1992. *Degrees of freedom: Word order in Pama-Nyungan languages*. Perth: University of Western Australia BA Hons thesis.
Pensalfini, Robert. 2003. *A grammar of Jingulu: An Aboriginal language of the Northern Territory*. Canberra: Pacific Linguistics.
Pensalfini, Robert. 2004. Towards a typology of configurationality. *Natural Language & Linguistic Theory* 22. 359–408.
Peterson, John. 2005. There's a grain of truth in every "myth", or, Why the discussion of lexical classes in Mundari isn't quite over yet. *Linguistic Typology* 9(3). 391–405.
Plank, Frans. 1992. Possessives and the distinction between determiners and modifiers (with special reference to German). *Journal of Linguistics* 28(2). 453–468.
Plank, Frans. 2003. Double articulation. In Frans Plank (ed.), *Noun phrase structure in the languages of Europe*. Berlin & New York: Mouton de Gruyter.
Ponsonnet, Maïa. 2015. Nominal subclasses in Dalabon (South-western Arnhem Land). *Australian Journal of Linguistics* 35(1). 1–52.
Postal, Paul M. 1970. On so-called pronouns in English. In Roderick A. Jacobs & Peter S. Rosenbaum (eds.), *Readings in English transformational grammar*, 56–82. Waltham, MA: Ginn.
Quirk, Randolph, Sidney Greenbaum, Geoffrey Leech & Jan Svartvik. 1985. *A comprehensive grammar of the English language*. London: Longman.
Reid, Nicholas. 1990. *Ngan'gityemerri: A language of the Daly River region, Northern Territory of Australia*. Canberra: Australian National University doctoral dissertation.
Reid, Nicholas. 1997. Class and classifier in Ngan'gityemerri. In Mark Harvey & Nicholas Reid (eds.), *Nominal Classification in Aboriginal Australia*, 165–228. Amsterdam & Philadelphia: John Benjamins Publishing Company.
Reinholtz, Charlotte. 1999. On the characterization of discontinuous constituents: Evidence from Swampy Cree. *International Journal of American Linguistics* 65(2). 201–227.
Richards, Eirlys. 1979. The Walmatjari noun phrase. In Christine A. Kilham (ed.), *Four grammatical sketches: From phrase to paragraph*, vol. 3, 93–128. Darwin: Summer Institute of Linguistics – Australian Aborigines Branch.
Riessler, Michael. 2016. *Adjective attribution*. Berlin: Language Science Press.
Rijkhoff, Jan. 2002. *The noun phrase*. Oxford: Oxford University Press.
Rijkhoff, Jan & Dik Bakker. 1998. Language sampling. *Linguistic Typology* 2(3). 263–314.

Romero-Figeroa, Andres. 1997. *A reference grammar of Warao*. Munchen: Lincom.
Round, Erich. 2013. *Kayardild morphology and syntax*. Oxford: Oxford University Press.
Rumsey, Alan. 1982. *An intra-sentence grammar of Ungarinjin (north-western Australia)*. Canberra: Pacific Linguistics.
Sadler, Louisa & Rachel Nordlinger. 2010. Nominal juxtaposition in Australian Languages: An LFG analysis. *Journal of Linguistics* 46(2). 415–452.
Sakel, Jeanette. 2004. *A grammar of Mosetén*. Berlin & New York: Mouton de Gruyter.
Sands, A. K. 1995. Nominal classification in Australia. *Anthropological Linguistics* 37. 247–346.
Sands, Anna Kristina. 1989. A grammar of Garadjari, Western Australia. Canberra: Australian National University BA Hons thesis.
Saulwick, Adam. 2003. Aspects of the verb in Rembarrnga: A polysynthetic language of northern Australia: Grammatical description, texts and dictionary. Melbourne: University of Melbourne doctoral dissertation.
Scancarelli, Janine. 1987. Grammatical relations and verb agreement in Cherokee. Oakland: University of California doctoral dissertation.
Schachter, Paul & Timothy Shopen. 2007. Parts-of-speech systems. In Timothy Shopen (ed.), *Language typology and syntactic description. Volume I: Clause structure*, 1–60. 2nd edition. Cambridge: Cambridge University Press.
Schebeck, Bernard. 1974. *Texts on the social system of the Atynyamathanha people with grammatical notes*. Canberra: Pacific Linguistics.
Schultze-Berndt, Eva. 2000. Simple and complex verbs in Jaminjung: A study of event categorisation in an Australian language. Nijmegen: Katholieke Universiteit Nijmegen doctoral dissertation.
Schultze-Berndt, Eva & Candide Simard. 2012. Constraints on noun phrase discontinuity in an Australian language: The role of prosody and information structure. *Linguistics* 50(5). 1015–1058.
Seifart, Frank. 2010. Nominal Classification. *Language and Linguistics Compass* 4(8). 719–736.
Sharp, Janet. 2004. *Nyangumarta: A language of the Pilbara region of Western Australia*. Canberra: Pacific Linguistics.
Sharpe, Margaret. 1972. *Alawa phonology and grammar*. Canberra: Australian Institute of Aboriginal Studies.
Sharpe, Margareth. 2005. *Grammar and texts of the Yugambeh-Bundjalung dialect chain in Eastern Australia*. München: Lincom Europa.
Siewierska, Anna. 1984. Phrasal discontinuity in Polish. *Australian Journal of Linguistics* 4(1). 57–71.
Silverstein, Michael. 1976. Hierarchy of features and ergativity. In R. M. W. Dixon (ed.), *Grammatical categories in Australian languages*, 112–171. Canberra: Australian National University Press.
Simpson, Jane. 1983. Aspects of Warlpiri morphology and syntax. Cambridge, MA: Massachusetts Institute of Technology doctoral dissertation.
Simpson, Jane. 1991. *Warlpiri morphosyntax: a lexicalist approach*. Dordrecht: Kluwer.
Simpson, Jane. 1998. Warumungu (Australian – Pama-Nyungan). In Andrew Spencer & Arnold Zwicky (eds.), *The handbook of morphology*, 707–736. Oxford: Blackwell.
Simpson, Jane. 2002. *A learner's guide to Warumungu*. Alice Springs: IAD Press.

Simpson, Jane. 2007. Expressing pragmatic constraints on word order in Warlpiri. In Annie Zaenen (ed.), *Architectures, rules, and preferences: Variations on themes by Joan W. Bresnan*, 403–427. Stanford: CSLI Publications.

Simpson, Jane & Jeffrey Heath. 1982. Warumungu sketch grammar. Manuscript.

Simpson, Jane & Joan Bresnan. 1983. Control and obviation in Warlpiri. *Natural Language and Linguistic Theory* 1. 49–64.

Singer, Ruth. 2001. A brief investigation of the inclusory construction in Australian languages. *Melbourne Papers in Linguistics and Applied Linguistics* 1(2). 81–96.

Singer, Ruth. 2006. Agreement in Mawng: Productive and lexicalised uses of agreement in an Australian language. Melbourne: University of Melbourne doctoral dissertation.

Singer, Ruth. 2016. *The dynamics of nominal classification: Productive and lexicalised uses of gender agreement in Mawng*. Berlin & New York: Mouton de Gruyter.

Smith, Ian & Steve Johnson. 2000. Kugu Nganhcara. In R. M. W. Dixon & Barry J. Blake (eds.), *Handbook of Australian Languages: Volume 5*, 357–507. Oxford: Oxford University Press.

Sneddon, James N. 1996. *Indonesian: A comprehensive grammar*. London & New York: Routledge.

Sommer, Bruce. 1970. Kunjen syntax: A generative view. Honolulu: University of Hawaii Doctoral dissertation.

Sommer, Bruce. 1976. Umbuygamu: The classification of a Cape York Peninsular language. *Papers in Australian Linguistics No. 10*, 13–29. Canberra: Research School of Pacific and Asian Studies, Australian National University.

Sommer, Bruce. 2006. *Speaking Kunjen: An ethnography of Oykangand kinship and communication*. Canberra: Pacific Linguistics.

Sommer, Bruce. 1998. Umbuygamu. Manuscript.

Spronck, Stef. 2015. Reported speech in Ungarinyin: [["..."] -ma-]: Grammar and social cognition in a language of the Kimberley region, Western Australia. Canberra: Australian National University doctoral dissertation.

Stirling, Lesley. 2008. "'Double reference'" in Kala Lagaw Ya narratives. In Ilana Mushin & Brett Baker (eds.), *Discourse and grammar in Australian languages*, 167–202. Amsterdam & Philadelphia: John Benjamins Publishing Company.

Stirling, Lesley & Brett Baker. 2007. Pronominal apposition and the status of "determiner" in Australian languages. Paper presented at the Australian Linguistic Society Annual Conference, University of Adelaide.

Stroomer, Harry. 1987. *A comparative study of three southern Oromo dialects in Kenya: phonology, morphology and vocabulary*. Hamburg: Buske.

Swartz, Stephen. 1982. Syntactic structure of Warlpiri clauses. In Stephen Swartz (ed.), *Papers in Warlpiri grammar: In memory of Lothar Jagst*, vol. 6, 69–127. Darwin: Summer Institute of Linguistics.

Terrill, Angela. 1998. *Biri*. München: Lincom Europa.

Terrill, Angela. 2002. *Dharumbal: The language of Rockhampton, Australia*. Canberra: Pacific Linguistics.

Thomas, Elaine. 1978. *A grammatical description of the Engenni language*. Dallas: Summer Institute of Linguistics.

Thompson, David. 1988. *Lockhart River "sand beach" language: An outline of Kuuku Ya'U and Umpila*. Darwin: Summer Institute of Linguistics.

Triffitt, Geraldine. 2006. *The OZBIB Supplement 1999–2006*. Canberra: Mulini Press.

Tryon, D. T. 1974. *Daly family languages, Australia*. Canberra: Pacific Linguistics.

Tsegaye, Mulugeta T., Maarten Mous & Niels O. Schiller. 2014. Plural as a value of Cushitic gender: Evidence from congruency effect experiments in Konso (Cushitic). In Greville G. Corbett (ed.), *The expression of gender*, 191–214. Berlin & New York: Mouton de Gruyter.

Tsunoda, Tasaku. 1981. *The Djaru language of Kimberley, Western Australia*. Canberra: Pacific Linguistics.

Tsunoda, Tasaku. 2011. *A grammar of Warrongo*. Berlin & New York: Mouton de Gruyter.

Van de Velde, Freek. 2009. *De nominale constituent: Structuur en geschiedenis*. Leuven: Universitaire Pers Leuven.

Van de Velde, Freek. 2010. The emergence of the determiner in the Dutch NP. *Linguistics* 48. 263–299.

van Egmond, Marie-Elaine. 2012. Enindhilyakwa phonology, morphosyntax and genetic position. Sydney: University of Sydney dissertation.

van Lier, Eva & Jan Rijkhoff. 2013. Flexible word classes in linguistic typology and grammatical theory. In Jan Rijkhoff & Eva van Lier (eds.), *Flexible word classes: typological studies of underspecified parts of speech*, 1–30. Oxford: Oxford University Press.

Van Valin, Robert. 2005. *Exploring the syntax-semantics interface*. Cambridge: Cambridge University Press.

Verstraete, Jean-Christophe. 2010. The noun phrase in Umpithamu. Paper presented at the Workshop on noun phrase structure, Aarhus Universitet.

Waters, Bruce. 1989. *Djinang and Djinba: A grammatical and historical perspective*. Canberra: Pacific Linguistics.

Weber, David John. 1989. *A grammar of Huallaga (Huánaco) Quechua*. Berkeley: University of California Press.

Wilkins, David. 1989. Mparntwe Arrernte (Aranda): Studies in the structure and semantics of grammar. Canberra: Australian National University doctoral dissertation.

Wilkins, David. 2000. Ants, ancestors and medicine: A semantic and pragmatic account of classifier constructions in Arrernte (Central Australia). In Gunter Senft (ed.), *Systems of Nominal Classification*, 147–216. Cambridge: Cambridge University Press.

Wilkinson, Melanie. 1991. Djambarrpuyngu: A Yolngu variety of Northern Australia. Sydney: University of Sydney doctoral dissertation.

Willemse, Peter. 2005. Nominal reference-point constructions: possessive and esphoric NPs in English. Leuven: KU Leuven doctoral dissertation.

Willemse, Peter. 2007. Indefinite possessive NPs and the distinction between determining and nondetermining genitives in English. *English Language and Linguistics* 11. 537–568.

Williams, Corinne. 1980. *A grammar of Yuwaalaraay*. Canberra: Pacific Linguistics.

Wordick, Frank. 1982. *The Yindjibarndi language*. Canberra: Pacific Linguistics.

Wulff, Stefanie. 2003. A multifactorial corpus analysis of adjective order in English. *International Journal of Corpus Linguistics* 8(2). 245–282.

Yallop, Colin. 1975. The Narinjari language 1864–1964. In A. P. Elkin (ed.), *Narinjari: An outline of the language studied by George Taplin, with Taplin's notes and comparative table*, 1–109. Sydney: University of Sydney.

Yallop, Colin. 1977. *Alyawarra: An Aboriginal language of central Australia*. Canberra: Australian Institute of Aboriginal Studies.

Zandvoort, Frank. 1999. A grammar of Matngele. Armidale: University of New England MA thesis.

Language Index

Alawa 11, 51, 152, 216, 223, 230
Alyawarra 9, 14, 31, 77, 101, 152, 214, 219, 238
Anguthimri 7, 69, 70, 78, 181, 200, 214, 230
Anindilyakwa 6, 12, 26–27, 28, 46–48, 51, 52, 55–58, 62, 64, 74, 76, 92, 106, 153, 155, 217, 224, 237
Arabana/ Wangkangurru 9, 13, 37, 38, 75, 90, 94, 103, 133–134, 147, 152, 181, 187, 216, 219, 229
Arrernte 9, 14, 34, 40–41, 43, 45, 69, 70, 78, 94–95, 103, 151, 182, 188, 199, 211, 214, 218, 231
Atynyamathanha 9, 152, 159, 215, 218, 226, 238

Bardi 12, 37–38, 50, 70, 72, 77–80, 94, 95–96, 103–104, 126, 130, 133, 142, 153, 154, 158, 160, 217, 218, 236
Bilinarra 9, 69, 75, 106, 113, 143, 150, 153, 155, 156–157, 217, 221, 225, 226, 237
Bininj Kunwok 3, 4, 12, 26, 46–48, 50–51, 54, 55, 57–59, 63, 64, 79, 92, 101, 113, 118, 123–124, 153, 155, 158, 194, 203, 211, 217, 224, 233, 236
Biri 7, 75, 139, 152, 215, 223, 229
Bundjalung 8, 49, 79, 152, 174, 200, 201–202, 215, 223, 229
Bunganditj 8, 92, 93, 153, 218, 224, 238
Burarra 12, 55, 77, 153, 155, 217, 224, 233

Dalabon 4, 12, 16, 46–48, 50, 69, 113, 152, 189–190, 191, 214, 218, 226, 227
Dharrawal/ Dharumba/ Dhurga/ Djirringanj 8, 95, 153, 217, 222, 237
Dharumbal 7, 69, 153, 218, 224, 238
Dhuwal 10, 13, 31, 79, 90, 93, 103, 152, 158, 172, 185, 189, 215, 223, 226, 228
Diyari 9, 48, 51, 63, 73, 75, 147–148, 151, 152, 181, 188, 216, 219, 229
Djabugay 7, 38, 44, 148, 152, 181, 216, 221, 229
Djambarrpuyngu *see* Dhuwal
Djapu *see* Dhuwal

Djinang 10, 153, 217, 219, 226, 233
Dutch 112, 155, 196, 213
Duungidjawu 8, 69, 147, 152, 177, 178, 200, 216, 221, 230
Dyirbal 1, 7, 49, 55, 73, 93, 152, 161, 167–168, 214, 223, 227

Emmi 11, 38, 40–41, 44–45, 50, 64, 75, 78, 126, 152, 216, 224, 230
English 66, 89, 97, 108–111, 114–115, 155, 193, 196

Fox 213

Gaagudju 11, 55, 58, 63, 69, 73, 75, 79, 91, 99, 101, 139, 152, 158, 164–165, 166, 171, 191, 214, 224, 227
Garrwa 10, 70, 98, 131, 143, 153, 206, 217, 221, 225, 227, 237
Gathang 8, 48, 49, 152, 216, 223, 229
German 163
Giimbiyu 11, 55, 57, 118, 153, 155, 217, 224, 233
Gooniyandi 12, 31, 45, 50, 91, 93, 102–104, 114, 119–120, 125, 127, 135, 139, 145–146, 152, 156, 158, 159, 166–167, 185, 189, 190–191, 194–195, 200, 214, 219, 227, 228
Gumbaynggir 8, 49, 70, 72, 77, 153, 155, 217, 223, 237
Gun-djeihmi *see* Bininj Kunwok
Gunin/ Kwini 54
Gurindji 105
Guugu Yimidhirr 7, 15, 72, 100, 152, 175–176, 181, 189, 216, 222, 229

Hixkaryana 117

Jacaltec 34
Jaminjung 11, 50, 69, 91, 120, 127, 153, 156, 158, 159, 205–206, 217, 222, 227, 236
Jaru 9, 45, 93, 114, 153, 161, 217, 223, 225, 233

Language Index

Jingulu 11, 25, 54, 55, 58, 99–100, 114, 153, 217, 222, 237

Kala Lagaw Ya 7, 48–49, 152, 165, 180, 182, 189, 215, 218, 232
Kalkatungu 2, 115, 118, 119, 124, 127, 154
Karajarri 9, 152, 215, 222, 238
Kayardild 10, 31, 38, 40–41, 42, 73, 86, 98, 103, 152, 158, 160, 182, 196, 214, 223, 231
Kugu Nganhcara 7, 23, 26, 37, 42, 44, 45, 77, 78, 97, 152, 180, 182, 215, 218, 232
Kuku Yalanji 7, 44, 69, 75, 79, 93, 100–101, 106, 152, 181, 182, 216, 221, 230
Kune: *see* Bininj Kunwok
Kungarakany 6
Kunwinjku *see* Bininj Kunwok
Kuuk Thaayorre 3, 7, 42, 43, 44, 70, 79, 86, 87–88, 96, 118–119, 134, 138, 148, 150, 152, 180, 182, 201, 209, 214, 218, 225, 227, 232

Lardil 10, 38, 148–149, 152, 182, 214, 223, 225, 231
Larrakiya 6
Limilngan 3, 11, 54, 55, 57, 58, 118, 152, 191, 214, 224, 227, 228

Malakmalak 11, 64, 69, 152, 215, 218, 238
Mangarrayi 11, 56, 59, 86, 87, 126, 152, 174, 175, 217, 223, 229
Margany/ Gunya 7, 13, 153, 218, 221, 238
Marra 11, 55, 92, 114, 153, 182, 184–185, 203, 211, 217, 223, 227, 233
Marrithiyel 11, 44, 60, 69, 77, 152, 178, 179, 182, 214, 218, 232
Martuthunira 10, 37, 38, 44, 95, 99, 100, 139, 152, 173, 181, 187, 192, 214, 223, 227, 228
Mathi-Mathi/ Letyi-Letyi/ Wati-Wati 8, 69, 77, 79, 152, 215, 220, 237
Matngele 11, 50, 152, 216, 224, 230
Mawng 12, 55–58, 60, 86, 90, 141, 152, 158, 185, 200, 217, 224, 228
Mayali *see* Bininj Kunwok

Mayi 8, 141, 152, 173, 217, 222, 228
Miriwung 12, 87–88, 153, 217, 224, 237
Mosetén 117
Murrinh Patha 44
Muruwari 8, 86, 147, 153, 217, 222, 236

Ndjébbana 12, 128, 152, 215, 226, 228
Ngalakgan 46, 57
Ngandi 46
Ngan'gityemerri/ Ngan'gikurunggurr 11, 16, 44, 60, 133, 153, 154, 168, 169, 205, 217, 219, 236
Ngarrindjeri 8, 99, 152, 214, 220, 225, 238
Ngiyambaa 8, 96, 99, 100–101, 152, 182–183, 215, 221, 225, 237
Nhanda 10, 86, 96, 152, 181, 217, 222, 229
Non-Pama-Nyungan languages 6, 13, 25, 29, 48, 49, 92, 95, 128, 143
Nunggubuyu 46, 51, 114–115, 118, 154
Nyangumarta 9, 44, 69, 153, 155, 217, 223, 237
Nyulnyul 12, 36, 50, 127, 139, 152, 185–187, 215, 220, 228
Nyungar 10, 138, 152, 177–178, 215, 219, 230

Oykangand 7, 37, 43, 44, 45, 127, 147, 152, 180, 182, 215, 220, 232

Paakantyi 9, 69, 87, 99, 100, 152, 157, 182, 216, 220, 227, 230
Pama-Nyungan languages 6, 13, 29, 48, 118, 143
Panyjima 10, 152, 168, 181, 215, 223, 228
Pitjantjatjara 14, 71, 118, 125, 146
Pitta-Pitta 9, 48, 113, 114, 152, 181, 202, 215, 223, 234
Polish 117, 118, 213

Rembarrnga 11, 46–48, 64, 87, 153, 157, 218, 220, 237
Rimanggudinhma 7, 37, 152, 215, 224, 237
Ritharngu 10, 94, 153, 218, 222, 225, 238

Scandinavian languages 110
South-American languages 117, 163, 213
Spanish 111

Swampy Cree 213
Swedish 111

Tharrgari 10, 152, 159, 216, 220, 238
Tiwi 11, 46, 55, 69, 94, 138, 152, 200, 215, 224, 228
Trumai 114–115

Umbugarla/ Ngumbur 6
Umbuygamu 7, 127, 152, 215, 219, 238
Umpila/ Kuuku Ya'u 7, 44, 45, 80, 87, 114, 132, 140, 150, 152, 157, 181, 193–194, 199, 209, 212, 216, 219, 227, 230
Umpithamu 7, 41, 44, 102, 131, 152, 179, 182, 209, 215, 219, 232
Ungarinyin 4, 5, 12, 23, 52, 55, 56, 79, 90, 114, 130, 153, 155, 201, 218, 224, 233
Uradhi 7, 78, 152, 170–171, 196–197, 215, 220, 228

Wadjiginy 11, 64, 69, 152, 217, 21, 229
Wajarri 10, 38, 80, 86, 149, 152, 217, 220, 225, 227, 230
Walmajarri 9, 38, 70, 75, 87, 149, 153, 218, 221, 225, 237
Wambaya 3, 11, 49, 54, 55, 56, 58, 74, 77, 79, 92, 94, 119, 153, 158, 211, 218, 223, 225, 234
Wangkajunga 10, 14, 31, 40, 44, 149–150, 153, 218, 223, 226, 227, 237
Wardaman 11, 38, 44, 64, 153, 158, 160, 204–205, 218, 223, 227, 234
Warlpiri 9, 34, 67, 101–104, 118, 123–124, 129, 133, 148, 150, 153, 154, 156, 160, 218, 222, 226, 237

Warray 11, 46, 58, 64, 76, 96, 97, 152, 215, 220, 227, 237
Warrongo 7, 132–133, 153, 155, 158, 218, 223, 236
Warumungu 9, 153, 218, 221, 226, 238
Wathawurrung 8, 153, 218, 223, 226, 238
Western Desert 13
– *see also*: Pitjantjatjara, Wangkajunga, Yankunytjatjara
Wik-Munkan 37
Wirangu 9, 145, 147, 153, 218, 220, 238
Worrorra 12, 54–55, 58, 93, 140–141, 152, 185, 216, 224, 230
Wubuy *see* Nunggubuyu
Wunambal 54

Yalarnnga 7, 90, 92, 94, 152, 182, 199, 216, 223, 231
Yandruwandha 9, 38, 41, 48, 63, 94, 127, 152, 181, 216, 220, 230
Yankunytjatjara 10, 13, 34, 45, 71, 152, 202, 216, 219, 226, 235
Yanyuwa 10, 49, 54, 92, 152, 215, 223, 229
Yawuru 12, 44, 50, 69, 71, 145, 152, 215, 219, 235
Yidiny 1, 7, 31, 43, 45, 152, 181, 202, 215, 223, 236
Yimas 116
Yindjibarndi 10, 86, 152, 181, 217, 221, 229
Yingkarta 10, 15, 102, 128, 139, 140, 152, 159, 180, 182, 215, 221, 226, 232
Yir Yoront 7, 71, 72, 76, 80, 109, 127, 152, 181, 216, 220, 226, 230
Yorta Yorta 8, 153, 218, 223, 238
Yuwaalaraay 8, 76, 87, 153, 155, 157, 218, 223, 238

Subject Index

Adjectival classifiers 28, 47–48, 64, 84
Adjective phrases 85–88, 134
Adjectives 16, 47, 49, 50, 66–83, 84–85, 106, 110, 196
– *see also* adjective phrases, word classes
Adpositions 126
Adverbs 75, 79–80, 81, 87–88, 103–104
Affix 26–27, 74–76, 87, 91–92, 106
– prefix 37, 50, 51, 57–58, 63, 92
– suffix 91, 100, 127
– *see also* agreement, bound pronouns, cross-reference
Afterthought 87, 156–157, 176
Agreement 24, 25, 48–51, 62, 79, 91, 95–97, 128, 133–134, 143–148
– *see also* case, noun class, number marking, word marking
Animacy Hierarchy 90–91, 94, 96
Apposition 32, 84, 91, 116–117, 127, 130, 133, 146, 150, 155, 180, 216
– *see also* juxtaposition
Article 184–186, 187–188, 198, 203

Behaghel, Otto 130
Body parts 33, 47, 50, 69
Bound pronouns 95, 148, 225– 226
– *see also* cross-reference

Case 51, 75, 79, 81, 126–129, 143–148, 179, 218–224
– *see also* adposition, phrasal marking, word marking
Classifying role 35–37, 111, 119–120
– *see also* generic-specific structures, functional structure
Class neutralisation 58–59, 63, 79
Clitic 91, 95, 148, 182–183, 225–226
Collective 51, 93, 99–100, 105
Comparative modifiers 194, 195–197, 198
Complementary distribution 63, 143, 169
Complex noun phrases 15, 134, 210
– *see also* adjective phrases, apposition, coordination, inclusory construction, quantifier phrases

Compounding 4, 23–24, 32, 37, 78–79, 84–85
Constructional class *see* structurally defined category
Coordination 33, 130, 176
Countability 52, 93, 97–98, 106
Cross-reference 50, 91, 95, 96
– *see also* bound pronouns

Definiteness 4–5, 97, 101–102, 108, 113, 182, 185–186, 187–188, 210–211, 216
Degree modification 68, 74, 79–80, 85–88
Demonstratives 50, 69, 94, 97, 147, 185, 188, 190–191, 198
Derivation 68, 74–76
Determiner phrase (DP) 110, 126, 179
Determination 97, 101–102, 108–114, 158–159, 210, 227–238
Determiner zone *see* multiple determiners
Diagnostic slot *see* second position
Diminutive 74, 100
Disagreement *see* variable assignment (classification)
Discontinuity 2, 87, 103, 115, 117–118, 120, 123–124, 130–131, 156–161, 162–163, 213
Dislocation 156
Distributive 93, 99, 104

Ellipsis 77
Embedding *see* complex noun phrases

First mention in discourse *see* reference management
Flexible class 67, 68–69, 81–83, 197–198, 209
Functionalist theory 3, 20
– *see also* functional structure, functional structure and category
Functional structure 35, 68, 77, 119–120, 164, 166–183, 202–206
Functional structure and category 5, 31–32, 85, 102–103, 111, 119–120, 135–136, 164–165, 183–198, 207, 208–209
– *see also* word class

Gender *see* noun class
Generic-specific structures 1–2, 26, 29–45, 61, 63–64, 79
Grammaticalisation 24, 33, 37, 48, 60–62, 93, 113, 162, 180, 185, 187–190, 191, 196, 210–211
Greenberg, Joseph 137, 206

Headedness 32–33, 77–78
– *see also* determiner phrase

Identifiability 102, 108, 164, 183–184, 186–187, 188, 190, 191, 193, 196
Ignorative 186–187, 198
Inclusory constructions 15, 33
Indefinite marker 102, 155, 166, 186–187, 195, 203
Information structure 51, 60, 117–118, 120, 130, 138, 140, 145, 147, 156, 159–160, 170, 180, 182, 184–185, 189–190, 201–202, 216, 219, 222
– *see also* reference management
Intensification *see* degree modification
Interrogative 72, 105, 186–187
– *see also* ignorative
Introduced items 40–42, 55

Juxtaposition 33
– *see also* apposition

Kin Dyad 93, 100
Kin terms 69, 100

Language sample XVIII–XX, 3, 5–14
Lexical-Functional Grammar 33, 46, 84, 156

Multiple determiners 5, 109–110, 165, 169, 198–202, 227–233
Multiple nominal classification 27, 43– 44, 47–48, 62–65

Nominal construals 155–156, 162–163, 203, 209–210, 211–212
– *see also* discontinuity, noun phrase constituency

Non-configurationality 2, 114–117, 124, 154, 210–211
Non-integral noun phrases *see* noun phrase constituency
Noun classes 1–2, 25–26, 48–60, 60–62, 63–64, 68, 79, 92, 96, 100
Noun classifiers *see* generic-specific structures
Noun incorporation 26–27, 45–48, 84–85
Noun phrase constituency 16, 114–120, 151–156, 162–163, 209–210
– *see also* nominal construals
Number Hierarchy 99
Number marking 4, 51, 52, 89–101, 189
Numerals 50, 85, 104–105, 158, 192–195, 198
Numeral classifiers 1, 26, 47, 98

Obligatoriness *see* optionality
Optionality
– of determiners 4–5, 109, 113, 182–183
– of generics 44, 61
– of number marking 91, 94, 96–97
Orthography 14, 16–17
Over-determination *see* multiple determiners

Part of speech *see* word class
Personal pronouns 48–49, 50, 69, 93, 94–95, 97, 180, 185, 187–190, 198
Perspectivisation 27, 47–48, 56–57
– *see also* variable assignment (classification)
Phrasal marking 95, 127, 143–148
Phrase fracturing 145–146
– *see also* case, word marking
Pointing 190–191
Possessive 15, 50, 85, 111, 191–192, 198
Predicative use of nominals 47, 69, 78, 81, 103–104, 176
Principle of Scope 112, 168, 199–200
Prosody 37, 129–130, 150, 226–227

Qualifying role 36, 85, 119–120, 171, 189–190, 190–191, 192, 193–195
– *see also* adjectives, functional structure

Quantifiers 50, 101–102, 105–106, 158, 192–195, 198
Quantifier phrases 103
Quantifying role 85, 102–103, 106, 135–136, 166–167, 194–195
– *see also* functional structure, numerals, quantifiers

Reduplication 74–75, 76, 87, 92
Reference management 44–45, 60, 188–189, 201–202
– *see also* information structure
Register and style 45, 148, 221

Secondary predication 84, 104
Second position 91, 129, 146, 148–150, 225–226
– *see also* bound pronouns
Semantic range
– of adjectives 68, 72–73
– of generics 38–40
– of noun classes 54–55
– of nouns (*see* subclasses of nominal)
– of quantifiers and numerals 104–106
Specialised categories 66, 68–69, 81–83, 114, 184, 197–198, 209
Specificity 4–5, 113, 188, 195
Structurally defined categories 34, 76–81, 81–83, 208–209

Subclasses of nominals 69, 82, 97–99
Substitution 130
Superclassing *see* class neutralisation
Suppletion 93

'Topic determiners' 113, 183, 204, 212
Tracking *see* reference management

Underdetermined category *see* flexible class
Unification 46, 84

Variable assignment 27, 42–43, 47–48, 55–58, 61–62
– *see also* perspectivisation
Verbal classifiers 26–27, 45–48, 64–65, 84
Verb classification 46

Wackernagel's position *see* second position
Word classes 16, 66–83, 213
– *see also* functional structure and category
Word marking 127, 143–148
– *see also* agreement, phrase fracturing
Word order 2, 31, 68, 78–79, 85–86, 112, 115, 119, 131–133, 135–143, 167–168, 199–200, 202–206, 214–218

www.ingramcontent.com/pod-product-compliance
Lightning Source LLC
Chambersburg PA
CBHW071815230426
43670CB00013B/2460